Holistic Emergency Care and Trauma Recovery for Animals

Restoring Divine Harmony

By Kathryn Shanti Ariel

Disclaimer : The author of this book is not a veterinarian and the ideas, procedures and suggestions in this book are not intended to be substituted for veterinarian advice, but are rather intended to augment such advice, or to be used as a bridge in times of emergencies when immediate veterinarian assistance is not available. The author and publisher disclaim any liability arising directly or indirectly from the use of this book, or of any products mentioned therein.

Copyright 2015

All rights reserved, including the right to reproduce this book or portions thereof in any form whatsoever. For more information see: www.holisticemergencycare.com .

Cover Design by Aaron Rose
Cover photographs by: Kathryn Shanti Ariel

Author's Note

From a very young age nature has been my friend, constant companion and teacher. The voice and power of the Divine through nature's kingdoms has been ever present in my awareness. These voices speak so clearly of the Universal truth that the question and the answer are created at the same time – no matter the topic. Thus in trauma, injuries and illness the means to correct them is always at hand in the energetics of nature and as direct energy from the Divine.

Early traumas resulted in imbalances in my body displaying as asthma and allergies. My parents were naturalists, but they had little natural medicine awareness beyond aspirin and basic vitamins from fruit and vegetables. Therefore, my treatment was allopathic/drug based, masking the symptoms and further depleting my immune system to the point of collapse over time. As a result, I spent my childhood physically compromised, but gratefully I retained my quick and inquisitive mind and ever present connection to the Divine.

The weakened state of my body was utilized by my Spirit to make me into a keen observer and listener in quiet presence. It was in the quiet that the Divine promptings of how to heal myself would come. And it was in this quiet space that I also heard the promptings to study first aide, emergency response, mountaineering medicine and all the holistic modalities that overtime became tools that I relied upon for myself, family and clients.

When I asked the Divine why it was so important for me to study emergency response and natural healing together, I was told that someday, with the assistance of others, I would share this wisdom and techniques with the world in a new format, and many – both human and animals would be blessed by the wisdom.

Although I have been teaching classes and doing consultations for years, *Holistic Emergency Care and Trauma Recovery for Animals (HECTR4Animals)* is the first of my publications containing the in-depth wisdom that I have gained over the years. I know in my heart that given the opportunity this wisdom can create a much more expanded, harmonious and empowering tool set for lay people and professionals alike when assisting animals and humans in emergencies, illness and trauma recovery.

It is the destiny of HECTR4Animals and Humans to be utilized in trainings worldwide – both in person and online. Please join me in making this destiny a reality.

For more information follow our websites: Earthwise.Institute, or www.holisticemergencycare.com .

The early years …
Shasta, Aslan and Isis … great teachers – great friends

DEDICATON and GRATITUDE

… First and foremost to God/Goddess/All there is, the LOVE, Light and Wisdom that they emanate.

… To the Angels, Elementals and Kingdoms of Earth who have been, and continue to be my teachers, friends and greatest support.

… To all of the glorious animals, companion and wild who have shared their lives, challenges, joy and wisdom with me.

… To my close animal friends in Heaven and on Earth: Bar Harbor, Spencer, Isis, Shasta, Aslan, Daunza, Thunder Rose, Spirithawk, Tuska, Sunny, Ishnahnay and Mitchel and my animal clients who have added so much to my knowledge of healing and magic who through their companionship, and who have given me the strength and courage to fulfill my destiny.

…To my parents Clifton and Jane Field for always encouraging me to study and share knowledge of emergency care and natural medicine, to improve my writing and speaking skills and to never be shy in speaking from my heart about what I know is important for the Earth.

…To all of my friends and associates who have continued to encourage me through the thick and thin of it all (Ruth, Akaysha, Maryann Frisbe, Dorothea …)

…To Sharon Callahan who is such an inspiration to many and who always told me this book was mine to write.

…To Mary Ann Simonds whose wisdom and encouragement helped me to complete this book and to take it out to the world in many applications and who honored me by writing its forward.

…To the many who assisted me in editing the work and taking it through the very demanding publication process (Mikaelah Cordeo, Akaysha Avila and Pamela West)

…To all my teachers from whom I learned the various holistic modalities which are contained with this work, and finally …

…To all my life experiences that provided me with living proof of the power of the Divine in physical form and beyond the physical plain of existence, that have so often come to my assistance in times of emergency and distress. And who are joyfully making themselves available to all who have the faith to call upon them in times of trouble.

Reviews & Testimonials

"Years ago I took a class from Kathryn on wild crafting herbs. She is devoted to the holistic way of healing and walks her talk. Her new book, Holistic Emergency Care & Trauma Recovery, is an introduction to the world of this woman's encyclopedic mind and deep understanding of animal well-being and care.

Written in a gently spiritual tone, a sense of all aspects of an animal's health is presented. With many lovely pictures and attention to details like what the vital signs for a cat or dog are, or what a correctly applied splint to a bird wing looks like, and lots of specific homeopathic and flower essence options for healing, as well as energy healing possibilities, this book is filled with practical wisdom." **Barbara J. Semple,** *Holistic Health Pioneer and Best Selling author of* **Instant Healing – Accessing Creative Intelligence for Healing Body and Soul**

__Kathryn Shanti Ariel__ has written a unique book that has been birthed from her ability to 'Hear the Whispers of Mother Earth's Voice.' It is rare meeting someone who has a deep passion, understanding, and practical knowledge for what is needed to live a conscious quality life. Mother Earth's natural elemental, mineral, plant and fruit kingdoms are Gifts given to us freely; Gifts that are life sustaining.

__Kathryn is an alchemist__, in that she has created tinctures from nature, and products to assist physical healing for animals. Going deeper, she invokes in the reader an in-depth awareness of how the animal, plant, and human kingdoms can interact to support each other through life's earth walk. Beneath the sound of language - there is that __Silence__ - the intuitive whisper - that connects us all.

As an __animal communicator__, Kathryn's Gift is to bring light to this. She attunes us to how the animal and plant kingdom have a special sensory intelligence that many humans are not truly aware of. Having experience working and training as a First Responder, Wildlife Rehabilitation consultant, Mountaineering 1st Aid trainer; Animal Rescue and Trauma Recovery consultant, and Holistic Wellness Consultant, Kathryn combines practical solutions with ways to open our Intuition, and to apply energy work to remove blocks to healing.

It is then that the flow of energy can move freely throughout the body system to induce healing. __As a modern medicine woman__, Kathryn facilitates healing to occur on many levels. Call it __integrative__ *medicine for the human and animal soul.* **Dorothea Joyce - Author of BEing 'In' CREATION/Performing Concert Artist for Inner Peace/ Energy Practitioner -**

♥♥♥♥♥♥♥

In this groundbreaking book, Kathryn issues a wake-up call to humanity to see all animals as worthy of respect and understanding as fully equal partners in sharing this planet. I was just delighted with all the information about herbs, homeopathy and flower essences. I've known about them for years, but never truly understood how to use them. This book is going into my library, and now I can use these tools for myself as well as my animals. **Mikaelah Cordeo, Ph.D. spiritual teacher, author and energy healer.**

Table of Contents

Book Forward 1-2
The Inspiration 3-4
Book Overview 5-7

SECTION I – WHAT IS HOLISTIC EMERGENCY CARE?

Chapter 1 – What Is Holistic Emergency Care? 9-10
Chapter 2 – Treating All Beings with Equality - Creating an Emergency Support System for Animals 11-13
Chapter 3 – Prevention – A Major Step in Wholistic Care 14-20
    General Nutrition 15-16
    The Importance of Super Foods 17-18
    Going Vegetarian 19-20
Chapter 4 – Injury and Acute Illness Prevention 21-23
    Choosing Wellness as Your Animals' True Expression of Self
Chapter 5 – Interspecies and Intuitive Communication 24-30
    Freeway Accident Intervention – My Guardian Angel in Action 28
    Incident in the Mountains – Where did Those People Come From? 29-30
Chapter 6 – Animals as Teachers and Assistants 31-34

SECTION II – HOLISTIC MODALITIES

Chapter 7 – What Is Homeopathy? 35-41
    Strength or Dilution Levels in Homeopathy 37-38
    Administering Homeopathy 38
    General Guidance 39-41

Chapter 8 – Homeopathic Remedies Most Often Utilized For Emergency and Trauma Recovery... 42-46

    Homeopathy Overview 42

    Homeopathic Remedies.. 42-43

        Apis Mellifica 43

        Arnica Montana 43

        Byronia 43

        Calendula Officinalis 43

        Cantharia 43

        Causticuma 43

        Hepar Sulph 44

        Hypericum Perforatum... 44

        Ledum Palustre 44

        Phosphorus 44

        Rhus Diversiloba 44-45

        Rhus Toxicodendren 45

        Ruta Gravelolens 45

        Silica 46

        Symphytum 46

        Thuja 46

Chapter 9 – Introduction To Flower Remedies 47-55

    What is a Flower Remedy or Essence? 47

    The Theory Behind Flower Remedies 48

    How Do Flower Remedies Work? 48-49

    Flower Remedies Most Utilized for Emergency & Trauma Care 50-54

        Love Lies Bleeding 50

        Arnica 50

        Borage 51

        Chamomile 51

        Penstemon 51

        Red Clover 52

        Self-Heal 52

        Snapdragon 52

        Star of Bethlehem 53

        Walnut 54

   Yarrow Special Formula 54

 Flower Remedy Blends 55

Chapter 10 – Herbal Medicine History 56-57

Chapter 11 – Basic Herb Terminology 58

 Signatures of Plants – A Sampling of the Doctrine of Signatures 58-60

  Flower Color and Shape
  Growing Conditions in the Wild
  Body, Leaf or Root Structure
  Plant Textures

Chapter 12 – Primary Properties of Herbs 61-65

 Alteratives 62
 Analgesics 62
 Antibiotics 62
 Anticatarrhals 62
 Antipyretics 62
 Antiseptics 62
 Antispasmodics 63
 Astrigents 63
 Carminatives 63
 Cholagogues 63
 Demulcents 63
 Diuretics 63
 Emollients 63
 Expectorants 64
 Hemostatic 64
 Nervines 64
 Parasiticides 64
 Sedatives 64
 Stimulants 64
 Tonics 65
 Vulneraries 65

Chapter 13 – Herbs Commonly Utilized For Emergencies, Acute Care And
  Trauma Recovery 66-79

 Alfalfa 68

- Aloe Vera 68
- Arnica 68
- Astragalus 69
- Burdock 69
- Calendula 70
- Chamomile 70
- Chaparral 70
- Chickweed 70
- Comfrey or Knitbone 71
- Dandelion 71
- Echinacea 71
- Goldenseal 72
- Horehound 72
- Horsetail 72
- Hyssop 73
- Lavender 73
- Marsh mallow... 73
- Milk Thistle 74
- Mullein 74
- Nettles (Stinging Nettles) 74
- Pau d' Arco 75
- Plantain 75
- Purslane 75
- Red Clover 76
- Rosemary 76
- Saint John's Wort 76
- Self-Heal 77
- Skullcap 77
- Slippery elm 77
- Tumeric 78
- Valerian root 78
- Violet (Sweet violet) 78
- Willow 79
- Witch hazel 79
- Yarrow 79

Chapter 14 – Energy Healing Techniques 80-86

    The Direct Linkup 80

Direct and Easy 82
Suggested Energy Healing Modalities 83-86
    Reiki 83
    Theta Healing 84
    Jin shin Jyutsu 85
    MAP (Medical Assistance Program) 85

Chapter 15 – Connecting With Divine Assistance 87-90
    The Premise 87
    Faith in Action 88
    Paying Attention and Receiving 89
    Calling Divine Assistance 90
    Gratitude as an Anchor 91

Chapter 16 – Basic Holistic Emergency & Trauma Recovery Kit 91-95
    Ready Made Remedies .... 91.
        Homeopathy 92
        Tincture and Herbs for Decoctions 93
        Flower Remedies 94
        General Kit Components 94-95

SECTION III – EMERGENCY RESPONSE TECHNIQUES

Chapter 17 – Emergency Response Techniques 97-98
    Emergency Response Overview

Chapter 18 – Being Prepared and Practice Scenarios 99-100
    Emergency Response Components

Chapter 19 – Detecting an Emergency 101-103

Chapter 20 – Physical Symptoms of Emergencies 104-111
- Body Wellness Signals 104
- Assessing the Situation 105
- Surveying the Scene 106
- Logging the Details 107
- Is It Safe to Proceed? 109

Chapter 21 – Does a Life Threatening Emergency Exist? 112-115
- Is the Environment Unsafe?
- Are There Any Life Threatening Injuries?
- If the Scene is Unsafe
- Moving an Animal Who is Injured

Chapter 22 – Types of Wounds and Their Care 116-124
- Bruises
- Scrapes
- Cuts
- Puncture Wounds
- Avulsions
- Amputations

Chapter 23 – Controlling Bleeding 125-127

Chapter 24 – Nose Bleeds 128

Chapter 25 – Eye Injuries, Impaled Objects & Mouth Injuries 129-133
- Eye Injuries
- Impaled Objects
- Mouth & Teeth Injuries

Chapter 26 – Internal Bleeding 134-135

Chapter 27 – Hypovolemic Shock 136-137

Chapter 28 – Allergic reactions and Anaphylactic Shock 138-140

Chapter 29 – Muscle, Joint & Bone Injuries 141-143

Chapter 30 – Head & Spine Injuries 144-146

Chapter 31 – Burns 147-157

    Burn Prevention 147

    Divine Assistance & Energy Healing for Burns 150

    First Degree Burns 151

    Second Degree Burns 152

    Third Degree Burns.. 154

    Chemical Burns 155

    Electrical Burns 157

Chapter 32 – Poisoning 158-172

    Poison Control Centers 159

        Poison Help Line – 800-222-1222

        AAPCC's – 888-426-4435

        Pet Poison Hotline – 800-213-8660

    Types of Poisonings and Basic Treatments 160

    Ingested Poisoning 161-163

    Absorbed Poisons 164-165

    Inhaled Poisons 166-167

    Injected Poisons 168-169

        Prevention – Bites & Stings
        Brown Recluse
        Black Widow

    Insect Bites 170-171

    Snake Bites 172

        Prevention
        Action

Chapter 33 – Sudden Illness 173-183

    When Illness Strikes 173-174

    Internal Cleansing 176

    Vomiting 177

    Diarrhea 180

The Danger

Characteristics of Diarrhea

Chapter 34 – Seizures 184-188

Chapter 35 – Element Exposure – Heat Emergencies 189-201

    Prevention of Heat Emergencies 191

    Heat Cramps 192

    Heat Exhaustion and Heat Stroke Prevention 194

    Heat Exhaustion 195

    Heat Stroke 198

Chapter 36 – Element Exposure – Cold Emergencies 202-210

    Prevention of Cold Emergencies

    Frostbite 204

    Hypothermia 207

        Hypothermia Prevention

Chapter 37 – Foxtails, Stickers and Seeds 211-215

    Foreign Object Awareness – The Hands on Approach
    Recognizing Foreign Object Emergencies
    Taking Action
    Nasal Passage Obstruction

SECTION IV – TRAUMA RECOVERY

Chapter 38 – Trauma Recovery Introduction 216-220

    My Philosophy on Trauma Recovery
    From Emergency to Recovery
    The Attitude Around Healing

Chapter 39 – Understanding and Supporting the Inner Healer 221-227

Why Does a Spirit Leave It's Body?
> Exhaustion Destruction and the Inner Healer

The Importance of Rest and Quiet in Trauma Recovery

The Discussion Continued

Chapter 40 – *Flower Remedy and Trauma Recovery* 228-229

    Flower Remedy Resources

Chapter 41 – *Animals Taking on Their Human's Diseases* 230-233

    But Are All Diseases That Animals Take On Due To Their Human?

Chapter 42 – *Post-Surgery Trauma Recovery* ……………………………………….. 234-237

    Pain Control and Transmutation
    Suggested Holistic Protocol
    The Importance of Blood Purification
    Administering Remedies

Chapter 43 – *Wound or Surgical Incision Repair* 238-240

    Herbal Healing Support
    Homeopathic Healing Support
    Flower Essence Support

Chapter 44 – *Disease Related Surgeries* 240-244

    Common Causes of Cancer in Animals
    Recovery

Chapter 45 – *Physical Rehabilitation* 245-251

    Whole Body Support
        Flower Essences → Herbs
        Energy Healing Options

            Theta Healing
            Quick Step
            MAP

Chapter 46 – *Mental and Emotional Trauma Rehabilitation* 252-257

Overview

Trauma in Rescued Animals

Main Sources of Stress or Trauma in Animals

Post-Traumatic Stress Syndrome (PTSD)

Recovery Necessities

Trauma and the Nervous System

Chapter 47 - Case Studies 258-272

Case One : Ishnahnay's Car Incident, Short & Long Term Recovery

Case Two : Daunza's Poisoning & Recovery

Case Three : Mitchel's Severe PTSD & Physical Trauma Rehabilitation

Case Forth : Tuska – Spinal Trauma & Recovery

Case Five : Case Study/Testimonial for Zella and Freebe : Physical
          Trauma & Recovery

Chapter 48 – Understanding the Lessons 273-274

Acceptance and Gratitude

Chapter 49 – The Journey, the Choices and the Lessons 275

APPENDICES

Appendix A: Poison Control Centers 277-279

Appendix B: Vital Signs for Horses, Cats & Dogs................................... 280-282

Appendix C: References ………………………….. …………………………… 283-284

Bibliography ……………………………………………………………………………… 285

FORWARD

Inspired from her own work over years of assisting animals, Kathryn Shanti Ariel shares her stories and process for helping animals.in emergencies and during trauma. You will find helpful insights on a number of topics from Flower Essences and Herbs to Hands On Healing and Nutrition. The reader will also gain a broad understanding of the various situations, which can cause symptoms and trauma in an animal.

Although various modalities are discussed, the real intent of the book is to give the reader the confidence and tools to access the healing energy in all life and allow this energy to be channeled in whatever way the animal wishes to use it. Bridging the various methods to treat an animal with the person's own ability to channel energy, Kathryn demonstrates how incorporating a variety of tools can bring wholeness to animals, as well as how animals in our lives often can reflect our issues.

Many of the case studies discussed employ more than one modality and there are a number resources provided for the reader who wants to learn more. Thus, there is a menu of remedies and protocols the reader can choose from in assisting an animal. Keeping in mind that veterinary attention is valuable, but not always available in emergencies; the book gives "first responders" and those working in rescues, humane centers or animal control options at their fingertips.

Emergencies have happened to everyone. Ever seen a dog get hit by a car and not known what to do first? Or worked at a rescue or humane shelter and watched animals come in with pain? Or perhaps your animal is dying from old age and you want to be able to assist them in their transition. These are real situations that many people who share their lives with animals face and this book will guide to have a better understanding of various situations as well as what options your can choose.

Being able to take action and have more than one way to assist an animal allows the person to be empowered to be a partner in healing. Realizing the animal's free will and knowing that healing does not always mean physical wellness, Kathryn takes the reader through a number of situations. From her own experiences helping people and animals, Kathryn offers options and suggestions of modalities and actions that have helped bring animals back into wellness.

Whether you are reading to validate your own experiences with healing, or you desire to learn various ways to assist our animal friends, this book will offer something to most people who are assisting animals. The book will not replace or contradict traditional veterinary medicine, but is will offer insights and new ways to assist animals. Think quantum physics or vibrational medicine layered on top of herbal medicine on top of nutrition and physical assistance and you will have a relative feel for the information presented in this book.

Mary Ann Simonds, MA
Ethologist & Holistic Health Consultant
www.maryannsimonds.com
www.mystichorse.com

THE INSPIRATION

In the beginning there was nature's medicinal garden. All life relied on its many gifts for wellness and healing and the great joy of her beauty. Then … we got busy. And in our busyness we demanded shortcuts because we did not wish to be bothered anymore with keeping healthy or using natural remedies or eating well. We wanted easy meals, and quick "cures" from illness and disease for ourselves and our animals and we wanted them now!

Then our health got worse, and with us, our animal's health got worse because we took them with us into the fast and furious life that we decided to experience. Fast food and fast remedies were great or so we thought for a while. Within the quick mix of life and "healing" we also simplified emergency care, from first responder skills to major trauma correction. Normal procedure has been to stabilize whoever is injured and transport to the closest veterinarian or medical facility. What had been household knowledge in the past regarding emergency or acute healing assistance was left to the medicine people and shaman.

The Holistic Emergency Care Project for Animals and Humans was launched on a wave of renewed interest in holistic and alternative care throughout the world. It was a time when people were beginning to seek more answers regarding overall wellness of their own bodies and that of their animals. The current mode of just using allopathic medicine was not working. There had to be better solutions.

So, on the energy of the desire for better solutions came a remembering of earth wisdoms and seeking new answers to old questions. How do we combine conventional or allopathic medicine with holistic / alternative medicine for the greater wellness of our animals and our own bodies? For truly, there are gifts in both.

Fields of study and practice in holistic healing have developed and are becoming more and more popular every day along with a greater awareness and appreciation within the veterinarian world and that of the AMA. Yet, there has maintained a gap in the sector of both veterinarian and allopathic medicine regarding the implementation of holistic healing in emergencies, acute illness and trauma recovery.

The purpose of *Holistic Emergency Care and Trauma Recovery for Animals and Humans* is to create a foundation of knowledge on how to utilize many of the holistic modalities such as homeopathy, herbology, flower essences and direct energy work in emergencies, acute illness and trauma recovery. In so doing our intention is to create a bridge of healing assistance that will ensure if the animal's Soul wishes to continue its embodied journey that it is given a much greater spectrum of tools to heal completely – body, mind & spirit that when the allopathic model of healing alone is utilized.

The books are but one part of a three part project which will contain an associated product line, clinics and online training through our website, in which the techniques in the book(s) will be taught in a more interactive format. It is my hope that in time these techniques will become accredited courses of study for those in health care for animals and humans, as well as being used in homes all over the world to bring a greater and greater success to healing and maintaining overall well-ness in to our families and the Earth as a whole.

To keep abreast of our progress please visit our websites:
- www.holisticemergencycare.com
- Earthwise.Institute or www.EarthwiseInstitute.com
- www.kathrynshantiariel.com
- and Like us on Facebook: Holistic Emergency Care and Trauma Recovery for Humans & Animals Alike

BOOK OVERVIEW

Emergency! Knowing where to find what information in an emergency is of immense importance. There is no time to waste when a life is at stake, and having tools to understand the dynamics of holistic trauma management and recovery is key to keeping such situations as stress free as possible for all involved; humans and animals alike.

It was with this intention in mind that I created the outline for *Holistic Emergency Care and Trauma Recovery for Animals*. Here the overview provides the reader with an easy to scan summation of what is where so that you can educate yourself in calm times and know right where to go in times of emergency or trauma.

In addition to the material in this book, case studies, remedy information and articles can be found on our website www.holisticemergencycare.com and Earthwise.Institute .

Section I – Holistic Emergency Care assists the reader in gaining a broad awareness of holistic living and healing philosophy. Many of these chapters have been written through direct experiences that I have had on my journey, both as an individual and with my animal companions. The initial chapter addresses the true meaning of "holistic" in emergency care and trauma recovery.

The second chapter addresses the importance of treating all beings with equality, unconditional love, caring and support during emergencies and traumatic situations. Whether the injured are two legged or four is of no matter to the healer and first responder. We have had many dramatic examples in recent years of how humans were put before their animals in emergency and disaster situations. The results have been traumatic and in many cases are still requiring rebalancing and reconciliation.

In this section you will also find an introduction to interspecies communication. It will assist the reader in opening up to a greater knowingness of communication with other species. A greater connection can be deeply helpful in emergency and trauma recovery situations, whether the animal is the one receiving the assistance, or by bringing your attention to another who needs help. Whether you are new or experienced at exploring a greater understanding of this ability, I hope that you find this chapter both enlightening and helpful.

Other chapters in this section will bring a variety of insights on how to serve all involved in emergencies for their highest and best good. The information also provides many tools for creating a healthier and happier world for all. Prevention is a major first step. Prevention and understanding the enormous co-creative power we all have through our thoughts and actions to create a more compassionate and harmonious world. I hope the readers enjoy and utilize the information within these chapters during leisure time. The intention is to provide healers and first responders with a broader scope in which to operate during an actual emergency.

Section II – Holistic Healing Modalities gives overview information on the various modalities utilized in the step-by-step directions. It is provided to allow the reader background educational materials for review and comprehension during calm times. What are homeopathy, herbology, flower essences, and essential oils, and which ones apply to first aid and acute care?

It is important to have a working knowledge of earth healing tools in order to make the best use of them in a stressful or crisis situation. While a person can make a career of studying and understanding these varied modalities, this section will provide the reader with the basics. Additional resources are also listed under Resources on our website: www.holisticemergencycare.com

Section III – First Responder Instructions is focused on particular first aid and acute illness situations. <u>Section III is the section to have at hand in case of emergency</u>. Each component contains basic information on the type of injury/illness being assisted, along with an explanatory scenario.

Following this are step-by-step first aid instructions that include holistic modality options and divine assistance instructions. Along with each step is a graph (see below) letting you know if the remedy shown is applicable to humans, dogs, cats, horses, and/or birds. This information will serve you best if you study and become familiar with it before actually needing it in a true-to-life situation. Having as much of this in your memory as possible is to your benefit. Then this book can be used as a reminder and guide during an emergency, keeping you on track if you are unsure about how to proceed.

Section IV – Acute Illness and Trauma Recovery is the last major section of the book. This section discusses the process of healing, once the emergency situation is stabilized and all life-threatening issues are well in hand. The information here addresses physical, mental, and emotional trauma, providing guidance on how to heal the whole body and being. It has been my experience that this part of the journey can be extremely rewarding and healing for all parties, for it is during this process that one realizes that the true healer is the one being assisted.

As healers we are facilitating the recovery of those we assist by providing tools that the inner healer of the wounded one requires to bring her back into wholeness. This part of the journey may be a full healing of all bodies, physical, mental, and emotional. However, the injured person or animal may find a new balance that allows her to continue in embodied form or to transition comfortably.

It is of deep importance to embrace the choice and free will of whomever is wounded and healing, or wounded and transitioning. Each situation we experience allows us to gain understanding of our lessons. I suggest during trauma recovery to spend quality time reviewing the situation and bringing intention to understanding what is being learned. Then, of most importance, be grateful for the knowledge and understanding that has come forth from you and all participants.

Section I
What is Holistic Emergency Care?

CHAPTER I
WHAT IS HOLISTIC EMERGENCY CARE?

What does holistic emergency care mean? How is it different from the traditional way that first aid is taught? Wholistic health embraces the whole being (body, mind & spirit), not just physical body. Holistic healing utilizes modalities that give assistance to the whole being, not just the part that hurts or seems to be ill. Together they recognize that all creatures have four energy bodies, which are the spiritual, emotional, mental and physical. And to successfully treat or facilitate lasting healing of any health imbalance all four bodies must be brought back into balance.

Many health problems, whether illness or "accident," begin with an emotional upset or imbalance of some type. If this is not corrected it can move into the mental body, and then eventually into the physical, where it manifests as an illness or bodily injury. This is as true of our animal companions as it is of us. It has been well-documented that animal companions will often take on the diseases of their humans in order to both assist them as well as mirror to them, to help in the learning of soul lessons. When an injury or acute illness occurs, the holistic caregiver will tend to all four bodies in the order of importance, to bring the one(s) being assisted into a state of calm and comfort as quickly and effectively as possible.

In addition to treating all bodies, the holistic healer/facilitator may utilize a variety of vibrational healing tools: herbs, homeopathy, flower essences, energy healing and working directly with healing Light Teams or Creator. Holistic care emphasizes treating the whole being through the understanding of the Oneness of everyone and everything. All things carry a vibration that can be beneficial or hazardous, dependent upon their nature and how they have been created. In holistic emergency care we are often called upon to utilize the beneficial to remove or rebalance the hazardous.

For example:

Assisting an injured animal has many similarities to that of a human. As a healer or first responder the holistic approach is to address all four bodies. The focus given to each body and the order that this occurs is sometimes different in animals, because they often deal with injury and disease differently than humans. In any case, it is our responsibility to treat all bodies to bring complete balance back into the animal, if that is her choice.

It is in the trauma recovery (Section IV) where the rebalancing and deep healing of all bodies can occur. It is here that the choice is made by the whole being to create a positive reality for itself, or remain stuck in negative thoughts and thinking that will attract more illness. In providing holistic tools to the human or animal to heal the deeper imbalances, the opportunity is given to return to wholeness and true health.

In an emergency situation we are seeking the stabilization of the bodies, and the correcting or containing of life-threatening situations. But we must remember that if one treats only the physical body and disregards the mental, emotional, and spiritual imbalances that created it in the first place, it is highly likely that continued imbalances or dysfunctions in the higher subtle bodies would once again be projected into the physical body in some form. This applies to humans and animals alike.

In summary, it is with holistic emergency care and trauma recovery that we address the whole by utilizing tools that serve and rebalance the whole. In so doing the causal energies that brought the situation into a physical manifestation may be removed or healed completely, thus eliminating the need for the human or animal to repeat the experience in any form.

CHAPTER 2
TREATING ALL BEINGS WITH EQUALITY - CREATING AN EMERGENCY SUPPORT SYSTEM FOR ANIMALS

What you do unto these creatures of God ... you do unto me - Jesus

The holistic (also termed wholistic) application of healing modalities for animals requires first and foremost the acknowledgement that animals, like humans, are Spirit in physical form. It requires the awareness the divine expressions that are animals are a combination of spirit, mental and physical bodies, and that like humans they are an equally important part of the whole that is Earth's community and the Earth experience that the Divine is having through us all.

In the years that I have been consulting and writing about holistic living and healing one of the greatest hurdles that I have had to overcome with people has been the way that people view animals so differently from themselves. This has been both spiritually and physically. Expressions of low worth such as "it's just a dog, cat, horse, etc." to the mental construct that wild animals are more to be feared than loved and seen as part of the Divine.

The philosophical conversation concerning the shift of consciousness to holistic towards all life is beyond the scope of this book. However, as it applies to the realm of emergency care, healing and overall well-being it is surely applicable. A greater understanding of the similar ways that animals can be assisted in emergencies and trauma recovery, especially holistically is one of the main focus of this book and my work overall.

Since the advent of the Hurricane Katrina and the disaster response that left companion animals behind as their humans were taken to shelters and rescue areas, a cry went up all over the world at this mishandling of the non-human members of our families. Now rescue teams are training to take humans and animals from disaster areas together when at all possible. This was a global marker of the consciousness shifting from animals being property to animals truly being a part of our families.

There is now a greater and greater awareness of treating companion animals and the animal kingdom in its entirety as the blessed sentient intelligent beings that they are, and to do so even in the midst of a major disaster. Granted there is still a long road ahead of us as we look around and see animals hit on the road and just left to suffer and die whether they are wild or domestic. Yet, as people learn more and more to look into the eyes of animals and see the Divine looking back, a greater willingness to embrace animals as equals worthy of equal care from nutrition to medical emergencies (from birth to death), is emerging and spreading throughout our global human society.

This said the development of a heart connection with animal that are either family members or under your care in another way is of key importance to the welfare of the individuals and of our planetary community as a whole. This is true in day to day life or during a trauma or emergency. Life is divine no matter its form. We are all Spirit, consciousness in form. Animals, like children newly born, are the innocents of the Divine who, given the chance, are teaching us how to return to living our lives through the heart – through LOVE.

Holistic living and medicine address the physical, mental and spirit of humans, animals, plants. Life in general brings with it a greater awareness of taking care of the whole being through the use of holistic modalities: the gifts that the divine provides us through food, alternative medicine, energy healing and loving kindness. ☺

When assisting an injured, ill or otherwise traumatized animal it is important to let go of the mindset that he cannot understand you, or that she cannot speak to you. If you are unable to make a telepathic link, then create a heart link instead. The language of Love crosses all boundaries. Holistic treatment is to *treat the animal as you would desire to be treated yourself.*

Breathing into peace and dropping into your heart is key in any situation that requires your focused attention. This can be an emergency, illness, trauma or learning to listen across the diversity of species. Drop into your heart and ask for Divine guidance on how best to assist in any given situation. For me I ask "Mother/Father/God/All that is, make me an instrument of your healing for this situation or being".... Then I wait, breathe and listen intuitively and through all of my senses for directions.

There is an additional step – a gap to fill – so to speak. This is the creation of emergency response teams or consultants for animals like that of the 911 system for humans. In some places there are organizations that will respond to emergencies with wild animals – Wildlife Rehabilitation Centers and branches of the Humane Society and Animal Control.

Yet for the general household or day to day emergency with animals where do you call for holistic emergency care? Where do you call when the veterinarian offices are all closed? What emergency teams in your community will respond to an emergency with your animal companion and have the tools – especially holistic tools to assist should you be unable to do so yourself?

Holistic Emergency Care and Trauma Recovery for Animals / Section I

CHAPTER 3
PREVENTION – A MAJOR STEP IN WHOLISTIC CARE

An ounce of prevention is worth pound of cure

*Ah, to walk in the grass on a spring day
and rejoice in the feel of nature
all around me and under my feet….*

*… To be allowed to play in the water, the mud and to roll in the grass.
This is the stuff that a good life is made of! - Luke*

General Nutrition

Let Food Be Thy Medicine and Medicine Be Thy Food
– Hypocrites

Hypocrites' statement is one of creating and maintaining well-being whether you are human, animal, or even plant. Eating natural, wholesome, high enzyme foods and drinking clean purified water are essential. Natural organic foods are high in enzymes and nutrients, and if prepared well also contain the variety that comes naturally when eating in harmony with nature.

Processed dog food was initially created by Mr. Stuart in England in 1860 but did not make its way to the U.S. in any significant way until after WWII ~ 1946 when Stuart's creation made its way into Purina's first dried dog/cat food. Since that time, dried dog and cat food and treats became the rave for companion animals and for a majority of households shifted the fresh nutrition given daily to our animals to processed food, primarily for the convenience.

What few people stopped to consider with the onset of this new fad was the consequences to our animals' health by replacing fresh foods with processed ones. A completely processed diet is one without enzymes or natural probiotics, both of which are key to anyone's health and well-being. The new venue of feeding also took the variety of a natural diet away and replaced it with the same food, every day; day in and day out. This in turn reduces the animals overall ability to deal with change, change in diet; change in environment, and so forth.

Eating the same food every day makes the digestive system weak and lazy at the same time. The saying "Variety is the spice of life" certainly applies to our animals' diet. A diet filled with healthy variety allows wellness and vitality to be ever present in an animal's (and human's) life. Allowing your animal to wild forage, either in your vegetable and herb garden or out in nature's garden, is also of keen importance. This is something that cats who are allowed to live indoor/outdoor lives do naturally. However, dogs who are held on lead and live in homes where there is no garden of fresh herbs and grasses to eat, pay the price with their health.

Lack of regulations regarding the quality of contents in animal food is also an enormous issue. In more recent years it has been disclosed that many of the ingredients were actually very unhealthy for our animals (corn and other grains) and the meat (meal) could consist of diseased animal remains.

Poor diet along with a dependency upon steroids and vaccinations have severely compromised the immune systems of our animals, creating greater and greater disease states rather than wellness. Fortunately the great awakening (return) on the planet to once again eating fresh organic foods is finding its way back into foods created for companion animals.

Juliette de Baïracli Levy was a noted herbalist and the first voice from the veterinarian profession to come forward and speak of the importance of natural animal rearing and nutrition once again. Her work was carried forward and dispersed by veterinarians such as Dr. Pitcairn and healing educators such as Diane Stein. Juliette wrote a multitude of books which can be found through Amazon: http://www.amazon.com/Juliette-de-Bairacli-Levy/e/B001KIVI1G , amongst other places.

Holistic Emergency Care and Trauma Recovery
for Animals / Section I

The Importance of Super Foods

Every day I thank God for the foods often referred to as superfoods or macro foods! In these days with the toxicity level of our environment, importance of macro foods in everyone's daily diet cannot be over emphasized. This of course includes our animal companions. Before our environment became so toxic and the soils used for farming became so depleted, all foods were – to a degree – superfoods. This is currently not the case.

Gratefully these amazing foods do exist in forms that are readily available in stores and cost effective as well. The primary super foods that I personally provide my animals on a daily bases are the ones I am sharing here. Others will be discussed on our websites: Earthwise.Institute (www.earthwiseinstitute.com) and www.holisticemergencycare.com and also in the *Holistic Emergency Care and Trauma Recovery for Humans* book.

Chlorella, spirulina and kelp all contain significant amounts of vitamins and minerals making them all macro foods of choice in our family. So what is so important about these superfoods?

Chlorella:
- This food is very low in Saturated Fat. It is also a good source of Vitamin B6 and Magnesium, and a very good source of Protein, Vitamin A, Thiamin, Riboflavin, Niacin, Iron, Phosphorus and Zinc. [1]

---

[1] (Read More http://nutritiondata.self.com/facts/custom/569428/2#ixzz37U2ZILSS)

- Chlorella's sodium level is also lower than Spirulina and other seaweed, which is important to be aware of with animals.
- It contains the full array of amino acids, which are the building blocks of proteins, and a must in healing and cellular regeneration.

Spirulina:
- This food is very low in Cholesterol. It is also a good source of Vitamin K, Pantothenic Acid, Magnesium and Potassium, and a very good source of Protein, Thiamin, Riboflavin, Niacin, Iron, Copper and Manganese. [2]
- It contains the full array of amino acids which are the building blocks of proteins and a must in healing and cellular regeneration.

Kelp and other Seaweeds:
- Seaweeds in general contain most if not all of the nutrients detailed for chlorella and spirulina
- Kelps have been repeatedly documented to be of assistance to the thyroid and now are also being shown to assist in strengthening the heart.
- Note, seaweeds tend to be high in Sodium. Some animals are troubled by high sodium foods, so be aware of the sodium level in the products you buy and use accordingly.

In their entirety these foods are all very powerful as detoxifiers, including for heavy metals and there is some evidence they are also good for removing radioactive chemicals from the body. They have also been shown to assist in balancing blood sugar levels (hyper and hypoglycemia) as well as being of benefit to diabetes type II (Diabetes mellitus).

In addition, studies are showing an improvement to digestive systems. This is a blessing if you have a dog or cat that likes to eat anything they find lying around and then end up with unhappy stomachs.

The tablets tend to be small and easy to just put in food or even directly down the throats of cats and dogs. For horses you can use powder or tablets. Either way it is best to mix them in their oats or supplementary foods as they will get lost in the larger foods such as hay and alfalfa.

---

[2] Read More http://nutritiondata.self.com/facts/vegetables-and-vegetable-products/2765/2#ixzz37U3U6bLG

Going Vegetarian / Vegan

With conscious living on the rise, the quality of processed foods for animals is also improving in many ways. Many new brands of dry food are now grain free, and also include a higher quality of ingredients. Also, due to a greater and greater movement towards vegetarian living on a planetary basis, there is a growing supply of organic and vegetarian foods and treats for both dogs and cats. These gems bring greater wellness to those who eat them and greater freedom to the animal kingdom of the planet overall.

Supplementary compounds such as *Platinum Performance* and *the Missing Link* provide the basic nutrients for the animal specified (dogs, cats, horses, etc.), thus allowing a greater flexibility to animals who have been omnivores in the past, to thrive as vegetarians. Superfoods as described above also play a vastly important role in both trauma recovery and overall wellness. Many of these foods are tasty, relatively inexpensive and thoroughly enjoyable by the animals to whom they are given.

Almonds and Other Nuts: These wonderful nuts are one of the three known nut species that are good for dogs and cats to eat. (Cashews and peanuts are the other two.) I provide my dogs raw, unpasteurized almonds on a daily basis in their food or as snacks. They are high in Omega 3 oils as well as protein making them another wonderful way to replace animal protein with vegetable protein in their diets.

Ready Made Foods: Several companies are now making either vegan or vegetarian food for dogs. These include Benevo, Ami, Halo, Pet Guard and Natural Balance.

Cats also have an array of vegan or vegetarian foods to choose from. The manufacturers that I found include : Evolution, Ami, VegiCat and Wysong.

There are also an array of vegan and vegetarian dogs and cat treats.

Holistic Emergency Care and Trauma Recovery for Animals / Section I

Take It In Stages

Like with shifting from an omnivore diet to a vegetarian and then vegan diet for humans, I suggest shifting your four-legged friends gradually. First off red meat, then off pink, then white to just fish and then vegetarian and down to vegan if you feel they are ready for it. I encourage you to have a conscious communication with your animals about making these choices.

With the great array of healthy premade vegetarian/vegan foods as well as the growing amount of books and websites offering menu's and wisdom about feeding your animals this way, allowing shifting off meat is safe and tasty.

I have been a vegetarian and now vegan for decades, but it is just recently that I have taken my animals in this direction. Animals more and more are choosing to release their participation in the killing and suffering of other animals through agribusiness and hunting. Educate yourself and assist them to make the shift in a manner that allows them to thrive. In doing so you are assisting animals at large to be free.

Thank you!

> *The ideology of Hypocrites:*
> *"Let food be thy medicine and*
> *medicine be thy food"*
> *is as applicable to the animal kingdom*
> *as it is to humans.*

CHAPTER 4
INJURY AND ACUTE ILLNESS PREVENTION

"An ounce of prevention is worth a pound of cure"

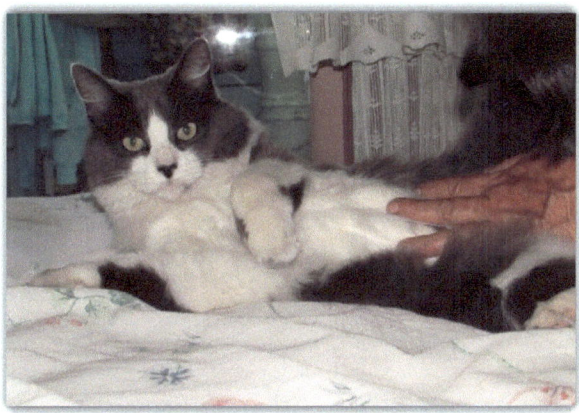

Choosing Wellness as Your Animals' True Expression of Self

We as humans have great capacity to choose our expression of self through the choices that we make each and every day from foods that we eat to thoughts that we focus upon and feelings that we create and embrace. Animals in our care are in a partnership of wellness or illness with us that can be highly affected by how we take care of them, from food to the environment that we create for them, to exercise, socialization and more.

Depending upon the frequency your animals have access to nature and the nutrition that exists there, they can be completely dependent upon your for their well-ness as associated with what they eat. As discussed in more detailed in articles on our website (www.holisticemergencycare.com), the nutritional essence of your animal's food is key to his or her well-being:

Think prevention, in health and well-being for you and your animal companions in your day-to-day activities. The holistic philosophy is that there is no such thing as an accident.

What many refer to as an accident occurs as a result of choices that we have consciously (or not so consciously) made. And in the case of our animals how those choices directly or indirectly affect their lives.

- For example: Feeding your animal(s) a natural or raw diet verses all processed. Dog and cat foods as they are called are relatively new in the world. Before they were created our companion animals were eating fresh food along with us on a daily basis.
- Making sure they get proper exercise each and every day. Running, playing, swimming are all keys to great health and longevity.
- Keeping their immune system strong through natural means rather than depending so much on vaccinations which in the long term can be very detrimental to the immune system.
- Keeping your and your animal(s)' living environment clean and safe. Be aware of toxins that you keep in your home and that are being used in your community and where you exercise your animals.
- Be an advocate for organic gardening and pesticide free community care in parks and public areas.
- Daily providing clean purified water indoors and outside for domestic and wild animal visitors.
- Including flower essences in your animals' water to assist them in maintaining or attaining optimum health.
- Keeping your animal(s) safety and well-being in mind when you are traveling or having outdoor adventures.
- Attaining knowledge on holistic wellness and healing so that you can provide the best care if illness or injury does occur.

Through our choices, we are largely in control and responsible for who, what, where and how we are as individuals and as a society. It is often said that this is the time of responsibility, that the problems we have as individuals and as a planet will not be rectified unless we all take **responsibility** for our actions, instead of placing the blame elsewhere. This is largely the case with our animals' care.

Your health and welfare along with that of your animals are the primary steps in this action. Learning about and taking care of the whole being is where this begins – body/mind/spirit.

It is also important to affirm wellness and to release all you and your animal(s) need to experience and learn from life through drama, pain and illness. As you make new choices for wellness and peace-filled lives, you give your animals, who sometimes assist in processing their human's "stuff," permission to let go of this process; simply because you are choosing to do so.

CHAPTER 5
INTERSPECIES AND INTUITIVE COMMUNICATION

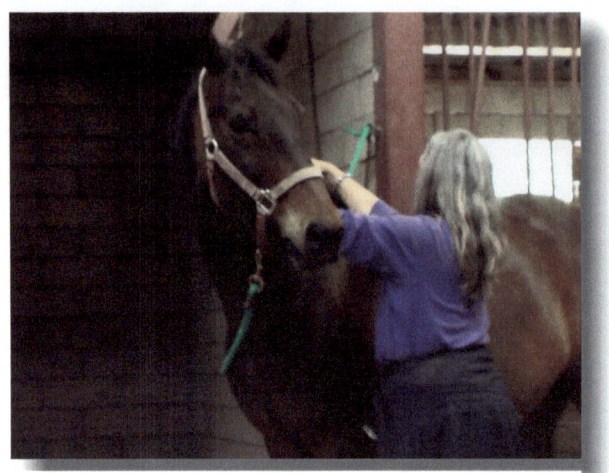
1JR confirming to Kathryn what his energy block was

Years ago when the idea of communicating with another species of Earth's inhabitants began emerging back into mainstream consciousness, it was primarily referring to the animal realm; companion animals to be exact. The people who could do this were often referred to as animal communicators, animal psychics, or more recently animal whisperers. From this point on, the awareness of the interconnectivity of all species, even all of creation, became part of humanity's conscious unfoldment.

As a part of this unfoldment it became recognized that the animal kingdom was stepping forward to help us understand that communication is just energy in organized form. It can be accomplished between any species or realm, seen or unseen, through the development of our senses to a higher and more sophisticated level, and in alignment with divine truth. The ability to communicate across species is in truth an innate ability for everyone.

As part of my early spiritual studies, a respected teacher told me the percentage figures of various forms of human conscious and unconscious communication. At the time these figures were quite surprising to me, however, in years since I have heard them repeated. There were as follows: audible communication is only 10-20% of total communication; body language generally ranges between 20-30%; and telepathy or energetic communication falls between 50-70%.

Thus for those relying only on audible communication, or even audible and body language combined, a majority of the true message is often being lost or misconstrued. It is no wonder that there are so many miscommunications between humans themselves and other species as well.

Holistic Emergency Care and Trauma Recovery for Animals / Section I

2 Thunder Rose communicating to me what she sees.

All animals and humans are born with an essence of intelligence and way of communicating that we call telepathy. It is innate in our Being. In the wild realms it is maintained as a prominent form of communication, interwoven with sound and body language.

For instance, it is known that a wolf pack can be dispersed over a five mile area and still be in full communication with each other through a combination of telepathy and sound. This is also true of whales, dolphins, and many other animals. Some humans enter their lives with these gifts and never completely allow society to turn them off. Of those who have quit their gifts, many are choosing to reconnect with them now to enhance their lives.

Those humans connected with their telepathic skills in mainstream cultures have often been dealt great judgment and criticism, causing them to hide away their awareness until the time that humanity is awake enough to embrace their gifts with open hearts and minds. This time is now. Through the combination of heightened conscious awareness within humanity and a drive to create a more sustainable world, the knowing that all Life truly can communicate is spreading globally.

The consciousness of humanity is returning back into oneness and unity, bringing along with it the ideas of quantum reality and the universal field of intelligence. (See Glossary for definitions.) These understandings bring forth a great foundation for telepathy to once again be utilized as part of normal day-to-day communication between humans as well as humans to animals, plants and the Earth herself.

We can see evidence of growing acceptance of these abilities in our television shows and movies, for example the television shows "Medium", "Ghost Whisperer", and the movie "The Gift." As time goes by we see more and more movies and television shows of this nature, showing a real change in American spiritual awareness and interest in this different way of interfacing with "reality."

In indigenous cultures, people with telepathic abilities are often revered as shamans, or medicine people, bringing great wisdom forth from other realms and species to assist the greater good. The understanding of plants and their gifts is an example of this communication. Often when a shaman is asked how she knows what plants are good for what uses, she will reply, "The plant told me."

Findhorn (www.findhorn.org) and other such communities have been founded on co-creative communication with the nature and devic realms. Another aspect of such communication, working with the spirit medical team (SMT) of a human or animal, will be discussed in detail within this book. Embracing such a relationship with the helpers of Creator may be a stretch for those new to interdimensional communication. However, as one's belief system is expanded and discernment is strengthened, such relationships as these become the Godsend that they are intended to be.

Many spiritual lessons over the ages have come through interdimensionally from those who have had open communication channels. Inventions, divine intervention in times of crisis, creations of music, art, and literature, are examples of receiving inspiration from other realms. It has been told that Walt Disney was creatively influenced by his telepathic connection to other realms of Earth and heaven. Edgar Cayce is another well-known example of a person who used his psychic abilities to enrich humanity.

In most human cultures telepathy has been ignored completely, preempted by verbal and visual communication. On top of this, a person's verbal communication is often seen as a mark of intelligence; a way of setting humanity apart from and above other forms of life. In truth, telepathic communication is much more sophisticated as it goes beyond the language barrier, allowing anyone to communicate at a level of unity and interconnectedness. There are some humans who have an innate gift of communicating between species and even realms (interdimensional communication). However, it is my belief that anyone can be assisted in learning or remembering how to communicate between species and dimensions.

The first step is to reconnect to our innate telepathic ability and utilize this in conjunction with the other primary senses. All life can communicate with you and you with it. And happily, most domesticated and wild animals are more than willing to help you along in your learning. Teachers indeed can come in many forms.

There are many references available for gaining greater understanding of this learning. The book *Animal Speak*, by Ted Andrews, has always been one of my favorites. Most animal totem teachings operate on the premise that each person's angels and guides utilize animals, birds, insects, and reptiles, to communicate specific messages at specific times to help us understand the events of our lives. The more we pay attention to these messages the more we will see them and the more help will be given.

It is worth noting here that discernment is one of the major skills that one must also develop in alignment with telepathic communication and communication in general. Webster defines discernment as "a power to see what is not evident to the average mind." A more spirit based accounting of discernment is the heightened ability to determine whether the source behind a text or teaching, an encountered problem, or a proposed course of action, is imbalanced or aligned, separated or whole, mischievous or divine in nature.

As part of this book and associated trainings, we will be addressing communicating with animals, as well as the interdimensional Light Teams and Spirit Medical Teams (the assistants of Creator) who will come forth to help you in times of crisis. However, you must ask them to help, and then know how to receive their assistance. Receiving of assistance comes in many forms: physical, mental, emotional and divine. How these come to you can be largely a result of your openness to and belief in certain levels of assistance from Creator God.

If you are open and have at least some level of belief in divine intervention, then Creator and the Angels have a much greater opportunity to provide you and others involved with deeply profound, co-creative assistance. I have enjoyed a great variety of divine incidences over the years of my awakening into full consciousness of asking for and receiving divine intervention. Instances of this type of assistance will be discussed in length within this book and the associated clinics. The chapter "Connecting with Divine Assistance" provides a much greater look at these methods.

Here are two examples that occurred to me early on in my holistic emergency care awakening process:

Freeway Accident Intervention – My Guardian Angel in Action:

I was on my way to the second half of my standard first aid training class down the I-5 from my home and place of work in southern California. Suddenly someone cut in front of a large truck in the lane next to me. The truck swerved and cut over into my lane to avoid the resulting collision of cars. As if by magic, my car moved into a parallel position next to the truck, gliding to the side of the road and parking itself inches away from the delivery truck. It was as though someone else of greater strength and understanding of the situation had taken over the steering of my car! A "normal" scenario could have caused me great injury or even my physical demise.

Everything had moved into a state of slow motion, like we see in the movies when the director wants us to understand the depth of an action. I stepped out of my car without a scratch and feeling fine. I then went to assist others who were in the crash before returning to my car and going on to class.

This type of assistance is referred to in general as divine intervention. It will occur without asking for help when your life is in jeopardy for a reason that is not part of your chosen soul's journey of learning.

Holistic Emergency Care and Trauma Recovery for Animals / Section I

Incident in the Mountains – Where Did Those People Come From?

I was hiking in the Laguna Mountains outside of San Diego with my three dogs, Shasta, Aslan, and Isis, enjoying one of our favorite retreats. Suddenly Shasta let out a howl and as I looked she showed me a long metal wire protruding from her front left paw. Upon close examination, I saw that it was an old hanger that someone had used for roasting food over a fire and then left behind.

The wire protruded more than three inches through the top of Shasta's paw and about two feet out the bottom. Due to the lumpy nature of the hanger's end and my emotional attachment to Shasta's pain, I could not pull it hard enough to get it back through her paw. I was greatly distressed and a bit paralyzed as what to do, and I called out to God, "Please send us help!" Then I surrendered into the situation and sat on the ground next to Shasta, holding her paw and sending her love.

Within a couple of minutes a man and a woman came down the trail, seemingly out of nowhere. This was an isolated trail where we would maybe see one other person all day long! The man was a doctor. He told me to hold onto Shasta, and then gave the hanger a good yank. Out it came! Giving both people great thanks, I gave Shasta some homeopathy and she rested for a couple of minutes. Then the couple drifted off down the trail in the other direction, like angels sent from God. We continued our hike, like nothing had ever happened. Yet something had, and for me it was an awakening to the unlimited possibilities of the divine.

Over years of sharing these stories with others, I've encountered many with similar experiences, which let me know that these are fairly common examples of divine intervention and receiving assistance in emergencies. Along with more unusual divine experiences, we will be discussing in depth how to receive assistance throughout this book.

The main pieces to understand and remember are:

- Due to humans having Free Will, humans must ask for Divine Assistance and then let it come forth in whatever way it is sent by Mother/Father/God. The accepting and following of that guidance or assistance is up to you.

- The exception to this is with your guardian angel interceding in a life-threatening situation not of your choice, with the direction of your God-Self, Christ Self or what some referred to your I AM Presence.

- The tools in this book are of great importance, providing you and your divine assistants more ways to help you, as well as those that you are attempting to assist. In the understanding of Oneness and the true energy of Divine Intelligence, we can utilize the frequency of thought and sound to communicate through time and space to all Light Beings, anywhere in Creation. The various clinic and training programs of Earthwise Institute take participants through the pathways of understanding to connect with this truth. (For more information see: http://holisticemergencycare.com/ and Earthwise.Institute)

CHAPTER 6
ANIMALS AS TEACHERS AND ASSISTANTS

A very wise friend of mine once said "Look into the eyes of unconditional love and you will find yourself." This friend's name was Spirithawk, a wolf dog and much honored part of my family. The animal kingdom as a whole embodies the energy of unconditional love, and as such are profound teachers to all of us as we find our way back to this pure and natural state held within our child self--our innocence.

Native Americans and other indigenous peoples have long acknowledged the messages and spiritual power of individual animals. Referred to as "totems," ceremonies have been developed in reverence to certain animals. Wolf is seen as master teacher, bear as healer, butterfly as transition, hawk as protector, and eagle as divine connection. Other more "gentle" totems include the skunk representing respect, the hummingbird as joy, dragonfly as inner world connection, and the list goes on.

Becoming aware of animals as messengers and totems of one's own inner essence can bring an enriching link to nature. As your awareness grows you may find that the synchronicity in which various animals come to you or pass in and out of your life may have deep significance to what is transpiring in your life at that moment.

For instance:

- Have you ever noticed butterflies flying around or even landing on you in a time of transformation in your life?

- A deer crossing your path can be telling you to reach within to your gentle power:

- An eagle flying nearby can be telling you that someone of the Heavenly Host is connecting with you or wishing to do so:

Skunk got your attention? This is a sign to respect yourself or give respect to others. The amazing ability of animals to speak to us through action and form is one of many ways in which they help us to understand our own deepest selves. In so doing, we are then challenged to embrace them and ourselves in unconditional love, or negate those feelings through fear and ignorance. The first, and for some more dramatic challenge, is to acknowledge the deep intelligence of animals. It is not the type of intelligence that will score high on a human IQ exam, but rather the intelligence of nature; of Knowing in its raw form that all of life is interconnected and speaks to us on a multitude of levels.

There are many references for learning more about animal totems and animal communication as a whole. Two of my favorites are *Animal Speak*, by Ted Andrews, and *Medicine Cards, The Discovery of Power Through the Ways of Animals*, by Jamie Sams, David Carson, and Angela C. Werneke.

The domestication level of an animal can often influence their connectivity with and awareness of their wild surroundings. This again is something they can teach or reflect to humans. A cat, horse, or dog that spends its life inside a house, pasture, or on a leash, tends to be much less connected with nature and aware of the environment than those who are allowed to be out interfacing with nature by exploring, eating, playing, and just being.

Likewise, a person who spends little time in nature being quiet, listening, and observing will have a much greater chance of putting himself in harm's way than one who has learned to connect with nature and listen, even beyond the chaos of the city, to hear what his environment is communicating and make decisions accordingly.

Many animals have been able to demonstrate their innate trust and knowingness of life in emergencies and other traumatic situations. Dogs and horses in particular have been called upon to assist and often take the lead in such situations to bring people to safety, or warn them off in the first place. In years past I learned to allow my dog (or dogs) to take the lead while out hiking so they could warn me of danger.

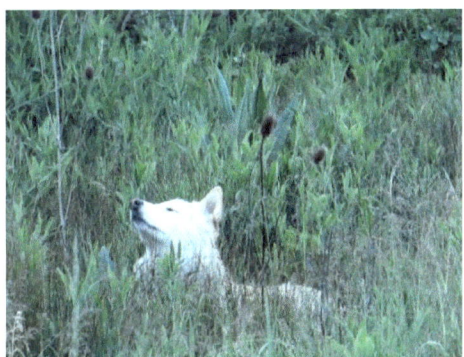

Ishnahnay: "Someone is coming – it's time to leave"

There has been many a time when I have taken a different path or been led home after taking a "wrong" turn in the forest by the natural guidance system of my dogs. Other animals have also been stepping forward to assist and to warn of danger. Dolphins, elephants, birds, cats and others have stepped in to warn humans of danger, or save a human life on many occasions. A well-documented example was the December 26, 2004 tsunami in Thailand and Sumatra when all the animals went inland before the wave hit indicating to humans who were paying attention to do the same.

One of the most dramatic lessons animals teach is to pay attention to what the Earth and those around us are saying, emitting, or suggesting through their actions. All of life, including the Earth herself, emits energies or frequencies of communication and intention.

When one is tuned in as consciously as most animals are, these energies can be read like a book, taking surprise out of most situations and instead allowing a partnership with life to be created. This tuned in state of being is augmented by animals being so masterfully in the now, or present moment.

We hear much of "being in the now" these days. This refers to emptying our heads of unnecessary clutter and not thinking of the past or future, so that we can be fully in the present moment to receive the gifts or danger alerts that are waiting for us. I have often sat and watched my animal companions or wild animals to learn from them how to better immerse myself in the present moment. Whatever the activity, animals are always present in the moment, while at the same time completely aware of their larger environment and beyond.

Part of this connectivity is seen in the animal's normal state of being. They are ever aware of what is going on around (and in) them. No to do lists, worrying about this or that, thinking ahead, or pining over the past while driving in rush hour traffic or hiking down a mountain trail. They listen to the heartbeat of the Earth, to the voice of nature, of Creation, that is in a constant state of motion and activity.

You may have heard the saying, "If you look into the eyes of an animal, you will truly see yourself." This truth is two-fold in nature. First, animals hold the energy of unconditional love, and through that they reflect yourself back to you through their eyes. Second, in any moment where you are truly looking into an animal's eyes, they are holding you fully in their presence, in the now, and asking you to do the same of them. See the teacher. Be the teacher. It is a partnership born of God.

Jessica Crabtree

Section II
Holistic Modalities

Holistic Emergency Care and Trauma Recovery for Animals / Section II

CHAPTER 7
WHAT IS HOMEOPATHY?

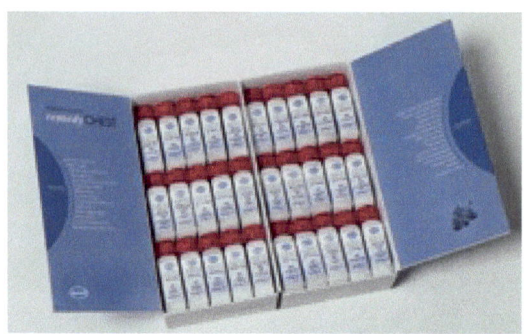

Homeopathy is considered by some to be the most effective form of natural medicine developed in the past 200 years. Discovered in the late 1700's by German physician, chemist and medical translator, Samuel Hahnemann, homeopathy has since been embraced as a valuable healing modality throughout the world. It uses tiny doses of natural substances from plant, mineral and animal kingdoms to stimulate the user's inherent ability to heal herself.

Homeopathy comes from the Greek words "homeo", meaning similar, and "pathy", meaning suffering. Treatments are based on the "Law of Similars" or "like cures like"; (similia similibus curantur). This law states that the same substance that produces disease symptoms in a healthy person or animal, when given in concentrated doses, can also cure a sick person or animal with similar symptoms when given in very diluted form.

Homeopathy is considered a vitalistic healing art; the theory is that homeopathic remedies are able to stimulate the body's own healing abilities, thus allowing the body to heal itself. Conventional Western, or allopathic medicine ("opposite suffering"), in contrast, is founded on a mechanistic viewpoint -- that an unhealthy body can be fixed with drugs. A drug is given that produces the opposite of the symptom. (e.g. decongestant to DRY UP a RUNNY nose).

According to homeopathic philosophy, the body works to maintain a balance, homeostasis, in order to promote health, in response to internal and external forces that cause the body stress. The maintaining of balance often takes the form of defense mechanisms. The body produces antibodies to combat the effects of foreign bacteria, for instance, and shivers to assist you in keeping warm.

Most people raised with the ideas of conventional medicine confuse symptoms of illness -- such as pain, rashes and discharges -- with the illness itself. Allopathic physicians give drugs to relieve the symptoms and when the symptoms are gone, presume the disease to be cured. In contrast, the homeopath believes (as do most natural healers) that symptoms are merely signs that the body's natural defense mechanism is attempting to restore balance internally.

For example, hives might indicate a particular kind of imbalance in the body. The homeopath would treat the imbalance, not the hives. Symptoms are utilized to understand what the body is attempting to accomplish. Conventional or allopathic medicine treats the symptoms and not the underlying cause of the disease. The symptoms may disappear but the health of the person is usually not enhanced. In fact, oftentimes it is actually weakened. Homeopathy corrects the underlying imbalance that caused the disease symptoms and allows the body to heal itself.

From the homeopathic viewpoint, the chronic use of most drugs, including cortisone and antibiotics, has a suppressive rather that a curative action. In other words, it temporarily fixes the condition without bringing the person to a balanced state of health.

Note: Caffeine and mint counteract or neutralize most homeopathic remedies. So avoid giving your animal anything with mint or caffeine in it during the use of these remedies.

Strength or Dilution Levels in Homeopathy

Homeopathic remedies come in a variety of dilution levels (6X, 30X, 30C, 1Mil, etc.). What these numbers represent is how many times the base material (arnica Montana, phosphorous, etc.) have been diluted. When choosing which dilution to utilize it is important to understand that the lowest level, 6X, works primarily on the physical body, while the higher dilutions also work on mental and emotional levels.

The highest 200C and 1mil are for deep healing, predominately addressing chronic or constitutional imbalances as well as severe emergencies such as poisonous snake or spider bites. In general, for acute or emergency challenges we only use 6X, 30X or 30C dilutions, and highly suggest that no one utilizes the higher dilutions without the guidance of a trained professional.

In general homeopathic dosing is every four hours, looking for improvement in the symptoms. If no improvement is seen after 3 doses then change remedies. In emergencies the dosing can be much more frequent, even up to every 5 to 15 minutes to assist with the immediacy of the situation. ***

(For more information on homeopathy refer to the books in the Reference List contained at the end of this book.)

Administering Homeopathy

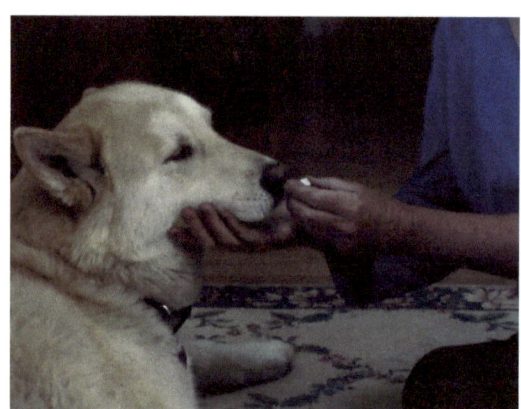

Showing Ishnahnay homeopathy & then administering it orally

Homeopathic remedies come primarily in tablet form, the individual pellets of which are called pillules. It has been my experience working with horses, dogs and cats, that the dogs are the easiest to give pillules directly to, while horses, cats and birds are amenable to a light dilution in water administered with an eye dropper or syringe.

Holistic Emergency Care and Trauma Recovery
for Animals / Section II

General Guidance[3]

- Homeopathic medicines are very delicate, therefore avoid touching the medicine with your hand.

- Do not return accidentally handled medicine to the bottle. Dispense just the required dose from the bottle at each dosage time.

- Keep the container tightly sealed at all times, except when actually dispensing. Do not open two containers of medicine at once.

- Store medicines away from sunlight, in a cool dark place and keep away from strong-smelling substances, especially camphor, embrocations, perfume etc.

- Do not refrigerate or freeze. If correctly stored, homeopathic medicines can survive for very long periods, so do not discard unused supplies; they could be useful to your animal (or for yourself) in the future. Those stored in glass bottles survive better.

- Pillules may conveniently be dispensed into the bottle cap, prior to dosing. It is not necessary to give an exact number of pillules. If the patient allows, the pills may then be tossed from the cap directly into the mouth (avoiding contamination of the cap with saliva etc.), to avoid handling of the pillules altogether.

- Drops may be given in water or directly onto the tongue. One to three drops is a usual dose. Drops should be water based, rather than alcoholic.

- Powders can be poured directly into the mouth from the paper.

- Pillules, powders or tablets may be dissolved in a little boiled, cooled water in a syringe and this provides a means of liquid dosing. This can work very well for cats, for whom a drop or two of liquid can be placed onto the front of the nose/upper lip or onto a front paw, for the cat to lick the dose promptly.

---

[3] Obtained from http://www.squidoo.com/how-to-give-homeopathic-medicines-to-dogs-cats-and-horses

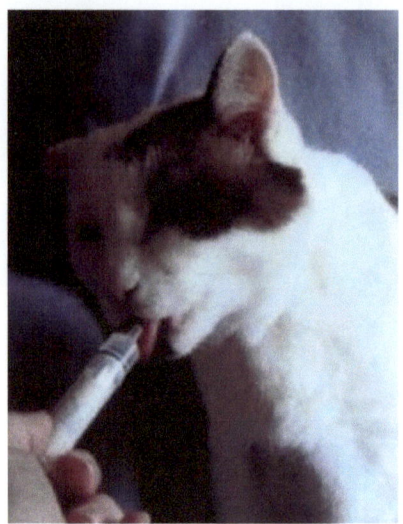

- Injections are available and, for farm use, in-water medication is commonly used.

- Lotions such as Arnica Montana cream are for external use only. These should usually be diluted prior to use (please check if not given clear instructions).

- For oral medicines, ensure that the dose is either swallowed or retained in the mouth for 30 seconds. Thereafter it may be ejected without diminishing the effect.

- When more than one medicine has been prescribed, please do not give them at the same time. If possible, allow a five-minute interval between different prescriptions. If possible, do not give doses within 15 minutes of food. For farm species and horses this is, of course, not possible, but try to avoid contact with "compound" feeds for at least five minutes. Homeopathy can be given to horses in a very little bland food (e.g. grated organic carrot or apple or a very small piece of bread).

Holistic Emergency Care and Trauma Recovery for Animals / Section II

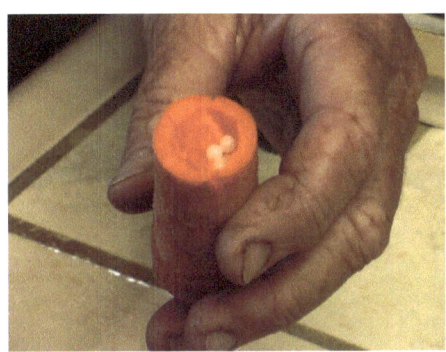 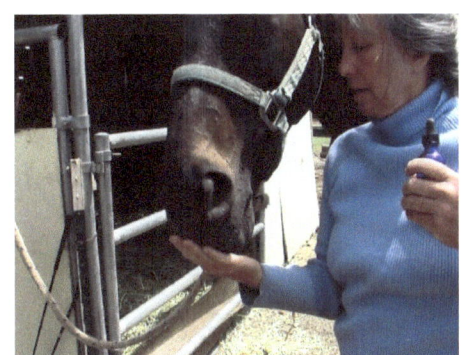

Using Carrot to hold homeopathy for administering to horse (Zella)

- In-water homeopathic dilution can be very useful for farm animals or groups of animals. In the case of cage birds and other small pets pillules may be added to the drinking water, freshly prepared each day. Be careful to avoid blockage of the water feeder nozzle.
- Avoid giving strong-smelling sweets or treats, mint family or anything with caffeine, to animals while they are on medication. These can neutralize the remedy.
- Adhere carefully to the prescribed dosage regimen and, if questions arise, please do not hesitate to raise them with the prescriber. If in doubt at any time, it does no harm to stop the homeopathic prescription, pending further advice.

Creating In Water Homeopathic Dilution

Some animals are happy to receive homeopathic pellets while others just do their best to spit them out. If you are assisting an animal who is in the spitting out category ☺ then creating a dilution in water may be the best route for all concerned. Making a water dilution is quite easy. Here is what you require:

- 2 – 4 ounce tincture bottle with eye dropper
- Distilled water
- Remedy to be diluted

Fill the bottle ¾ with distilled water. Add 3-5 homeopathic pellets. Close bottle. Strike bottle against the palm of your hand 80 times; 1, 2, 3, 4, … steady rhythm.

CHAPTER 8
HOMEOPATHIC REMEDIES MOST OFTEN UTILIZED FOR EMERGENCY AND TRAUMA RECOVERY

Homeopathy Overview

The following homeopathic remedies are ones that I have used successfully in emergencies as well as trauma recovery. Some are also used as constitutional remedies by professional homeopaths [4]. The remedies are listed in alphabetical order, rather than according to use. However, Section III of the book breaks emergencies and traumas down into actual situations (i.e., wounds, burns) and provides the correct remedies to utilize.

Thus, this section is for the reader to become familiar with the remedies and to gain a working knowledge of them to aid in the understanding of the applications if the need arises.

Homeopathic Remedies

APIS MELLIFICA (Honey Bee):
  Indications: Bee stings, insect bites, hives, jelly fish stings, stinging nettle rash, mosquito bites.
  Symptoms: Swelling, itching, redness; painful stinging and burning; puffy swelling -eyes, throat, tongue, face. Little or no thirst. Symptoms get better with cold applications, and open air; worse with heat, touch or pressure.
  Dosage: 30X every two hours up to four doses a day. (In extreme cases, such as allergic reactions, 30C may be necessary, but always start with 30X and increase to higher dilution if necessary).

ARNICA MONTANA (Leopard's Ban):
  Indications: Give immediately for any injury or accident for bruising to soft tissues, sore muscles, shock, falls, head injuries, contused wounds, black eye, or shock due to burns.

---
[4] A constitutional remedy is one that is used to heal chronic illness and overall body imbalances.

Holistic Emergency Care and Trauma Recovery for Animals / Section II

Symptoms: Soreness and bruised feeling, shock, bleeding caused by injury, muscle soreness from over exertion, bruising. For pain from sprains, blows and fractures. Speeds healing of injuries.

Dosage: 30X every two hours up to four doses a day.

NOTE: If Arnica fails, look at Ledum, Hypericum, and Ruta Graveolens.

BRYONIA (Whit. Bryonia):

Indications: Sprains, joint pain.

Symptoms: Joint pain is worse with movement; better lying still. Joint near injury is swollen with pain on least movement.

Dosage: 30X every two hours up to four doses a day.

CALENDULA OFFICINALIS (Calendula):

Indications: Abrasions, scratches, burns, superficial wounds, gnat bites, incised wounds, eye irritation. Calendula cream can be used as a lotion, for cleaning wounds and for 1st or 2nd degree burns. Creams are more often used on humans than animals due to presence of fur & feathers.

Symptoms: Skin irritation or injury requiring a soothing lotion or cleansing. Protects skin and promotes healing. Prevents infection. _Not to be used for puncture wounds_.

Dosage: As ointment or tincture, apply topically as needed. As lotion - 10 drops to 8 ounces water - to clean wounds. In tablet form, 6X, 2-3 times day as needed up to 4 days.

CANTHARIS (Spanish Fly):

Indications: Burns; Second degree burns; burns with blisters; Extreme sunburn. Also, acid or chemical burns.

Symptoms: Burning pain, heat, redness, or blistering.

Dosage: 30X every 15 minutes up to four **doses.** If no improvement use CAUSTICUM.

CAUSTICUMA (blending slaked lime and sulfate of potash)

Indications: Burns with extreme pain; blistering; Electrical burns

Symptoms: pain with restlessness; slow healing burns

Dosage: 30c to 200x or 200c

HEPAR SULPH (Calcium Sulphide):
   Indications: Wounds prone to infection - Promotes suppuration.
   Symptoms: Wounds that become swollen, red and tender (that become infected) with pricking pain.
   Dosage: 6X or 30X to promote suppuration every two hours up to hour doses per day.

HYPERICUM PERFORATUM (St. John's Wort):
   Indications: Nerve end injuries - crushed fingertips, tailbone injuries. Puncture, incised or lacerated wounds. It is also good for dental work, and recovery from any form of surgery.
   Symptoms: Pain along nerve root; Coccyx pain from injury; Pains shooting up the limb or pains shooting centrally in the limb. In spinal injury, pain moves up and down the spine. Symptoms worse from touch, cold, dampness, fog. Better from bending head back.
   Dosage: Use topically as lotion as needed, or internally - 30X every two hours up to four doses a day.

LEDUM PALUSTRE (Marsh Tea):
   Indications: **Puncture wounds from** sharp objects, bee or mosquito stings, animal bites and scratches, black eye from blow, long lasting bruises, and splinters. (See also SILICA)
   Symptoms: Injured area is cold and numb, relieved by cold. Worse at night, from warm applications, and from heat of bed. <u>Always give Ledum for puncture wounds</u>.
   Dosage: 30X every two hours for up to four doses a day. Note: It has been my experience that utilizing Ledum Palustre along with other good healing techniques (see section on Puncture Wounds) can eliminate the need for tetanus vaccinations. However, due to the serious nature of tetanus (lock jaw) if you have any doubt, get your animal a tetanus shot!

PHOSPHORUS (Phosphorus):
   Indications: **Hemorrhage. Nose bleeds. Give** prophylactically before surgery to prevent bleeding complications.
   Symptoms: Extensive bright red bleeding.
   Dosage: 30X every 10 minutes to every two hours depending on intensity of symptoms.

RHUS DIVERSILOBA (Poison Oak)
   Indications: California Poison-oak antidote to Rhus;

Holistic Emergency Care and Trauma Recovery for Animals / Section II

Symptoms: Violent skin symptoms, with frightful itching; much swelling of face, hands and genitals; skin very sensitive; eczema and erysipelas, great nervous weakness, tired from least effort; goes to sleep from sheer exhaustion.

Note: It is commonly thought that dogs and other companion animals can carry poison oak/ivy oils in the hair but not get infected. This is not entirely true. There have been cases of the oils getting onto the skin of an animal resulting in eruptions just like those that occur on a human. Key – wipe your animal's hair down thoroughly if you suspect that she has been romping through any poison oak or ivy.

Remember – Homeopathy is about Like healing Like – so homeopathic dilution of poison oak actually helps the body to heal poison oak. Truly ☺

RHUS TOXICODENDREN (Poison Ivy)

Indications: Sprains or strains of joints, muscles, tendons, or ligaments; torn ligaments and tendons; blistering, itching, burning and swelling of skin (poison oak/ivy). Also, hives and allergic reactions to medications.

Symptoms: Painful when beginning to move - better after continued motion, better from heat. Thirsty. Restless. Injured area is hot and swollen. Worse from cold, damp weather. Blistering red bumps with intense itching.

Dosage: For strains, use after Arnica. 30X every two hours up to four doses a day.

RUTA GRAVELOLENS (Rue):

Indications: Sprains close to the bone and periosteum (membrane that covers outer surface of most bones) or involving tendons or ligaments and not helped by Rhus Toxicodendren (Rhus Tox). Also, bruised bone, shin splints; Carpal Tunnel syndrome.

Symptoms: Sprains, whose symptoms are worse from cold, lying down, wet weather, being at rest.

Dosage: After Arnica initially. 30X every two hours up to four doses a day.

Note: I have had great success giving animals with chronic muscular-skeletal issues a combination of Rhus Tox and Ruta Gravelolens on a periodic basis, such as after extreme exercise that leaves them achy and sore.

SILICA (Silica):
Also known as Nature's Surgeon
Indications: Foreign objects broken off under skin; (i.e. tick heads, foxtails, thorns, splinters. Problems with vaccinations -- possibly impure. Know as *Nature's Surgeon*, due to its ability to promote expulsion of foreign bodies from tissues.
Symptoms: Swelling and possibly redness, indicating something is trapped under skin. (These symptoms can also indicate the onset of infection. So if unsure of the cause, treat for both).
Dosage: 30X every two hours up to four doses a day.

SYMPHYTUM (hedgerow plant — comfrey):
Indications: Wounds, fractures, non-healing fractures, nerve pain of knee.
Symptoms: Wounds and fractures that are slow to heal. Pricking pain of periosteum.
Dosage: 30X every three hours up to three doses per day.

THUJA OCCIDENTALIS (evergreen coniferous tree):
Indications: Negative symptoms after vaccines (referred to as vaccinosis)
Symptoms: Signs of vaccinosis can include large, hard lumps that remain days after the vaccination; warts, sarcoids, general fatigue or lack of health that comes on after vaccinations. This may also include the sudden appearance of allergies and skin eruptions following immunizations.

It has been my experience that many holistic veterinarians recommend that Thuja be given concurrently with any vaccination but it probably is better to handle each dog as an individual and give the remedy if any signs of vaccinosis occur as sometimes Silica or in the case of rabies vaccinations another protocol is desirable.
Dosage: 30X every three hours up to three doses per day.

(For more information on vaccinosis treatment see chapter in Section IV on Vaccinosis).

Holistic Emergency Care and Trauma Recovery for Animals / Section II

CHAPTER 9
INTRODUCTION TO FLOWER REMEDIES

What is a Flower Remedy or Essence?

Flower remedies are the energy of certain flowers captured in a water base/alcohol tincture. They are created through a process of decoction. Put the flowers (preferably buds or partially opened blossoms) into water held in a glass bowl, the combination is then placed in the sunlight for 2-3 hours to allow the warmth of the sun [for 2-3 hours] to cause the decoction to occur. Once this process is complete the flowers are removed and the liquid is combined with bourbon for preservation. Some essences are combined with glycerin instead for easier consumption by animals and children. However, their shelf life is shorter and thus they require refrigeration. Those preserved within bourbon (or vodka) have an unlimited shelf life when stored in moderate temperatures.

There are several major flower essences/remedy lines available on the market. In addition more and more cottage industries are creating essences with flowers and also crystals to create healing essences. The two main types of flower essences that I refer to in this book are Bach Flower Remedies and Flower Essence Society, which covers a combination of the English (Bach), and American flower essences (www.flowersociety.org). Also, an organization local to Mount Shasta where I live makes essence combinations specifically for animals, although they are great for people as well. This is the Anaflora line and can be found at www.anaflora.com.

The Theory Behind Flower Remedies

The emotions play a crucial role in the health of the physical body. Flower remedies directly address an animal or person's emotional state in order to help facilitate both psychological and physiological well-being. By balancing negative feelings and stress, flower remedies can effectively remove the emotional barriers to health and recovery.

"Behind all disease lie our fears, our anxieties, our greed, our likes and dislikes," wrote English physician Edward Bach in the early 1930's. Dr. Bach based his revolutionary belief upon his personal observations of patients whose physical illnesses seemed to be predisposed by negative psychological or emotional states such as fear, anxiety, insecurity, jealousy, shyness, poor self-image, anger, and resentment. Today, numerous studies conducted at major universities and medical centers have verified Dr. Bach's early conviction, revealing a definite connection between negative emotional states and a reduction of the body's natural resistance to disease.

Many around the world have continued the work of Dr. Bach. One of the foremost organizations is the Flower Essence Society: www.flowersociety.org, and as previously mentioned Anaflora for animals.

How Do Flower Remedies Work?

"Think of the patient, not the disease," was Dr. Bach's motto concerning health and the use of his flower remedies. The physical condition of the patient was not the primary focus in his opinion. "The main reason for the failure of modern medical science is that it is dealing with results and not causes," said Dr. Bach.

In contrast, flower remedies set out to affect physical problems of the body by addressing their emotional and psychological causes. As the emotions stabilize and general health (especially emotional outlook) improves, the illness begins to dissipate. This seems to be accomplished by the triggering of mechanisms that stimulate the internal healing processes.

During the past 20 years, these "mechanisms" that represent the link between the mind and the body have received intense scrutiny from the scientific community. This has led to the emergence of a new field called psychoneruoimmunology. Clinical studies have confirmed that the psychological and emotional state of a person influences a myriad of bodily processes, for better or worse, by stimulating or suppressing immune cell activity, adrenal gland hormones, and neurotransmitters.

"Unlike most pharmacological drugs, flower remedies have a subtle effect, gently resolving underlying emotional stress by triggering mechanisms which serve to mobilize the body's own internal healing processes," says Leslie Kaslof, researcher, writer, educator, and authority on Bach remedies. Most often, as the remedies take effect, one will not even have a sense of having had an emotional problem.

With people, only in retrospect, will she(one) be able to determine where attitudes have changed or resolved themselves. However in assisting an animal in healing through the use of flower essences, the human caregiver has the opportunity to notice the shift in behavior and overall health as a result.

Flower Essences Most Utilized For Emergency & Trauma Care

Bach Rescue Remedy: This is one of the most widely used Bach flower remedies. It provides great relief from any kind of stress, emotional, mental or physical, and can assist in keeping shock and other dangers from developing into life threatening situations. The components of Rescue Remedy are:

- Star of Bethlehem - For 'trauma' and numbness.
- Rock Rose - For terror and panic.
- Impatiens - For irritability and tension.
- Cherry Plum - For fear of losing control.
- Clematis - For the tendency to 'pass out', the sensation of being 'far away' that often precedes unconsciousness.

Love Lies Bleeding (Amaranthus flower):
Animal/Human: utilized for a wounded or deeply suffering animal that may not live. Enables the soul to encounter and transmute pain and suffering by lifting the soul above the personal experience to a higher conscious level of the experience.

Arnica (*Arnica Montana***):**

Animal/Human: used along with Rescue Remedy or Five Flower Remedy for shock, trauma, illness, injury or after surgery. Arnica helps to heal deep shock or trauma which may become locked into the body (cellular memory) and prevent full healing or recovery.

Holistic Emergency Care and Trauma Recovery for Animals / Section II

Borage (*Borago officialis*):

Animal/Human: used to assist in lifting the heart of a human or animal who may be disheartened, due to disease, old age or other factors. It can also be utilized for grief depression or despair to assist in overall upliftment and encouragement of the soul.

Chamomile (*Chamomillia recutita, etc*)**:**

Animal: for barking dogs or distressed animals, emotional upset that may be accompanied by vomiting or gastrointestinal upset.
Human: utilized for humans (especially children) who allow stress and tension to accumulate in their abdominal area causing stomach upset or vomiting.

Penstemon *(Penstamin family)*:

Animal/Human: utilized during illness or trauma. It provides inner strength during adverse circumstances such as loss of home, job or loved ones.

Red Clover *(Trifolium pratense)* :

Animal (esp cats): utilized in calming hysterical animals; i.e. taking to vets, or other traumatic situations (in the eyes of the animal).

Human: utilized for maintaining calm especially in situations of mass hysteria or panic such as natural disasters, war or economic crisis.

Self-Heal
(Prunella officiallas):

This essence (and herb in general) is one of the most diversely utilized for soul balance and overall healing. It amplifies the truth that the individual (animal or human) is her own healer and no amount of outside tools can assist without her willingness to heal from within and to recognize the wholeness of all life. In essence, Self Heal activates the animal or person's inner healer.

Animal/Human: Self-heal can be mixed with any other essences for maximizing their effectiveness. It is especially helpful for chronic or long-term illness or slow healing injuries where the animal/human has lost faith/belief in her ability to heal.

Holistic Emergency Care and Trauma Recovery for Animals / Section II

Snapdragon:

Animal: utilized for animals that bite out of aggression; especially horses with aggressive tendencies acting out through biting and sucking.

Human: can be utilized for humans who have very strong energy – especially in the lower chakras that when out of balance is acted out through sarcastic, aggressive or violent verbal expression.

Star of Bethlehem:

Part of both Rescue Remedy and Five Flower Remedy, this flower essence assists in the healing of current or past trauma.

Animal/Human: Utilized in the healing of anyone who has experience abuse of any kind. Also as part of the healing of traumatic injuries or other experiences, emotional or physical.

Walnut:

This essence is especially helpful for support during change. With animals this can include moving, new family members, going on road trips and more. I jokingly say that the entire planet should be on a Walnut essence I.V. during these changing times.

Animal: Helpful before and after moves to assist in the breaking of emotional attachments to old residences and adjustment to new environments. Walnut is also helpful for animals during birth.

Human: To assist in making choices and change based on one's own guidance; breaking the influence of family, friends or past experiences where they are not for the person's highest good.

Yarrow Environmental Formula:

Yarrow (Achillea millefolium) with Arnica (Arnica montana or Arnica mollis) and Echinacea (Echinacea purpurea) flower essences in a sea salt water base, combined with the fresh plant tinctures of these three plants. Originally developed due to practitioner requests after the Chernobyl nuclear plant disaster in 1986.

Animal/Human: Utilized for exposure to nuclear radiation or other forms of poisonous environmental or geopathic stress. Other examples include: video-display terminals, X-rays, radiation therapy, high-altitude radiation, detection devices at airport terminals and invasive electromagnetic fields.

Flower Remedy Blends

Flower essences like homeopathy and herbal products come in single form and in blends with a particular healing focus. There are several companies of which I am familiar that create such blends for animals in particular.

A few other companies also create blends, but often opt instead to have trained practitioners who can be hired to create personalized flower essence blends for a particular persona or animal. Two of the best known of these are:

- Flower Essence Society: http://www.flowersociety.org/Animals.html
- Bach Flower Remedies: http://www.bachflower.com/bach-animals/
- Anaflora Flower Remedies: http://www.anaflora.com
- Mystic Horse Flower Remedies and Vibrational Remedies: http://mystichorse.com/

CHAPTER 10
HERBAL MEDICINE HISTORY

People of various cultures have recognized herbs for their spirit and power for thousands for years. Wild and domesticated animals past and present also take advantage of the natural pharmacy available to them. As part of their utilization of herbs, indigenous people worldwide honor both the spirit and the physical being of these wonderful plants for their culinary and medicinal uses by including gratitude ceremonies in their harvesting.

Much of this wisdom had been put aside by modern cultures, exchanging herbs for human derivatives initially made from the plants and more recently made synthetically in laboratories creating a gap between drugs and the true healing medicine of nature.

The true power of the herbs is only really obtained when the entirety of the plant's medicinal parts (leaves, flowers, roots, etc.) are utilized, not just their active ingredient(s) as is the case with so many modern day pharmaceuticals. When used properly, herbs rarely have side effects, again in contrast to pharmaceutical drugs that often have side effects that may seem worse than the illness that they are supposed to be assisting.

Many different herbs can be combined together to form powerful healing teams. There are also many herbs that are system tonics and highly nutritional for strengthening and cleansing the body overall when eaten on a regular basis whether you are animal or human.

Also in the wild it is found that herbs that cause a challenge of some kind and herbs that heal that same challenge often grow close by one another. An example of this is the stinging effects of Nettles can be neutralized by rubbing broad leaf plantain leaves on the skin where the stinging symptoms are acting out, and they often grow in the same ecological niche as one another. This relationship of effect and healing is also demonstrative of what is referred to as part of the *Doctrine of Signatures*.[5]

It is this power and wisdom that so many people desire to reconnect with, and when used with love and respect this power can be a big piece of bringing people once again into harmony with themselves and the wonderful nature realms of Earth that support us all.

---

[5] The doctrine of signatures, dating from the time of Dioscurides and Galen, states that herbs that resemble various parts of the body can be used by herbalists to treat ailments of that part of the body. A theological justification for this, as stated by botanists like William Coles, was that God is showing humans what plants are useful for… - Wikipedia

Holistic Emergency Care and Trauma Recovery for Animals / Section II

CHAPTER 11
BASIC HERB TERMINOLOGY

Signatures of Plants –
A Sampling of the Doctrine of Signatures

The physical appearance and growing environment of a plant often denotes its nutritive or healing properties. This is referred to as the plant signature or the Doctrine of Signatures. Here is a sampling of various types of signatures to give you an idea of what to look for in the plants that grow in your garden and local environments:

Flower Color and Shape

- <u>Blue / purple</u> – sedative or calming herbs; also good blood purifiers when used in tonics. Examples include: blue valerian, purple passion flower, lavender

- <u>Red</u> – blood purifiers or alteratives (see section entitled *The Properties of Plants* below); also often antibiotic in nature. Examples include: Echinacea, Red Clover and beets.

- <u>Yellow</u> – generally utilized for liver, gallbladder, urinary tract problems and detoxification and infection fighting tonics. Examples: chamomile, eyebright, dandelion.

Holistic Emergency Care and Trauma Recovery for Animals / Section II

Growing Conditions in the Wild

With all life forms, the environment in which we live and grow dictates to a degree who we become. Thus the environment of plants contributes to their overall properties and qualities.

- Plants that grow close to water are usually diuretic in nature. Examples include: stinging nettle and broad leafed plantain

- Plants growing in gravel based soil generally are good for assisting with illnesses that cause stones or gravel in the body. They cleanse the alimentary and bronchial systems of harmful accumulations and can assist in dissolving or preventing kidney stones / gallstones. Examples: parsley, peppergrass, shepherd's purse, sassafras and mullein.

- Herbs growing in swampy or wet ground are good for assisting with the balancing of excessive mucous excretions in the respiratory or other body systems. Examples: Willow, Verbena, Boneset, Elder

Body, Leaf or Root Structure

Medicinal herbs may display a body, leaf, flower or root structure that provides hints as to its medicinal powers. Having a working knowledge of anatomy – human or mammal – can be of great assistance in observing these natural hints.

Examples include:
- Skullcap, whose flower is the shape of the cap of a skull
- Horehound, whose leaf shape is similar to that of a lung
- Juniper Berries, shaped like kidney stones
- Hypericum perforatum (St. John's Wort) stem configuration resembles the nervous system

Plant Textures

- Soft textures indicate an aid for treating inflamed or swollen areas. They are also good for "wet" colds and respiratory ailments. (*Emollient herbs*) Examples include: horehound, mullein, hollyhocks

- Smooth, silky textures can indicate assistance in beautifying the skin or assisting the mucous membrane of the body. Examples: aloe vera family; mullein

- **Rigid leaves** suggest the plant is high in silica and therefore helpful to bones and teeth. Examples: horsetail

CHAPTER 12
PRIMARY PROPERTIES OF HERBS

*The properties of a plant is vital to knowing its gifts
for healing – its gifts to life...*

A good example of holistic healing is the benefit of using an entire plant (as opposed to just parts like in most pharmaceutical drugs). Whole plants offer a variety of healing and healthful properties that when matched with symptoms being treated can often deal with the entire scope of a disease at one time, quickly and with minimum dosage. All plants have a multitude of chemical constituents that may have an effect on one's body. The physiological effects or "properties" are descriptions that these chemical constituents lend themselves to.

As stated in the overview, originally pharmaceutical drugs were created from plants and other naturally occurring elements. However in most cases, pharmaceutical drugs were created using only the active ingredients of a plant leaving behind the elements within the plants that provide buffering and balance to the healing properties. Using just the active ingredients within a plant is one of the main reasons for side effects with such drugs.

There are over 36 categories that define herbal properties - what they do and how they do it. They are listed below with examples of each, and are also listed in the chapter on <u>Herbs Used in Emergencies, Acute Care and Trauma Recovery</u>. For clarity I have underlined those that are most likely to be helpful with animals:

Alteratives: Blood purifiers; agents that gradually and favorably alter the condition of the body. Examples include: red clover, echinacea, sarsaparilla, cascara sagrada, and dandelion root. The one that is chosen to utilize has to do with the other properties contained in the herb.

Analgesics: Herbs that are taken to relieve pain while upholding consciousness. Some analgesics are also antispasmodics (see definition). Examples include: cramp bark, dong quai, cloves, kava kava, lobelia catnip, chamomile, wild yam, skullcap and valerian root.

Antibiotics: Inhibit the growth of or destroy bacteria, viruses or amoebas. These natural antibiotics often have direct killing effects while simultaneously bolstering the immune system response. Extensive use of antibiotics (herbal and other types) will destroy the beneficial bacteria of the intestinal and GI tracks. Thus it is suggested to augment the diet with fresh yogurt, miso or tamari to rebuild this natural defense system. Examples of herbal antibiotics include: chaparral, echinacea, garlic, goldenseal, myrrh, juniper berries, thyme, and yarrow.

Anticatarrhals: Herbs that counteract or eliminate the formation of mucous in the body. It is often beneficial for these herbs be utilized in conjunction with those that aid in the elimination of mucous through sweat (diaphoretics), urine (diuretics) or feces (laxatives). Examples of anticatarrhals include black pepper, cayenne, ginger, sage, cinnamon, anise, gota kola, mullein, comfrey, wild cherry bark and yerba santa.

Note regarding diaphoretics: these are not useful for animals that do not sweat, such as dogs, cats and birds.

Antipyretics: Herbs that are cooling in nature and are used to prevent or reduce fevers. This cooling may also apply to the neutralization of harmful acids in the body (excess heat) as well as reducing physical body temperature. Examples include alfalfa, boneset, basil, gotu kola, skullcap, chickweed, aloe vera and seaweeds.

Antiseptics: Substances that can be applied to skin to deter the growth of bacteria. Astringents are included in this category. Examples include: witch hazel, goldenseal, calendula, chaparral, and myrrh and the oils of garlic, thyme, pine, juniper berries and sage.

Antispasmodics: These prevent or relax muscle spasms both internally and externally. They may be applied externally (poultices) or taken internally. They can be included in most herbal formulas to encourage the body to relax and utilize its full energy for healing. Lobelia is one of the most important antispasmodics. Others include dong quai, black cohosh, blue cohosh, skullcap, valerian, kava-kava, raspberry leaves and rue.

Astringents: Astringents are nature's cleansers and are antibiotic in nature. They have a binding or constricting effect and are commonly utilized to check hemorrhages. They include: witch hazel, bayberry bark, white oak bark, yellow dock, calendula, myrrh, horsetail, juniper berries, prince's pine, and stoneroot.

Carminatives: Assist in the relief of gas and griping in the GI tract. Examples include: anise, caraway, fennel, cumin, dill, ginger, peppermint and calamus.

Note: Gas in dogs and cats is more often than not due to poor diet.

Cholagogues: Herbs used to encourage the flow and discharge of bile into the small intestine. Such herbs are also laxative in nature since bile stimulates elimination. Examples include aloe vera, barberry, Oregon grape root, culver's root, mandrake, goldenseal, wild yam and licorice root.

Demulcents: Soothing substances, usually mucilage used internally or externally to protect damaged or inflamed tissue. Such herbs are often used in conjunction with diuretics to protect the kidney and urinary tract. Examples include marshmallow, comfrey, Irish moss, slippery elm, chickweed, licorice, psyllium, flax, chia seeds, aloe vera, burdock and fenugreek.

Diuretics: Increase the output of urine, assisting in the removal of harmful & toxic substances from the body. Common members include: shepard's purse, watercress (water nasturtium), nettle, some sage, carrot, comfrey, heartsease, dandelion, and lemon.

Emollients – herbs that are softening, soothing and protectiv'e to the skin or mucus membrane. Examples include: olive, almond, apricot kernel, sesame, linseed, flaxseed and wheat germ oils; and herbs such as marshmallow, slippery elm, comfrey root and chickweed.

Expectorants: Expectorants cause the expulsion of mucous and the breakup of congestion in the lungs. Examples include: horehound, slippery elm, comfrey, marshmallow, Irish moss, hollyhock (in the mallow family) and nettle.

Hemostatic – substances that stop hemorrhaging. Hemostatic herbs can be of great assistance for internal bleeding as well as external and include astringents and herbs that assist in the coagulation of blood. Examples include: yarrow, horsetail, bayberry, blackberry, cayenne, cranes bill, mullein, goldenseal, white oak bark, and witch hazel.

Nervines: These relieve nervous irritation caused by strain and tension. These herbs have become rather popular herbs among humans in this day and age of hustle and transition and can also be helpful to animals who are feeling the effects of their human counterpart's stressful lives. Some of the more common ones include: heartsease (pansy or viola), chamomile, rosemary, skullcap, willow, yarrow, lavender and motherwort. Also see Tonics (below).

Parasiticides: Destroy parasites in the digestive track or on the skin. Examples include: chaparral, garlic, tee tree, rue, thyme oil and cinnamon oil.

Note: Tea Tree is very strong and must only be used in very small amounts for animals and not at all for cats or birds

Sedatives: Herbs that quiet the nervous system with a strong action (more so than nervines). Examples include: valerian root, chamomile, skullcap, catnip, passionflower and wood betony.

Note: Herbal sedatives can be helpful especially during healing directly after surgery or trauma that requires a great amount of rest for healing. Best to use decoction or diluted tinctures.

Stimulants: Increase stimulus to the system (nervous, lymphatic, circulatory, etc.) energizing the body, driving the circulation and breaking up obstructions. Some members include: all members of the mint family, calendula, parsley, red clover, yarrow (white), comfrey, nettle, valerian, sage (salvias not sagebrush), and ginger.

Reminder: The mint family can neutralize homeopathic remedies when taken in the same duration of time.

Tonics: Benefit the entire body by strengthening the organs that are affected by the action of the digestive system. Tonics are generally done over a period of time to allow time for them to work. These include: nasturtium, dandelion, comfrey, rosemary, parsley, goldenseal, burdock, lavender, mints, red clover, yarrow, raspberry, and violet.

Vulneraries: Herbs that encourage healing of wounds through promoting of cell growth and repair. Examples include: **comfrey**, **calendula**, aloe vera, cayenne, fenugreek, garlic, rosemary, thyme, marshmallow, **yarrow** and slippery elm.

Holistic Emergency Care and Trauma Recovery for Animals / Section II

CHAPTER 13
HERBS COMMONLY UTILIZED FOR EMERGENCIES, ACUTE CARE AND TRAUMA RECOVERY

There are a large variety of herbs that can be utilized for emergency and acute care. The ones you choose may have more to do with where you live and what is available than anything else. One of the rules of thumb that I learned from a wise teacher long ago was to use herbs that grow close to where you are living or traveling as they generally contain properties more in alignment with your body's requirements. For the most part, the ones that I have listed below are commonly found in North America. If you live in other parts of the world you would do well to research the local flora, and cross-reference that information with the properties of local herbs.

If you are purchasing herbs of choice to create your own apothecary, then you can choose from the great array available through on-line herb stores that either you or your local herb store can access. If you have a garden you may choose to grow those herbs that you find a resonance to, for one reason or another. This is also true of wild crafting, which is the art of gathering your own herbs from the wild. You will most likely be drawn to gather some herbs over others. I suggest that you have on hand an apothecary of 12-20 herbs to fill the needs of your family and yourself.

As we discussed in Signatures of Plants earlier in this section, the environment in which herbs grow directly affects their properties and medicinal components, which in turn influences our bodies when we ingest them. Thus, by utilizing herbs that grow in your own climate and geographical environment, you are more likely to have a greater success rate with what you are attempting to heal and bring back into balance and wellness.

If you are planning to do wild crafting, or are going into the back country and wish to be able to recognize the medicinal plants available, then I highly recommend you spend time learning the flora through books, the Internet, and the herbalists/botanists in your area before venturing to collect in the wild. It is necessary to have references and knowledge that will assist you in discerning how to identify herbs and plants correctly. There are many wonderful references to assist you in this self-education, some of which are listed under Appendix C - References at the back of the book, as well as under Resources on our website: www.holisticemergencycare.com

I also encourage you to spend time communing with the plant life that lives in your area, both in the wild and in your town/city. Many of the most powerful herbs will be found growing in the local watershed, vacant lots, playgrounds, and your own yard. This is a great way to get practice at identifying various herbs and how their appearance varies from place to place. Just be certain that if you are going to collect any of these, you know if they have been sprayed with pesticides.

> Many, if not all, of these herbs may grow naturally in your garden, neighborhood or surrounding parks and open spaces when left undisturbed by people who mistake them for weeds.

The following herbs are a combination of those used for nutritive, acute, and emergency functions:

Alfalfa (Medicago sativa)

Part used – above ground portions
Energy and Flavors – sweet, neutral to cool energy
Properties – nutritive tonic, restorative (Yin) tonic, alterative, hemostatic, diuretic
Dosage – one cup decoction /3t daily; 2 capsules/day
Used for – wasting, improving digestion and assimilation, weight gain, increase in strength and vitality, lowering fevers, and regulating the bowels.

Aloe Vera (Aloe Vera)

Part used – mucilaginous gel found inside the leaves and the dried powder of the leaf
Energy and Flavors – cold, bitter
Properties – the gel is a vulnerary, "Yin tonic" and the dried leaf is a laxative
Dosage - gel, topical, or two tablespoons three times daily in juice; powder, ½ to 1 teaspoon
Used for – burns, injuries, skin tonic, laxative, female hormone balancing

Arnica (Arnica montana)

Part used – flower heads
Energy and Flavors – poisonous, warm energy
Properties – stimulant, analgesic
Dosage – <u>External Use Only</u> in herb form: Use freely as an oil, liniment, or poultice **(Internally in homeopathic form)**
Used for – bruises, painful injuries, shock

Holistic Emergency Care and Trauma Recovery for Animals / Section II

Astragalus *(Astragulus membraneceus)*

Part used – root
Properties – stimulates cells and gland activity
Dosage – 1-2 tsp. of root 3xday
Used for – restores red blood cells, stimulates natural production of interferon, good for the immuno-compromised.

Burdock *(Arctium lappa)*

Part used – root, seeds, leaves
Energy and Flavors – bitter, slightly sweet, cool
Properties – Alterative, diuretic, diaphoretic, nutritive.
Dosage – grated fresh in food according to animal's weight of the crushed seeds make an decoction; and of the root; a strong decoction or tincture is preferred
Used for – Skin diseases, blood purification, urinary problems – overall blood tonic.

Calendula *(Calendula officinalis)*

Part used – flower heads
Energy and Flavors – spicy, bitter, neutral
Properties – vulnerary, diaphoretic, astringent
Dosage – decoction (1 tsp / cup); tincture 10-30 drops; poultice; salves.
Used for – bruises and injuries, burns (good with aloe vera), earaches, shingles, eruptive skin diseases.

Holistic Emergency Care and Trauma Recovery for Animals / Section II

Chamomile (*Chamomilla recutita*)

Part used – flower heads
Energy and Flavors – bitter, spicy, aromatic, neutral.
Properties – calmative, nervine, antispasmodic, diaphoretic
Dosage – standard decoction as desired; tincture 10-30 drops; externally in baths, salves, creams, etc.
Used for – nervousness and irritability, digestive disorders, teething and irritability, menstrual cramps, back pains, etc.

Chaparral (*Larrea tridentata*)

Part used – leaves
Energy and Flavors – bitter, acrid, slightly salty, cool
Properties – antibacterial, antiseptic, expectorant, diuretic.
Dosage – ½ oz. infused in a pint of boiling water, 3xday
Used for – infection prevention or healing in salves, liniments or tonics; arthritis and rheumatic pains, colds and flus, diarrhea, urinary tract infections.

Chickweed (Starweed) (*Stellaria media*)

Part used – aerial portion
Energy and Flavors – sweet, mildly bitter, cool
Properties – diuretic, alterative, mild astringent
Dosage – standard decoction using 1 ounce of dried, 2 ounce fresh herb 1cup 3x day;
Used for – externally: skin irritation, itch and rashes; internally: weight loss, as a potherb, demulcent for sore throat and lungs.

Comfrey or Knitbone (*Symphytum officinale*)

Part used – leaf and root
Energy and Flavors – bitter, sweet, cool energy
Properties – tonic, demulcent, expectorant, vulnerary, astringent
Dosage – standard decoction, or one teaspoon of tincture 3 times/day; also used externally in poultices, salves, etc.
Used for – promoting healing, broken bones, lungs, diarrhea, hemorrhage and bleeding.

Dandelion *Taraxacum officinale*

Part used – whole plant
Energy and Flavors – leaves are cool and bitter, root is bitter, sweet and cool
Properties – alterative, diuretic, tonic,
Dosage: standard decoction; fresh, 10-30 drops tincture, powder in capsules 2x/day
Used for – liver problems, urinary tract infections, skin eruptions, stomach pains, breast cancer, beverage

Echinacea (*Echinacea angustifolia* and other species)

Part used – root, leaves
Energy and Flavors – bitter, pungent, cool
Properties – anti-inflammatory, alterative, antimicrobial
Dosage – of the tea, ½ cup; liquid extract, 10-30 drops; for chronic conditions, 3x day
Used for – all inflammatory conditions; internally over short term to stimulate the immune system

Goldenseal *Hydrastis canadensis)*

Part used – rhizome and root
Energy and Flavors – bitter, cool
Properties – alterative, antihistamine, anti-inflammatory, bitter tonic, hemostatic, astringent
Dosage – 1 teaspoon / 5-30 drops of the tincture
Used for – gastritis, colitis, ulcers, general tonic for female reproductive tract, skin disorders, including allergies. Generally used in the onset of an issue for the short term to boast immune system.

Horehound (*Marrubium vulgare*)

Part used – leaves, flowers
Energy and Flavors – bitter
Properties – expectorant
Dosage – decoction; cough drops
Used for – respiratory support
Note: best combined with raw honey and other herbs such as mullein to sooth its bite

Horsetail (*Equisetum arvense*)

Part used – stem
Properties – silica based;
Dosage - decoction, ½ ounce of the dried herb added to 1 pint of cold water, soak for 2 hours; boil, simmer 20 min., cool. 2 fluid ounce 3 or 4x day
Used for – tonic for skin, nails, hair; stops bleeding inward or outward, as well as inward ulcers.

Holistic Emergency Care and Trauma Recovery for Animals / Section II

Hyssop *(Hyssopus officinalis)*

Part used – leaves, flowers
Energy and Flavors – bitter
Properties – expectorant
Dosage - decoction; cough surly
Used for – respiratory support, digestion and urinary track tonic

Lavender *(Lavandula angustifolia, L. officinalis)*

Part used – flowers
Energy and Flavors – spicy, fragrant, mildly bitter, cool
Properties – aromatic, carminative, antispasmodic, antidepressant
Dosage – standard decoction; 10/30 drops of tincture; externally in baths, creams, salves, etc.
Used for – calming, balancing, antidepressant, releasing tension, enjoyment

Marsh mallow *(Althea officinalis)*

Part used – leaves, flowers and root
Energy and Flavors –cool energy, sweetish, bland taste
Properties – demulcent, nutritive, diuretic, mild laxative
Dosage – 2 ounce covered, steeped in a qt. of hot water; or as a poultice to heal wounds, sores, burns, and bruises
Used for – tonic to soothe mucous membranes of body and skin; inflammations, irritations, ulcers and sores. Combine with other herbs to aid in healing wounds other herbs in poultice or salve form.

Milk Thistle *(Silybum marianum, Carduus marianus)*

Part used – seeds and aerial portions
Energy and Flavors – bitter, sweet, cool energy
Properties – bitter tonic, antidepressant
Dosage – 420 mg/day; best used fall through spring
Used for – protects and regenerates liver, effective against liver cirrhosis, hepatitis A,B

Mullein (*Verbascum thapsus*)

Part used – leaves, flowers
Energy and Flavors –cool energy, sweetish, bland taste
Properties – demulcent, nutritive
Dosage – Standard Decoction for internal or external use; also great in salves
Used for – tonic to soothe mucous membranes within body and skin; inflammations, irritations, ulcers and sores, urinary and gall stones. Also helpful in healing wounds especially combined with such herbs as yarrow.

Nettles (Stinging Nettles) *(Urica urens and other species)*

Part used – Leaves
Energy and Flavors – Bland, slightly bitter, cool
Properties – diuretic, antihistamine, tonic, hemostatic, expectorant, nutritive
Dosage – Standard Decoction
Used for – allergy relief, chronic and acute urinary complaints, cystitis, urinary stones; additional uses include taking for hemorrhoids and chronic arthritis;

and rheumatic problems.

Pau d' Arco *(Tabebuia heptaphylla, T. impetiginosa and other species)*

Part used – inner bark of the Tabebuia tree
Energy and Flavors – cool energy, bitter flavor
Properties – antifungal, antidiabetic, digestive, antibacterial, antitumor
Dosage – 1 cup tea, 3 to 4x day for acute conditions; ½ cup 3 to 4x day for chronic conditions
Used for – slowing and inhibiting the growth of cancers and tumors; for skin diseases; lymphatic system stimulant and tonic.

Plantain (Narrow leaf)
(Plantago species)

Part used – leaves and seeds
Energy and Flavors – bland, somewhat bitter, cool
Properties – diuretic, alterative, anti-inflammatory
Dosage – standard decoction, poultice, salves
Used for – urinary tract infections, hepatitis, stings, bites and wounds

Purslane *(Portulaca)*

Part used – whole plant
Energy and Flavors – Bitter but tasty, nutritive
Properties – nutritive, antioxidant, omega-3 fatty acids, beta carotene
Dosage – fresh as desired
Used for – culinary, medicinal; for good health. Highly nutritive

Red Clover *(Trifolium pratense)*

Part used – blossoms
Energy and Flavors – sweet, salty, cool
Properties – anti-tumor, alterative, antispasmodic, expectorant
Dosage – standard decoction; 10-30 drops of the tincture
Used for – cancer and tumors, skin diseases, fevers, colds, coughs

Rosemary *(Rosmarinus officinalis)*

Part used – leaves
Energy and Flavors – spicy, cool
Properties – anti-inflammatory, tonic, nervine, diaphoretic, astringent, antiseptic
Dosage – 1 teaspoon as decoction (1 cup)
Used for – headaches, indigestion, colds, inflammation of the joints, scalp and hair growth and stimulation; also in decoction spray for flea and bug repellent.

Saint John's Wort *(Hypericum perforatum)*

Part used –herb
Energy and Flavors – cool, bitter
Properties – sedative, anti-inflammatory, astringent, antidepressant
Dosage – standard decoction or 10-30 drops of the tincture
Used for –nerve pains, neuralgia, depression

Holistic Emergency Care and Trauma Recovery for Animals / Section II

Self Heal *(Prunella officiallas)*

Part used – flower & leaves
Energy and Flavors –
Properties – Supports the body's inner healer to activate and accept other healing support
Dosage – As needed in tincture or decoction form preferably but can also be eatten directly.
Used for – Activating the body's inner healer to receive healing assistance from within and outer sources as well.

Skullcap *(Scutellaria lateriflora and other species)*

Part used – aerial portions: It consists of stem, leaves, flowers and fruit and seeds.
Energy and Flavors – bitter, cool
Properties – sedative, nervine, antispasmodic
Dosage – standard decoction; 10-30 drops of tincture
Used for – nervousness, insomnia, epilepsy/seizures

Slippery elm (Red elm) (Ulmus rubra; Ulmus fulva)

Part used – inner bark
Energy and Flavors – sweet, neutral
Properties – nutritive demulcent, yin tonic, expectorant, emollient, mild astringent and vulnerary
Dosage - 9-30 grams of the cut and sifted bark; poultice component to assist in healing and holding other herbs together
Used for – sore throat, nutritive anti-nauseous food, gastrointestinal ulcers, dryness of the respiratory tract,

externally to heal ulcers, sores and wounds.

Turmeric (Curcuma longa)

Part used – Rhizome
Energy and Flavors – Spicy, bitter, warm
Properties – Alterative, analgesic, astringent, antiseptic, blood thinner
Dosage – Internal Use: Never use before surgeries or if severe bleeding is present either internally or externally.
Used for – Internally for hepatitis, digestion and assimilation, externally for bruises and injuries

Valerian root (Valeriana officinalis and other species)

Part used – rhizome
Energy and Flavors – spicy, bitter, warm
Properties – sedative, hypnotic, nervine **??**, antispasmodic, carminative, stimulant
Dosage – standard decoction; 10 drops to 1 tsp tincture; externally in salve or oil
Used for – insomnia, stress and nervousness, pain relief

Violet (Sweet Violet) (Violet odorata)

Part used – leaves and flowers, either dried or fresh
Energy and Flavors – Sweet, mild but pleasantly bitterish, cool
Properties – Demulcent, expectorant, alterative, antipyretic, antiseptic, vulnerary, antispasmodic
Dosage – Standard decoction; fresh in food
Used for – Dry coughs and sore throats, softening of hard cancerous masses, as a potherb and in food.

Holistic Emergency Care and Trauma Recovery
for Animals / Section II

Willow (*Salix alba*)

Part used – bark
Energy and Flavors – bitter, cold
Systems Affected – liver, kidneys and heart
Properties – Analgesic, alterative, astringent,
Dosage – Dependent upon animal size: One – three teaspoons of the bark soaked in cold water for two to five hours. **Used for** – Willow bark is the herbal component of aspirin and can be used as a substitute with less side effects. This is very helpful with animals as it is best not to give them aspirin overall.

Witch hazel (*Hamamelis virginiana*)

Part used – mainly the bark, secondarily the leaves and twigs
Energy and Flavors – bitter, astringent, neutral
Properties – astringent, hemostatic, anti-inflammatory
Dosage – bark internally; leaves and twigs, which contain more tannins, are used externally
Used for – diarrhea, dysentery, hemorrhages, excessive mucous discharge, externally as on wounds, inflammations, etc.

Yarrow (*Achilles millefolium*)

Part used – whole herb
Energy and Flavors – warm bitter, spicy
Properties – diaphoretic, anti-inflammatory, antipyretic, carminative, hemostatic, astringent, antispasmodic, tonic
Dosage – standard décoction; poultice/direct application; salve, etc.
Used for – colds, flues and fevers, painful or suppressed menses, to stop bleeding, hemorrhoids, blood

purification.

Holistic Emergency Care and Trauma Recovery
for Animals / Section II

CHAPTER 14
ENERGY HEALING TECHNIQUES

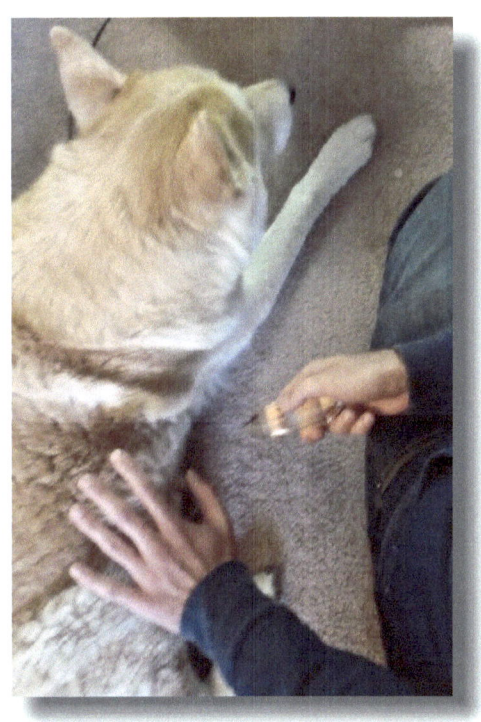

The Direct Linkup: …. If you are in an emergency situation and have nothing but your own self to assist those who are injured or traumatized having a knowledge of energy healing techniques can facilitate a direct link up with the Divine/Mother/Father/God that otherwise would not be available to you.

For those who are open to and understand such techniques there are many energy healing modalities that can also be of great assistance at such times and are also a blessing acute illness, trauma recovery and everything in between. These tools do not require anything except your knowledge of using them and your faith in their ability to facilitate healing.

A great blessing of energy healing techniques is that they can be used alone or in partnership with other holistic and even allopathic modes of healing. And in some cases they will facilitate healing when nothing else will.

For example, several years ago a friend came to me with her dog whose hip was dislocated. She had been to the veterinarian and was told that surgery would be required to correct the issue. My friend (Jill) was an advocate of alternative healing and told the veterinarian that she was going to go a different route, and then she brought Casey to me. Utilizing my knowledge as a Theta Healing practitioner I was able to connect with God/Goddess and facilitate the reintegration of Casey's hip within a few minutes time. Casey got up and then walked, gingerly at first, and off he and Jill went.

My understanding is that this was such an easy and successful occurrence in part because we all had such great faith in the ability of this type of healing to occur. It was just one example of how we as holistic or allopathic practitioners are truly facilitators for the divine inner healer within the animal, human, or any other life form to correct the imbalance.

Direct and Easy

It's as complicated as you need it, or as simple as you can stand it – Mary Burmeister

Although I encourage everyone to receive training in energy healing techniques such as those listed below, energy healing can be facilitated through anyone trained or otherwise. What is important is for people to understand the basic concepts of energy healing.

A primary component is unconditional love (LOVE). Other activities are contained in activities of Divine Light (golden sun) and what is referred to as the Sacred Fire in many spiritual circles. A simple explanation of the Sacred Fire is an etheric rainbow; each color band having a specific activity. This is similar to color therapy in the physical realm. Yet the frequency of the Sacred Fire rainbow is higher and cannot be seen unless you are clairvoyant.

Animals can see (generally in grayscale) and feel the energies being transmitted in energy healing due to their heightened awareness of other realms. These include:

Emerald Green	**Healing**
Violet / Blue Violet	**Purification**
Pink	**Unconditional Love (LOVE)**
Light Blue	**Purity and Peace**
Cobalt Blue	**Protection**
Yellow	**You and Illumination**
Dark Blue	**Communication**
White	**All Rays Combined**

So how do you bring forth energetic healing without formal training such as Theta Healing, Reiki or Jin Shin Jyutsu®? The key is to keep it simple and remember you are just the instrument. Example:

1. Close your eyes *(unless you are in motion)*

2. Breathe and focus into your heart. Then while maintaining your heart connection,

3. Focus upward to your pineal gland and the area above it (this includes the crown chakra) seeing the channel between the heart and crown open and filled with white light.

4. Say silently or out loud "God/Goddess (Creator or Mother/Father/God) make me an instrument of your peace, healing and LOVE to assist this animal(s) (or whomever / whatever is in need)

5. See and feel the LOVE, Light and Sacred Fire (rainbow) come into you, your immediate surroundings and all that you are assisting be they human, animal, plant element (water, earth, etc.) and so on.

6. Remember to breathe, and relax while doing this, following your intuitive guidance of what else to do one step at a time. If need be ask for greater clarity of action to come to you in a way that you will understand.

7. Call for a healing of the highest good. "Beloved God/Goddess… I call forth healing assistance for the highest good of all effected now and ongoing as necessary"

    It is important to understand that this assistance may come in the restoration of the body(s) of those you are helping or it may lead to the graceful transition if the animal (or person) is complete with her current body experience. Your role when assisting is to be the "instrument" or facilitator and to trust in the outcome.

8. Always complete your call with "I Thank you", "So Be It! It is so done." Saying these statements confirm to the Universe that you know your call has been heard and is being responded to.

Direct energy healing can be combined with the administering of other assistance both general first aid and holistic. But if you do not have any physical tools then make the calls for divine assistance as exemplified above and trust that great assistance can be given in this way.

Holistic Emergency Care and Trauma Recovery for Animals / Section II

More specific details are given in Sections III and IV of this book and on our website http://holisticemergencycare.com/emergency-training-scenarios/

If you are a medical intuitive you may be guided to see within the body of the one your are assisting to see the imbalance (injury) being corrected. This is the way with Theta Healing (see below) and other modalities. Again, ask to be the instrument for healing and peace on for the highest good.

Practice :
- Non-attachment
- Mindfulness
- Harmlessness
- Peace
- Gratitude
- Humility

Never force your assistance on anyone or anything. Always ask permission. If the animal or human are unconscious then permission is considered given, however if the animal/human are awake and either do not give you permission or in the case of an animal you cannot understand him, then just intend an unconditional love healing to occur. Again state "Dear Mother/Father/God or Jesus/Mary or Creator … Make me your instrument of healing through unconditional love (LOVE)".

Suggested Energy Healing Modalities

A few examples of these methods include Reiki, Theta Healing, Jin Shin Jyutsu, and MAP (Medical Assistance Program). I am only mentioning these methods briefly here as each have their own training programs or books which provide those interested the details and skills required.

Reiki: The word Reiki is made of two Japanese words - Rei which means "God's Wisdom or the Higher Power" and Ki which is "life force energy". So Reiki is actually "spiritually guided life force energy."

Holistic Emergency Care and Trauma Recovery for Animals / Section II

As stated on the International Reiki Training website (http://www.reiki.org/faq/WhatIsReiki.html) Reiki is a Japanese technique for stress reduction and relaxation that also promotes healing. It is administered by "laying on hands" and is based on the idea that an unseen "life force energy" flows through us and is what causes us to be alive. If one's "life force energy" is low, then we are more likely to get sick or feel stress, and if it is high, we are more capable of being happy and healthy.

I will add here that low life force energy is often present when a severe injury, illness or other trauma has occurred. Thus the use of Reiki and other energy techniques that release impediment to the life force and open channels for it to be restored in the body is of great benefit.

Theta Healing: Theta Healing fits into the mind/body therapies as a complementary or alternative health modality. It is both therapeutic and self-help and aims to assist with physical, spiritual and emotional well-being. Theta Healing is not a replacement for conventional medical treatment, but rather is supplementary to it.

Using a meditational process that accesses the "theta' brainwave, we pray for our clients to receive unconditional love to assist in the healing changes they desire. Another way of expressing this is that we ask God, The Energy That Moves in All Things, Source or The Creator for the healing to take place.

Despite Theta Healing being an intangible spiritual healing process it could best be described as "focused thought and prayer bringing healing and transformation through unconditional love". The processes of Theta Healing are not specific to any age, sex, race, color or creed or religion. Anyone with a pure belief in God or the Creative Force can access and use the branches of the Theta Healing tree." Source founder Vianna Stibal, http://www.thetahealing.com/about-thetahealing.html

Animals of course have a pure belief in God or the Creative Force as it is intrinsic in their nature and unswayed by the vast religious teaching that humans are subject to. This enables animals to receive and utilize the unconditional love and divine intelligence that is brought forth through Theta Healing without question.

Holistic Emergency Care and Trauma Recovery for Animals / Section II

Jin Shin Jyutsu®: This is a system of Japanese acupressure that has gained world-wide recognition. It is designed to have some very simple and easy to use Self-Help techniques that anyone can learn and use as well as more complex amd in-depth approaches for those who choose advanced training.

Japanese-American Mary Iino Burmeister brought this ancient, universal healing art of gentle touch acupressure out of obscurity and into the Western world in 1950. Since then it has gained world-wide recognition and a growing numbers of devoted practitioners. The art of Jin Shin Jyutsu can be quite complex or amazingly simple. It is also adapted for use with animals. You may find the book, Jin Shin Jyutsu for Your Animal Companion by Adele Leas, very helpful. For information go to link: http://amzn.to/1tAS4VU

Healing activist and author Barbara J. Semple has written a book Instant Healing - Accessing Creative Intelligence for Healing Body and Soul ... and a deck of Heal Now cards introducing Healing Touch Quick Steps. These tools are designed to introduce the self-help methods based on Jin Shin Jyutsu® principles in a simple and straightforward manner that anyone can use immediately. You can also access the multimedia Healing Touch Quick Steps HOME GUIDE - 42 Powerful Things You Can Do Instantly to Bring Your Body into Harmony. For more information go to www.instanthealingzone.com

MAP (Medical Assistance Program of the Great White Brotherhood): This program was given to Machaelle Small Wright who published it in book form in 1990. The following is taken from the Preface of Machaelle's book on MAP: "MAP is not allopathy, homeopathy, naturopathy, or any other conventional medical specialty. Nor is it related to alternative health modalities or holistic health. And it is not esoteric, occult, new age, or spiritual. All those approaches to health are essentially evolutionary developments by man.

MAP is qualitatively different because, like co-creative science of which it is a part, it integrates the involutionary input of nature with man's evolutionary development. The healthy human being" or animal "is a balanced combination of these two dynamics. We do not need to know anatomy, physiology, biochemistry, pathology, psychology, etc. to use MAP effectively. As in the case of co-creative science, the only credentials we need are intent, sincerity, commitment, and the information and processes in Machaelle's book."

To speak of more details of this process outside of Machaelle's book is not my place. However, as with the Theta Healing, I have successfully utilized the techniques given in her book on animals, humans and other kingdoms of Life. As such, I encourage those who are open, to read her book and applied the techniques in your life and the life of your companion animals for everyone's benefit.

In summary, energy healing and co-creative healing techniques such as these can be of great assistance in our lives and the lives of our animals for day to day issues through to dire emergencies and traumas. I encourage all who feel in your heart to learn about these to do so, as the benefits are too extensive to express in anyway other than direct experience.

CHAPTER 15
CONNECTING WITH DIVINE ASSISTANCE

The Premise

The premise for connecting/communing with God, the angelic realms and other Light assistants is twofold. First, the knowingness that every being in creation has divine assistants assigned to oversee and support them through their journey, no matter what species or realm they are incarnated in (human, animal, plant, etc.). The second, is the truth of the phrase "Ask and you Shall Receive". This is a law of the Universe as is the necessity of asking to receive help.

The necessity of asking comes from humanity and our experience on Earth being based in Free Will, thus creating the dynamic that Divine assistance or Intervention cannot be given without a request being made from Earth to Heaven so to speak. There are a few exceptions to this when your Guardian Angel is given leave to step in to minimize the danger of a situation, especially if not doing so would end up in your early demise and sufficient incompletion of your reason for being here.

Divine Assistance and Intervention are part of Divine Will. Yet, Free Will oversees us here on Earth, thus, resulting in both the power of asking and the importance of asking for assistance

Holistic Emergency Care and Trauma Recovery for Animals / Section II

in emergencies and all other aspects of our lives.

Faith in Action

The next step believes in the divine and in divine assistance without actually being able to see who or what is providing you with assistance.

Believe that it is and there it shall be.

Taking believing a step further and you have:

Knowing is Divine Wisdom Fulfilled

And Making the Call for Divine Assistance is:

Embracing that Divine Assistance is Real and Your Call Will Be Answered

It may be that the response to your call will come in the form of one or more humans in form, or it may be directly through divine energy that simply creates a change in circumstance or feeling, creating the change that you have requested. There are unlimited ways in which the Divine can respond to a call for help. The main requirement for you is to believe and better yet, know that you can receive Divine Assistance for it to arrive.

Paying Attention and Receiving

There is an old story about a person sitting on his house in a flood asking for help from God. The story goes that he called to God for help. "Please God send me help so that I do not drown." Then several means of assistance came his way; a raft, a boat and a helicopter. Each time the help was offered, the person on the roof proclaimed, "No I don't need your help, God will save me."

Eventually the help stopped coming and the man drowned as his house went completely underwater. So what is this story telling us? Asking for help is the first step. Believing it will come is the second. And then it is our "job" to pay attention, so that we recognize the gift when it arrives and say *Yes* and *Thank you*!

Calling Divine Assistance

In most towns and cities there is not a 911 system for animals in place as there is for humans. Thus, making a call for Divine assistance can be of even greater importance than when assisting humans.

Calling for Divine Assistance *is* a step that can be taken in the immediate moments of an emergency while you are assessing the overall situation. The call can be made silently or out loud.

The initial call can be generic applying to the entire situation:

> *I call forth a Divine 911 Emergency Team into this situation Now – Please help! Thank you!*

or specific to a specific individual (animal, human, tree, etc.), illness or injury.

> *I call forth a Divine 911 Emergency Team to assist this injured animal Now – Please help! Thank you!*

By making such a call right away you are allowing for Divine assistance to manifest and join you and those involved (responder or those in need) from that moment forth. This can create a much improved outcome for everyone involved whether professional medical or emergency assistance are available or not.

More detailed explanation and examples of making such calls is contained in Section III – Emergency Response Techniques

Gratitude as an Anchor

One of the keys to success in visioning or intending anything into manifestation is to be GRATEFUL for it BEFORE it has actually come into being. What this does is anchors the fulfillment of the request through your knowing that it is already completed. Some personal examples of this process are:

> I now intend that my day be filled with harmony, unconditional love and peace.
> I ask that the angels of harmony, unconditional love and peace
> overlight everything in my day and in the day of my family.
> Thank you, thank you, thank you. It is so done!

Another example could be:

> Mother/Father/God I command a healing of my body/mind/spirit
> on all levels of all grief, sorrow, despair and related energies
> that I am experiencing from the death of my friend ….
> Thank you, thank you, thank you! It is so done!

Or

> Mother/Father/God I ask that all grief, sorrow, despair, anguish, or trauma energies
> that are still resident in my body/mind/spirit in any form be completely transmuted
> and transformed into unconditional love and divine light.
> Thank you (3x). It is done!

CHAPTER 16
BASIC HOLISTIC EMERGENCY & TRAUMA RECOVERY KIT

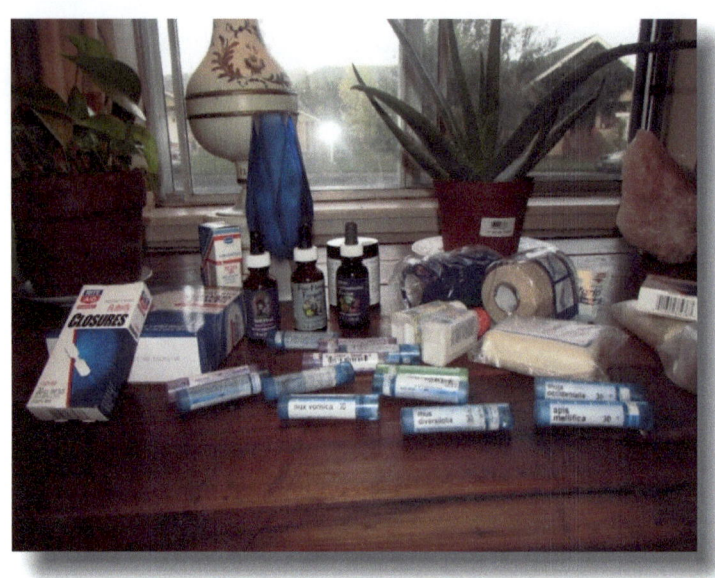

Section II of our *Holistic Emergency Care and Trauma Recovery for Animals* book contains a detailed layout of the remedies and Western herbs most often used in emergencies, trauma recovery and acute illness. As the list is quite extensive, I have been prompted to provide a basic list of what to have on hand that will provide *you* with greater ease of responding to emergencies or illness. I have derived this list from my most often used list of remedies over the past 20 years for both animals and humans.

Having as extensive a healing kit on hand as possible is always a blessing in emergencies and acute illness. It allows you to respond quickly and more decisively on your own or through the assistance of a veterinarian, poison control, holistic practitioner or comprehensive reference guide such as my book. Calling for assistance from a professional does you little good if you do not have the supplies required on hand.

Of course it is in these times that a comfort level with energy healing and calling in Divine assistance can be an immense blessing. (Reference *Connecting with Divine Assistance* in Section II of *Holistic Emergency Care and Trauma Recovery for Animals* and on our website http://www.holisticemergencycare.com .

Ready Made Remedies

Homeopathy

The following are the homeopathic remedies that I have used most frequently over the years and therefore make a point of having on hand in my home and travel emergency kits:
- April Mel – bites and stings
- Arnica Montana – bruising and hypovolemic shock
- Calendula – skin & eye irritation and minor burns
- Cantharas – burns : 1st to 3rd degree
- Hypericum – nerve damage either crushed or cut
- Ledum Pal – puncture wounds: heals from the inside out thus preventing abscesses; also for bites of any kind
- Rhus Toxicodendron – ligament and tendon injury; muscle pain due to overuse, etc.
- Ruta Graveolens – soreness in bones, tendons, ligaments and cartilage

Herbs for Decoctions or in Tinctures

Many of these herbs can be grown in your garden and are also found in the wild. But in lieu of this having them on hand in either bulk – cut & shifted form or in tincture can be of great assistance:

- Aloe vera – skin or mucous membrane assistance
- Astragalus – immune system, upper respiratory assistance
- Burdock – blood purifier
- Calendula – skin irritation; eye tonic
- Chamomile – digestion; calmative
- Comfrey – bone and overall cell repair
- Dandelion – liver tonic
- Echinacea – blood purifier and initial immune system booster
- Lavender - astringent
- Ginger – digestion challenges
- Plantain – immune support; skin irruptions; kidney and urinary track challenges
- Witch hazel - astringent

Holistic Emergency Care and Trauma Recovery for Animals / Section II

- Yarrow – overall healer for wounds & immune system

Flower Remedies

The three main flower essences that I carry with me at all time are:

- Bach Rescue Remedy or FES Five Flower Remedy
- Self Heal
- Yarrow Environmental Formula

In reviewing the Flower Remedies chapter of our book you may choose to have others on hand as well that resonate to you and your family's needs.

Basic First Aid And Emergency Kit List

The following list is the basic components to have in your first aid kit, minus the holistic remedies outlined above. This list is similar to what you will find on the American Red Cross website and other emergency care sites. The items included are for humans and animals alike.

NOTE: You should add to your first aid kit any special medications or items you or a family member might personally need. Remember to check your first aid kit regularly for expired medications, missing or consumed items. Replace as necessary.

____ Sterile adhesive bandages in assorted sizes and shapes

____ 2-inch sterile gauze pads (4-6)

____ 4-inch sterile gauze pads (4-6) ___ Splints (3, various sizes)

____ Hypoallergenic adhesive tape

Holistic Emergency Care and Trauma Recovery for Animals / Section II

____ Triangular bandages (3)

____ 2-inch sterile roller bandages (3 rolls)

____ 3-inch sterile roller bandages (3 rolls)

____ Scissors

____ Tweezers

____ Needle

____ Tongue blades (3)

____ Moistened towelettes

____ Rubbing alcohol or hydrogen peroxide

____ Antiseptic (towelettes, cream or liquid)

____ Oral thermometer

____ Medicine droppers

____ Petroleum jelly or other lubricant

____ Safety pins, assorted sizes

____ Razor blade or small, sharp knife

____ Cleansing agent/soap

____ Latex gloves (2 pair)

____ Face mask/shield - breathing device

____ Chemical cold pack (2)

____ Space blanket-to treat shock, warmth

____ Pen, paper and emergency contact information

____ Flashlight and batteries

____ Matches (preferably waterproof)

____ Distilled water (for flushing eyes, emergency drinking)

____ Paper drinking cups

____ First Aid Book

____ Plastic bags (assorted sizes, with fasteners)

____ Baking soda

____ Epson Salts

____ Hard candy or sugar granules (helps with dehydration, diabetic emergencies)

____ Activated charcoal (to neutralize poisons in the body)

____ Calendula lotion

SECTION III
EMERGENCY RESPONSE TECHNIQUES

Holistic Emergency Care and Trauma Recovery for Animals / Section III

CHAPTER 17
EMERGENCY RESPONSE TECHNIQUES

(When Play – Turns into Injury)

Emergency Response Overview

Now here we are at the guts of the book – the How To section for emergency care. This is the section that is important to have bookmarked for easy access in an emergency or sudden illness. Sections I and II were the what, the understanding and the overview. Section III is the how and the when. You can certainly study it ahead of time and get familiar with the key components. The more you know and can remember in an emergency, the better.

Yet, having this reference information close at hand is critical until you do know the material automatically. Studying the material in the book – running scenarios in your mind are all deeply important to being able to respond successfully in emergencies. This is what professionals, such as fire fighters and emergency responders do. Imaging *the what if's* and your response. By being at ease with the response material as detailed in this section, you can be more peaceful regarding an emergency occurring. If one does – you will be ready.

Holistic Emergency Care and Trauma Recovery for Animals / Section III

Note: additional scenarios and case studies will be available on our website www.holisticemergencycare.com.

The backbone of this section was taken from the California approved Standard First Aid as it was taught by the America Red Cross and other organizations that I taught for in the nineties. The holistic additions have been added through my wisdom gained through education and actual life application. Through choices that my animal companions and I have made over the years, I have had extensive opportunity for taking the holistic wisdom I have learned and apply it to real life.

A note of caution, unless the cause and solution to a situation is obvious, I recommend obtaining a diagnosis from a veterinarian or holistic animal consultant before doing extensive emergency or trauma recovery treatment. This is especially true for traumas where breaks or severe soft tissue injuries are indicated, and of course for any situation that may in any way be life threatening. More and more veterinarians are becoming open to a cooperative relationship of providing diagnosis or trauma support along with the animal's caregiver (you) providing holistic home care yourself or with the assistance of a trained holistic animal care consultant.

CHAPTER 18
BEING PREPARED AND PRACTICE SCENARIOS

When reading through the application instructions in Section III and IV of this book do so with the intention of understanding what you would do if an animal that you are assisting had an emergency and you were:

1. Too far away from the veterinarian to make the journey with your animal friend in her current condition.
2. Getting assistance from a vet, poison control or emergency consultant such as myself over the phone or through chat.
3. Unable to get to a veterinarian at all (such as being in the mountains camping)
4. At the scene of an emergency with no first aid kit or such tools of any kind.
5. Having fairly easy access to a vet or holistic practitioner
6. Or you feel competent with the material in this book to manage the situation successfully on your own.

Through the consideration of these items you will understand more the importance of either :
1. Understanding how to Call in Divine Assistance and doing Energy Healing, especially when your body, mind & spirit are the only tools you have with which to give assistance, or
2. Having easy access to holistic remedies and the knowhow of using them on your own, or with someone giving you basic guidance. Having the knowledge, but not having the remedies is only going to get you so far when an emergency occurs.

So I suggest studying the material in this book and on our website (www.holisticemergencycare.com), along with putting together a holistic emergency and

Holistic Emergency Care and Trauma Recovery for Animals / Section III

trauma kit of the remedies and other materials that might be required in the immediacy of an emergency, acute illness, and to lesser degree trauma recoveries. Also, learn Energy Healing techniques and if you are comfortable doing so, Divine Assistance Calls.

Being prepared both in mind and in physical preparation can make all the difference to your success in an emergency, sudden illness and trauma recovery.

Emergency Response Components

Throughout Section III you will be given an array of options for assisting with particular emergency situations. The basic outline of these options will be as follows:

- Divine Assistance
- General Treatment
- Flower Remedy Treatment
- Homeopathic Treatment
- Herbal Treatment
- Energy Healing

Calling for Divine Assistance and Energy Healing techniques are relatively the same throughout the various applications. However, you will find a few specifics where the author felt is was applicable. The General, Flower Remedy, Homeopathic and Herbal Treatments may vary considerably for the various emergencies, traumas or illnesses. So learning the different applications as well as carrying this book with you (e-book or paperback) can be of great help during an emergency situation.

Side Note regarding Homeopathy: Homeopathic symptom descriptions for keying out are generally written with humans in mind. So the language is given as if you have a human (adult or child) in front of you whom you are determining what remedy to use.

Holistic Emergency Care and Trauma Recovery for Animals / Section III

CHAPTER 19
DETECTING AN EMERGENCY

A crash, a scream, a howl, a cry, animals fleeing en mass, or a flash of fire, all these things can be indications of an emergency. Emergencies can also be indicated when there is sudden and complete silence where perhaps there shouldn't be: i.e., a child and puppy playing in the water together, someone working on your home on top of a ladder, or the incredible quiet that can occur before the onset off an intense storm. Being attuned to our environment and what is going on around us is a key element to determining when something is out of kilter.

Watch animals and you will see that even while they are resting, they maintain sensory awareness of their environment. This innate skill is one which we humans can develop, allowing us to be fully engrossed in what we are doing in any given moment, while still having "an ear on the world" so to speak. Now, as part of as your reading this section, pause and make a mental (or written) list[6] of changes in your environment to be aware of. Develop an animal-like awareness of your surroundings. What changes (subtle or sudden) in your home or community environment could indicate an emergency is at hand?

---

[6] *Writing* the list is vital. The information is more quickly accessible at a later date both to your mind and physically in the book. In times of trauma, it will be smarter to rely on your list than your memory. So go ahead and get started. Grab your phone book, you'll need to get some information.

Holistic Emergency Care and Trauma Recovery for Animals / Section III

Expand that to include your family, community, and environment. What kinds of emergency alarm and communication systems does your community have? Who do you need to communicate with immediately if an emergency is serious and widespread? What's your family's plan? How about more acute situations like a serious injury to immediate people and animals?

Does your community have emergency alarms of some kind for large storms or earthquakes? Some communities have CERT programs (Community Emergency Response Teams). CERT is a FEMA based project and includes training of willing residents to create and maintain response teams to assist the professionals in times of disaster. To find out more visit their website at http://www.fema.gov/community-emergency-response-teams.

What kind of emergency detection communication does your family, human and animal, have that would indicate that something is amiss? This awareness includes everything from the incoming of a major disaster to something amiss in your home, office or a potential danger when you are out of doors. Much of emergency or danger awareness really does occur on an intuitive or inner sense level. This is especially true of animals, but can also be true of humans. Your inner sense, if you listen to it, will always give you warning of an impending danger, be it an illness or potential injury.

Here are two examples:

Are you tuned-in and aware of your angelic guides and what they are telling you? Develop that intimate relationship with your animal companions and guides as it will serve you and your family in all emergencies.

For example, Spirithawk, one of my wolf-dog family members, is very adept at telepathically signaling me when there is something he believes requires my attention. It's energetically like a "Kathryn, hey Kathryn, pay attention!" Then I will look at him and he will often look in the direction where he wishes my attention to go by lifting his nose and pointing and saying "over there", "listen", and "pay attention". By becoming still and "listening", I too can detect what is going on and what we need to do in accordance with the situation.

Go inward with these questions. Be quiet; listen to yourself, your intuitive connection with your family, nature, and community. Journal what comes to your mind or heart. Is this an area that requires improvement in your life, the lives of your animals and your community? What can you do today that will improve that communication mechanism within your family and perhaps community?

Another question: If you got an emergency evacuation call from your home right now, would you be ready? Do you have evacuation kits for your animals and your human family that you can jump in your car and leave right now and have what you require with you to survive for a few days if need be? For suggestions on what to put in your kits see: First Aid and Emergency Kit Check List on our website : www.holisticemergencycare.com

Holistic Emergency Care and Trauma Recovery for Animals / Section III

CHAPTER 20
PHYSICAL SYMPTOMS OF EMERGENCIES

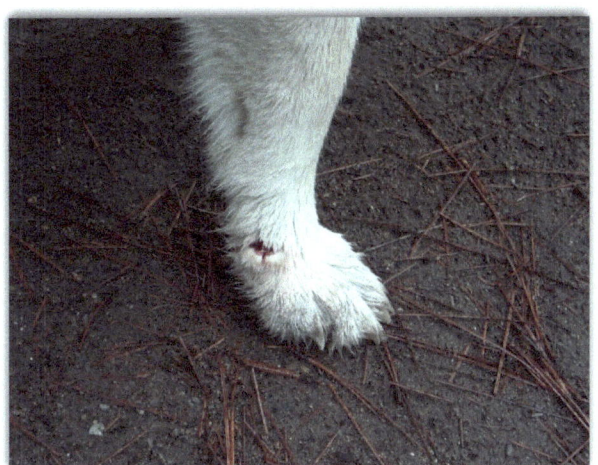

Emergencies and acute illness for humans and animals manifest in many different forms: physical, mental and emotional. Some are obvious, such as someone lying unconscious or an open wound. Others are not so obvious, such as heat exhaustion, internal bleeding from a trauma, or emotional lashing out from past abuse.

Body Wellness Signals

One's ability to detect the less obvious emergencies is enhanced by having a basic understanding of human and animal anatomy, physiology, and mental or emotional trauma characteristic signals. Knowing body wellness signals characteristics *is* a great part of this understanding. Examples include:

- Normal skin color and feel
- Normal blood pressure
- Normal pulse
- Normal breathing, panting (in cats and dogs primarily) verses stressed panting
- Normal body appearance and feel. For animals, lightly running your hands along their

body on a daily basis can create a knowingness of what their body normally feels like. If there is something amiss this allows you to more easily detect it.

Regular visual and intuitive examinations are also useful for the body's overall wellness: checking ears, feet, paws, hooves, eyes, abdomen, lymph nodes, checking for unwanted objects (stickers, ticks) and again, skin coloring, temperature, and moisture.

Doing a similar check of your own body and that of your partner, and other family members are of great benefit in being able to detect unusual or sudden changes. Doing these types of checks with a human or an animal, also allows for a deeper, more loving and wholesome relationship to ensue between you and your family.

Assessing the Situation

No matter how large or small an incident or emergency situation there are several components to assessing what happened and how to proceed:

- Surveying the scene to see if it is safe for you to enter
- Getting permission to assist those who are injured. With animals this can be a bit tricky if you are not consciously aware of how to speak to them. However, if it is a domestic animal and her guardian is present then begin with getting her permission. If her guardian is not present or if it is a wild animal, then do your best to intuit whether the animal wishes your assistance or not.

Holistic Emergency Care and Trauma Recovery
for Animals / Section III

- Determining if a life-threatening situation exists
- Calling in Assistance (Emergency care for animals and Divine Assistance)
- Understanding when it is necessary to move an injured party
- Doing triage if necessary. This is in the case of a large accident or disaster where there are many injured or traumatized.

Surveying the Scene

Think Respond rather than React…. Be it large or small, once you have detected an emergency or injury, the next thing you do is to survey the scene. No matter if the incident is your home or in some other environment, it is key to assess what has occurred and why to the best of your ability before responding.

Stop, Look, Listen, Breathe … all are active ingredients in surveying the scene. Doing so will:

♥ Allow you time as a rescuer or first responder to become centered, balanced, and focused in the present moment. Stop moving, breathe at least three deep breaths, and ask for Divine guidance.

This Extremely Important!
If you are not clear, how can you assist another who is in trouble?

♥ Assist you to gain vital information as to what occurred. (This is a good time to be logging details for future use in explaining what happened to others who may assist such as emergency workers, veterinarian(s), etc.

♥ Assist you to locate all those needing help, be they human or animal. Remember, treating all equally in an emergency is the holistic way.

- ♥ Assist you to quickly evaluate what must be done first, and to request God or the Angels to stabilize the situation and bring aid to those who require and desire it.
- ♥ Assist you to assess whether the scene is safe to enter and work in, or requires evacuation before providing any in-depth assistance to the animal(s) or human in need.

Surveying the scene and becoming centered is a good preventative for jumping into a situation without thinking. *Assessing whether a scene is safe is one of the most important things you need to do. You must be proactive rather than reactive.*

Think Respond rather than React.
Stop, look, listen, breathe, center, evaluate
and then enter – if it is safe to do so.

Logging Details

While surveying the scene, or checking an animal(s) directly, have a notepad and log the who, what and where, of any injury, trauma or sudden illness. Logging details is helpful for whoever is doing the immediate and long term treatment, whether you are doing it at home, or for providing a veterinarian or holistic practitioner valuable background information.

For ease of access, keep a notepad in your first aid/emergency kit, car, purse, or backpack. If you do not have one, then be creative. One other option is to send yourself text messages or a voice mail from your cell phone if you carry one.

In the case of an accident or disaster where there are multiple animals, or animals and people involved it is suggested to record the following:

- Number of injured – remember include humans and animals and a basic assessment of the severity of their injuries.
- Location of the emergency – note the streets and the address. If you are in the country

Holistic Emergency Care and Trauma Recovery
for Animals / Section III

use very specific geographic landmarks. GPS cell phones come in handy in these cases, as does an in-depth knowledge of your surroundings.

- A brief assessment of what has occurred to the best of your ability in the immediate moment and ongoing if things shift before professional assistance arrives, or you arrive at your destination.

- Is there anything involved or close by that is considered life threatening (fire, downed power lines, etc)?

- Also write what you do to assist, such as the administering of holistic remedies.

If you are at home or are the initial first responder to arrive at the scene in another environment, you, by default, will be in charge of organizing the "rescue" process unless one of two things is present:

- You feel unqualified and a more qualified person arrives and is willing to take the lead.

- Professional fire, medical, wildlife rescue, FEMA or CERT (Community Emergency Response Team) personnel arrive and take over the lead.

In the event that there is a second responder, allow that person to log the details and call for help, where available, while you continue forward with what is required.

Is It Safe To Proceed?

There are many reasons why a first responder or rescuer would be ill advised to enter an emergency site. Examples include if an animal or person is or has:

- Caught in a rushing river
- Fallen over an unstable cliff
- Trapped in the middle of a busy highway
- Caught in a car with a power line down across it.
- In a burning building that is unsafe to enter

… and so on.

Be Proactive, Not Reactive – Prevention is a Key Element:

If you are in an area where the environment is potentially dangerous, keep your dog or cat on a leash and watch your horse or other animals to keep them A safe distance from potential dangers.

It is easy in the stress or excitement of the moment to react to before thinking about the consequences. This is one of the major disciplines that a first responder or rescuer must develop. **It never does any good to become one of the ones who requires rescuing.** This is true even if the one in need of assistance is a loved one.

Remember. Stop, look, listen, breathe, center, evaluate, call for help, and then enter – if it is safe to do.

Proceed only once you feel that doing so could be of benefit to the situation and all involved.

Here is a true story to emphasize the importance of resisting going into an unsafe situation:

My mother and I were visiting Monterey, CA on a casual trip up the coastline. We were driving up Hwy 101 and came upon a spot by the ocean where many police and fire trucks were parked. People were staring into the water and an ambulance was pulling away. Later, we read in the paper that three members of a family of four, visiting from out of the country drowned.

What had happened? The family was standing on the low-lying rocks watching as the waves crashed into the shore. Suddenly a large wave reached up beyond the others and scooped the mother off the rocks and into the water. The father then jumped in, attempting to rescue the mother. Seeing him disappear, the son then followed suit. In the end, only the young daughter remained. Note that this could just have easily involved a beloved animal companion at the onset or a child with the same outcome.

So what do you do in such a situation?

- Keep yourself out of jeopardy by using tools at hand: rope, a long pole, rescue tubes, etc. (photo – stable body positioning of person rescuing with pole)

- Call for help and organize others to create a human chain of assistance.

This type of rescue chain can be used in oceans, lakes, rivers or even on land is deemed necessary.

And it can be utilized effectively whether the one being rescued is a human or an animal.

- If you are in alignment with calling to and receiving assistance directly from the Divine, then call in Angelic assistance to protect or assist whoever is injured or in danger in whatever way they can. Also, ask that they fill everyone with divine grace by moving through the situation in a manner that is for the highest and best.

- For example: God/Goddess/All That Is, Beloved Archangel Michael, please send assistance immediately to *the one in need* and assist the rescuers too. I thank you!

- Another example: Beloved I AM, I am making a 911 call for Divine Assistance in *this situation*. Please send the assistance that you know he/she/we require now. I thank you!

Holistic Emergency Care and Trauma Recovery for Animals / Section III

CHAPTER 21
DOES A LIFE THREATENING EMERGENCY EXIST?

Understanding how to detect a life-threatening emergency is of key importance to a first responder and trauma caregiver. When you come upon the scene of an emergency, have a checklist of questions in your mind. Here is a list of the main items:

Is the environment unsafe? Examples would include:

- In the path of fire
- Severe flooding
- Poison fumes
- Violently aggressive persons or animals
- Earthquake: unstable buildings, unstable landscape
- In the path of a tornado
- Downed power lines impeding your path

Are there any life threatening injuries?

- Heart attack or cardiac arrest (no pulse)
- Respiratory arrest (no breathing)
- Electrocution
- Shock (both hypovolemic and anaphylactic)
- Water in lungs; possible drowning
- Severe bleeding (internal or external)
- Poisoning
- Severe burns, especially in infants and the elderly. Many multiple injuries combining to create life-threatening situation, especially those involving organs

If the scene is unsafe, requiring those who have been injured to be moved, stabilize them to the best of your ability.

(Remember you can ask for divine assistance in this area.) Then move the animal or animals to safety as quickly as possible while doing the least amount of damage to them in the process

Holistic Emergency Care and Trauma Recovery for Animals / Section III

(see section "Moving an Animal Who Is Injured"). **If the scene is safe,** proceed to assist the animal or animals proceed to assist/treat him/her to the best of your ability using your knowledge, wisdom and if you are comfortable doing so calling on Divine Assistance as well.

Once you have determined that the scene is safe for you, you can begin checking animals in earnest. In many cases you can determine with a quick survey if any of the injuries is life threatening. If a life threatening injury or illness exists, proceed to "Calling in Assistance," while at the same time obtaining permission to assist. If others acting as first responders are there a veterinarian or emergency assistance of some kind is going to be called, let them do this while you proceed with calling in divine assistance and continuing with the procedure checklist.

In the case of disasters, where the infrastructure in your community may be completely disrupted, or emergencies that occur out of the range of conventional assistance, your responsibilities may take on a fairly long-term time line. This is important for every person to consider during these times of great Earth shifts and changes. Being prepared physically, mentally, emotionally, and spiritually is very important to a potential emergency/trauma first responder and caregiver. Having holistic training as well as the partnership that is provided through divine assistance may make the difference between life and death.

Holistic Emergency Care and Trauma Recovery for Animals / Section III

Moving an Animal Who Is Injured

Moving an injured animal can cause further injury, therefore only move an injured animal if the scene becomes unsafe or to transport to a place where care can be provided, be that your home or a professional/medical facility. Since calling 911 for animals is generally not available, decisions to move must be based on what care must be given and where, rather than waiting for professional care to arrive.

The exception is for equines or other large animals who are injured in such a way that transportation is considered to be unsafe or may cause additional injury. Then a veterinarian or caregiver must come to wherever you and the animal are.

To move an animal with a possible head, neck or back injury, gently but firmly grab the animal's shoulders and carefully drag the animal while supporting the head and neck with your arms. Try to keep the head and neck in line with the back. For animals that are too large to carry easily, the blanket pull is done using a blanket, board, small rug or large piece of cardboard under the injured animal assisting in moving the animal, while also helping to avoid further injury.

- To place the blanket under the animal, fold or pleat the blanket into thirds and place beside the animal against her body.
- Grasp the animal by the hip and shoulder and roll as a unit about 1/8 of a turn away from the blanket.

- Push the blanket as far as possible under the animal then carefully roll the animal an 1/8 of a turn the opposite direction and slowly pull the blanket through.
- This procedure works best when others are available to assist. <u>This is not to be used if there are suspected head, neck or back injuries.</u>

If an animal is trapped in a confined space or pinned in an automobile or by machinery, you must remember to check the area for safety before approaching. If you can safely reach the animal in need, provide life support until trained emergency or medical personnel arrive and extricate the animal(s). Do not try to remove her yourself as doing so could complicate any injuries. If at all possible, this is best done by trained medical or emergency personnel.

More harm can be done through the improper moving of someone who is injured than any other emergency assistance procedure. As a general rule, in severe cases, rescue and transportation should be carried out by trained emergency or medical personnel.

Holistic Emergency Care and Trauma Recovery
for Animals / Section III

CHAPTER 22
TYPES OF WOUNDS

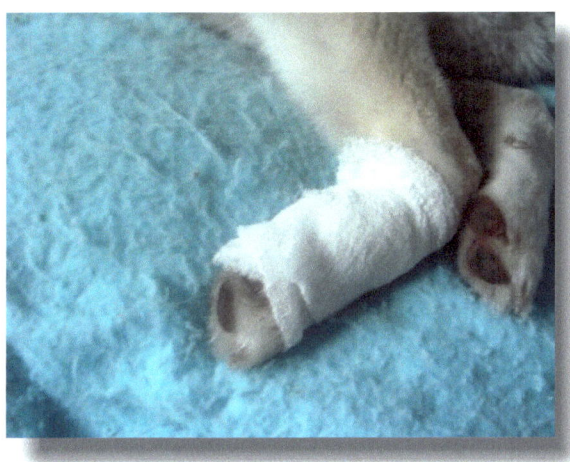

There are six different types of wounds that you are likely to encounter. Their descriptions and the appropriate first aid steps include:

BRUISES

These occur when soft tissues and blood vessels are damaged and there is bleeding under the skin. This causes the black and blue appearance. Bruises can signal more severe damage that is not obvious on the surface. This can include internal bleeding, bone bruises, organ damage, sprains, strains or even broken bones.

Types of Bruising - There are two main types of bruising. That which involves soft tissue, and that which includes bone (bone bruises). Bone bruises can result from intense trauma – generally from impact and are very painful. General bruising can result from many different injury scenarios; mostly involving physical impact of some kind. However, most surgeries also create bruising and of course the accompanying inflammation.

Note that internal bruising is treated more effectively through homeopathy and herbs rather than through the general methods. (Also see Internal Bleeding)

Divine Assistance

The necessity of calling in Divine Assistance for bruising or wounds of other kinds, has primarily to do with their severity and what other healing tools that you have on hand. My motto is "ask for Divine Assistance, it can't hurt".

God/Goddess/ All That Is I command a complete and immediate healing of this animal's injuries, bruises, all that is injured, now. I thank you. It is so done!

Once done visualize the animal's injuries being healed. Remember Gratitude is a very powerful component of all healing.

Energy Healing

Remember, energy healing can be utilized on its own or along with other modalities if you have them available. If you are trained in Reiki, Theta Healing or other energetic healing follow your guidance for facilitating the healing of bruising or any other kind of wound. If you do not have specific training, the following is suggested:

- Request: God/Goddess, make me your instrument of healing for this animal. You may see white, emerald or rainbow colored light coming into the animal either directly the animal, or indirectly through you to the animal. If you don't see it, then feel the energy

- Hold the vision of healing and allow the energy to continue until you are prompted within your heart or by the animal that it is enough.

- Say thank you & then relax.

General Treatment

- Apply cold pack or ice – cold pack is preferable. (Be sure to separate the ice from the injury with some type of barrier, such as a thin towel.)

- Elevate bruised area if this can be done without impeding overall healing.

Homeopathic Treatment

Arnica Montana is a must for bruising-- 6X to 30X for general bruising; 200x for bone and internal bruising and/or hypovolemic shock/ bruising from major surgery. (See chapter on Shock for more details)

Herbal Treatment

- Turmeric (either in tincture or capsule form)
- White Yarrow (decoction, capsule, or tincture)
- Calendula

SCRAPES

These are not as common in animals as in humans due to their fur coats and feather protection. However, they can result from being hit by a car or dragged for any reason. Scrapes are when the top layers of skin are scraped away. This is usually very painful and can become easily infected if not cleaned promptly and properly.

General Treatment

- Clean thoroughly with liquid soap or witch hazel and lavender blend.
- You can also disinfect with diluted hydrogen peroxide or Betadine.
- Bandage to prevent further damage if possible or practical.
- Provide clean bedding and resting places for your animal to relax and heal while keeping the injury site as clean as possible.

Homeopathic Treatment

- Administer *Homeopathy Remedy:* Hepar Sulph 6X - 30X and Calendula Officinalis 30X.
- Calendula Officinalis lotion can also be used for cleaning wounds

Herbal Treatment

- Yarrow (Achillea millefolium) is top of the list for wounds in general. It can be applied topically as a poultice or salve, or administered systemically through decoction or tincture.

- Comfrey, calendula, plantain and lavender in decoction, salve or tincture can all assist in cellular regeneration and inflammation.

- Wound Repair Salve (see Products)

Holistic Emergency Care and Trauma Recovery for Animals / Section III

CUTS

Cuts are usually caused by sharp objects like knives or glass. Sometimes a cut can occur when a blow is strong enough to split the skin. Nerves, soft tissue and large blood vessels may also be damaged. Cuts can bleed freely and, if deep, severely.

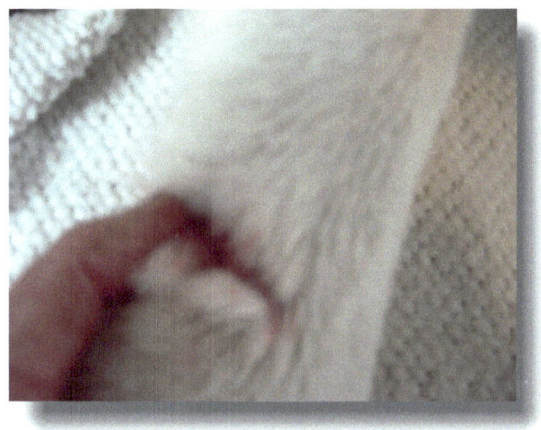

General Treatment

- Stop the bleeding (See Controlling Bleeding)

- Clean the wound if necessary with clean warm water, witch hazel and lavender or castile soap. Be gentle and listen to your animal to see if the cleaning process is causing more pain. If so, back off, administer Homeopathic Remedies or Wound Repair salve.

- Determine if stitches are required. (Two reasons for stitches: 1. To promote healing and minimize chance of infection. 2. To minimize scarring.

- If you feel the wound requires stitching then loosely wrap the area and transport to your veterinarian.

- If not, wrap or cover the wound and administer herbs for promoting healing.

Homeopathy

- Treat for shock if necessary with Rescue Remedy.
- Phosphorus for bleeding
- Hypericum perforatum if nerve damage is suspected. 6X - 30X.

Herbal Treatment

- Yarrow (Achillea millefolium) is top of the list for wounds in general. It can be applied topically as a poultice or salve, or administered systemically through decoction or tincture.
- Comfrey
- Wound Repair Salve (products)

PUNCTURE WOUNDS

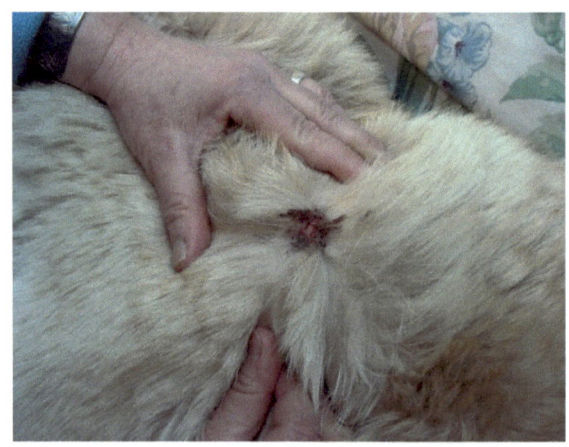

Punctures occur when a pointed object pierces the skin leaving a hole that is longer than it is wide – like a tube. Some of the things that can cause this type of wound include a nail, claws, teeth, pen, pencil, thorn, stick or knife. Punctures usually do not bleed freely and can easily become infected. The threat of tetanus infection is very serious and should always be a consideration when an animal has sustained an injury that punctures the skin.

General Treatment

- Cleanse the wound by soaking it in warm water with Epson Salts or Betadine for 10 to 20 minutes.

Homeopathy

- *Always* administer *Homeopathy Remedy:* Ledum Palustre; 6x or 30x, 30c.
- Add *Homeopathy Remedy:* Hypericum Perforatum if nerve involvement is suspected. 6x or 30x

Herbal Treatment

In my studies there is no clear cut herb for assisting in the healing of puncture wounds specifically. Rather there are herbs such as comfrey that induce accelerated cellular regeneration that should be avoided until the puncture wound in well into its healing stage. This is because any healing agent that causes the puncture wound to heal more quickly on top than within may result in the formation of an abscess.

Homeopathic Ledum Palustre (Ledum Pal) is my treatment of choice along with flushing or soaking of wound area with a cleaning agent such as betadine solution or diluted hydrogen peroxide.

AVULSIONS

This is when a large portion of skin or tissue is torn away either partially or completely. This will often include damage to deeper tissues and can cause severe bleeding.

Call veterinarian if deemed necessary. Stop the bleeding. Treat any completely severed body pieces as amputations. Administer *Bach* Rescue Remedy for shock; *Homeopathy Remedy:* Arnica Montana, Phosphorus, and Hypericum Perforatum 30X for the injury itself.

AMPUTATIONS

An amputation is the complete removal of a body part, such as a finger. Tissues will close around the vessels at the injury site which may help control the bleeding.

Call a veterinarian if deemed necessary. Control any bleeding first, and administer *Bach Rescue Remedy* (to the animal and anyone else who needs it) and *Homeopathy Remedy:* Hypericum for nerve damage. When the bleeding is controlled, attend to the amputated body part. In many cases, it can be reattached to the animal through surgery.

To save an amputated body part:
- Wrap in moist, sterile (or as clean as possible) gauze or cloth.
- Place in a plastic bag or plastic wrap.
- Put on ice or keep cold and dry.
- Transport with the animal to emergency animal care facility.

Never place an amputated body part directly on ice without protective wrapping because the tissue may freeze and then be destroyed.

CHAPTER 23
CONTROLLING BLEEDING

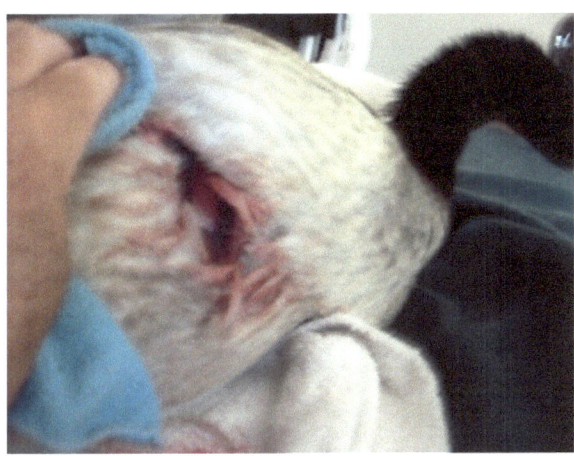

To care for a major open wound, you must first control bleeding. There are five steps that should be followed when controlling bleeding:

General Treatment

1. If desired and practical, protect yourself with latex gloves or some other type of protective barrier. If gloves are not available, use plastic wrap or a clean cloth. (This is more an issue with humans than in helping animals.)

2. Cover the wound with dressing or a suitable substitute and apply direct pressure. If no dressing is available, just use your hand(s). Use firm, steady pressure - being certain to do so without further injuring the area. The purpose of direct pressure is to slow the flow of blood enough to allow it to coagulate.

3. If possible, elevate the wound above the level of the heart.
   Contraindications: if you suspect a fracture or head/neck injury. Elevation is, of course, simpler on a human than most four legged animals. However, dependent upon the level of consciousness of the animal, it may be possible (The purpose is to use gravity in slowing the blood flow to assist with the blood clotting).

4. Both herbs and homeopathy can be utilized to assist in the coagulation and healing process. For internal bleeding or hemorrhaging homeopathy is recommended in the immediate emergency and will not interfere if the animal requires surgery.

    a. Homeopathic Arnica Montana: 6x, 30x or 30c
    b. Homeopathic Phosphorus: 6x, 30x or 30c

    Hemostatic herbs such as yarrow can be administered in decoction, diluted tincture or in salve form (some animals will eat it) if surgery is not indicated.

5. Cover with a roller bandage, applying more dressings if necessary. Do not remove old dressings or bleeding will start again. It is during this step that you can use either of the herbal supports listed below. Either the poultice or salve are placed within the bandage, preferably right next to the wound. In the case of a severe bleeder, leave the gauze closest to the wound in place, placing the poultice or salve on top of it and then adding additional gauze and completing the bandaging process.

If bleeding continues...

6. Squeeze the main artery to that limb against the bone. Pressure may be continued from 5 to 20 minutes dependent upon need. The circulatory system of vertebrates is generally the same.

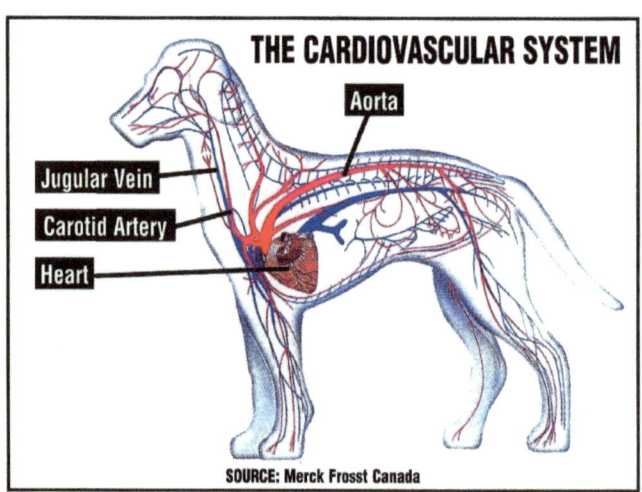

Holistic Emergency Care and Trauma Recovery for Animals / Section III

Flower Essence

- Bach Rescue Remedy or FES Five Flower Remedy liquid or cream to help reverse or prevent hypovolemic shock.

Homeopathy

- Homeopathic Phosphorus for hemorrhaging, recommended along with Arnica Montana; 30X to 30C
- Homeopathic Hypericum for nerve damage, 6X - 30X.

Herbal Treatment

- In conventional treatment, no fluids are to be giving to someone where internal bleeding is possible, especially if a veterinarian has been called and surgery is indicated. However, in the case of animals or even humans if conventional medical facilities are not readily available, homeostatic herbs can be given internally as decoction or salve/liniment to assist in stabilizing or correcting the imbalance.

- Herbal remedies in the form of decoctions or Wound Salve (see appendices) can be taken internally, after the immediate emergency is stabilized.

CHAPTER 24

NOSE BLEEDS

Prevention

Many chronic nosebleeds are due to dry mucous membranes in the nose. One remedy for this is saline nose spray, which is available in most drug stores. It is also helpful for these people to use a humidifier in the home/office.

High altitude nosebleeds are also helped by saline spray, as the air gets dryer and dryer as the altitude increases. Nosebleeds can also be a result of traumatic injury. Again, be aware of your surroundings, wear proper gear for sporting activities, and be nice to your neighbors so they don't punch you in the nose!

General Treatment

- To control a nosebleed: if possible, pinch the animal's nose and put head forward. (This prevents the blood from going down the back of the throat and into the stomach.)

- Other effective methods include rolling a small piece of gauze or paper towel and placing it between the upper lip and gum, which acts as a mini pressure point, or placing a cold compress on the bridge of the nose.

- **Do not attempt to control bleeding if you suspect a head, neck or spinal injury.**

Homeopathy Treatment
- Administer *Homeopathy Remedy:* Phosphorus 6X - 30X

Herbal Treatment
- Yarrow

Holistic Emergency Care and Trauma Recovery for Animals / Section III

CHAPTER 25

EYE INJURIES, IMPALED OBJECTS & MOUTH INJURIES

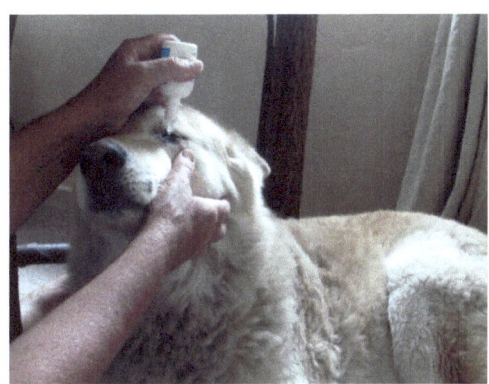

Eye Injuries

Because of the importance of vision for any animal, eye injuries or illness must be taken seriously and treated with as much mastery as possible. It is imperative for responders to remain calm and centered. These can often be unsightly injuries which create great distress in the one experiencing them, so as a first responder it is your calm approach to assisting that will help the animal experience less trauma at least on the feeling and mental levels.

Divine Assistance

I highly recommend calling in Divine Assistance for eye injuries, impaled objects or mouth injuries. Due to the nature of such injuries the trauma can easily expand to the mental and emotional bodies on the animal and become stuck there without multi-level assistance. Here are general examples of how to do this:

- God/Goddess/All that is please make me your instrument of healing and peace to assist this dear animal who is suffering. I thank you. It is so done.

- Beloved I AM Presence; through you I call a Divine 911 Emergency Healing Team to provide this animal (and myself) assistance immediately.

Eye injuries such as a foreign object entering the eye or scratching the eye can also be aided greatly by the holistic modalities below. Another example of Divine Assistance in such a case is:
- Angels and elementals please remove (etherealize) the foreign object(s) in this animal's eye(s) and heal the damage fully. I thank you.

Energy Healing

If a foreign object enters the eye and cannot be easily removed by rinsing, bandage both eyes and administer

Homeopathy Treatment

- Ledum Pal 30X
- Calendula 6x or 30x

Flower Essence

- *Bach* Rescue Remedy

Take the animal to a medical doctor if deemed necessary

If an object is impaled in the eye, NEVER try to remove it. Bandage both eyes and take the animal to a medical doctor. If chemicals enter an animal's eyes, immediately begin flushing both eyes, always flushing from the good eye to the injured eye & continue flushing with water until trained medical personnel arrive and take over. Never apply any type of cream or ointment to the eyes without medical direction.

Holistic Emergency Care and Trauma Recovery for Animals / Section III

Impaled Objects

If there is an object impaled in the animal, **do not remove the object**. Control bleeding around the area and bandage with bulky dressings around the object to support it and keep it from causing further damage.

Communicate with the animal to the best of your ability, both to explain what you are doing to help and to aid in calming the animal down. It is natural for animals to attempt to get the impaled object out of their body if they can reach it. This, along with the shock that usually ensues can make the animal very unstable, or at least very restless.

When possible, stabilize the animal and seek medical attention immediately

Veterinarian assistance is always recommended for such situations. So the key is to stabilize the animal, activate Divine Assistance, treat for shock and transport. Performing energy healing before and during transportation is also highly recommended.

Divine Assistance / Energy Healing

- First objective is to calm the animal down and to call in divine healing energies – Divine Love – being the most important. Like with any situation you can facilitate the calling in of Divine Love and an Divine Emergency Team (Divine 911) whether you are directly hands on with the animal(s) or assisting from a distance.

- The second objective is to decrease the pain being caused by the injury through Divine and direct hands on assistance as suggested below.

- Energy healing such as Reiki, and Theta can be of great assistance in facilitating the minimization of pain and commencement of healing, even while the impaled object is still present. If you do not have these skills then speak the following:

Say silently or out loud "God/Goddess (Creator or Mother/Father/God) make me an instrument of your peace, healing and LOVE to assist this animal(s)"
(or whomever / whatever is in need)

Holistic Emergency Care and Trauma Recovery for Animals / Section III

- Breathe, connect heart to heart with the animal(s) and allow the Divine energies to be emanated through you to all in need while envisioning the Divine Highest and Best of all being served.

General Treatment

- Stabilize impaled object to the best of your ability WITHOUT creating more pain for the animal. Dependent upon the size, a paper cup and gauze can be used to place over the object (punching out the bottom of the cup first) and then wrapping the cup in place around the animal to hold it in place. Dependent upon when the object is will dictate the way the wrapping must occur. General practice is to place the cup (or whatever you are using to stabilize the object) over the impaled object, stabilize it with gauze and then wrap it in figure 8 pattern around the body part that where it is located.

  This can require a lot of wrapping. Ace bandages can be utilized as can vet tape. Caution with the vet tape not to put it on too tightly. Remember the goal is to do no more harm!

- If the object is affecting an eye, it is important to stabilize the object and then tape both eyes shut to minimize their movement.

Flower Remedy

- *Bach* Rescue Remedy or Five Flower Remedy, if deemed necessary.

Homeopathic Treatment

- Administer *Homeopathy Remedy:* Ledum Pal 30X
- Administer Homeopathic Arnica Montana: 30C or higher for bruising and shock.
- *** Liquid dilution is suggested for such traumas, again to minimize further agitation or discomfort to the animal.

Mouth & Teeth Injuries

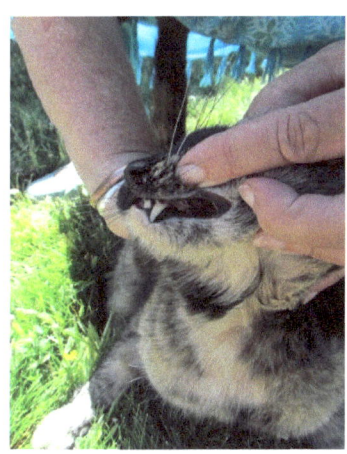

Bleeding in the mouth can usually be controlled by direct pressure with a sterile or clean cloth or gauze. More serious lacerations of the skin, mucous membranes and tongue may require stitches by a medical doctor.

A knocked-out tooth can sometimes be replanted by a dentist. Have the animal place the tooth back into its socket if she can so without pain and then have him/her bite down on gauze or clean cloth with gentle pressure to hold it temporarily in place. If the tooth cannot be placed back in its socket, place the tooth in milk or water for transportation. In either situation, get the animal to a veterinarian/dental specialist as soon as possible.

- Administer *Homeopathy Remedy:* Hypericum 30X for pain and nerve damage.
- Call in Divine Assistance using Theta Healing or MAP coning to promote immediate healing and pain relief.
- Seek veterinarian assistance if possible.

Holistic Emergency Care and Trauma Recovery for Animals / Section III

CHAPTER 26
INTERNAL BLEEDING

If an injury is caused by a strong force, it could result in serious damage and internal bleeding. The nature of the injury and the following list of signals will help you to determine the possibility of internal bleeding.

Symptoms include:

- Tender, swollen, bruised or hard areas of the body, such as the abdomen.
- Vomiting, coughing up or passing blood.
- Fast, weak pulse.
    - Strong thirst.
    - Confusion, loss of consciousness, dizziness, drowsiness or fainting.
    - Cool, moist, pale or bluish skin (

Divine Assistance

If internal bleeding is suspected I always call for Divine Assistance & an Emergency 911 Healing Team. In such situations you may be guided to perform energy healing as part of what else you are facilitating even if you have other assistance.

Energy Healing

If transport to medical facility is imminent: Administer *Homeopathy Remedy:* Phosphorus for hemorrhaging, Arnica Montana for soft tissue damage and *Bach* Rescue Remedy for Shock. Call your veterinarian or emergency animal care center and assist the animal to rest while you monitor breathing and pulse. Avoid giving the animal anything to drink in case surgery is required to correct the problem.

Note: administering homeopathy tablets or Rescue Remedy topically is acceptable even if surgery is suspected. These remedies do not interfere or endanger the animal in any way.

Holistic Emergency Care and Trauma Recovery for Animals / Section III

If no conventional medical facilities are available (for whatever the reason) then utilize flower essence, homeopathy and herbal treatment as deemed appropriate through these guidelines.

Flower Essence Treatment

- Bach Rescue Remedy or FES Five Flower Remedy liquid or cream to help reverse or prevent anaphylactic and hypovolemic shock.

Homeopathy Treatment

- Homeopathic Phosphorus for hemorrhaging, recommended along with Arnica Montana; 30X to 30C

- Homeopathic Hypericum for nerve damage, 6X - 30X.

Herbal Treatment

- In conventional treatment, no fluids are to be given to someone where internal bleeding is possible, especially if 911 has been called and surgery is imminent. However, in the case of animals or even humans if conventional medical facilities are not readily available, hemostatic herbs can be given internally as decoction or salve/liniment.

- Hemostatic (assist in blood coagulation) herbs include: yarrow, horsetail, goldenseal, white willow bark, bayberry, blackberry, cayenne, cransbill, mullein, uva ursi, and witch hazel. Yarrow is my preference with animals.

- Wound salve or liniment – see our website
  http://holisticemergencycare.com/category/products/

CHAPTER 27
HYPOVOLEMIC SHOCK

Hypovolemic shock is a reduction of blood flow throughout the body tissues that, if untreated, may lead to collapse, coma and death. Shock in this sense is physiological shock- different from the mental distress that may follow a physically or emotionally traumatic experience.

In animals as well as humans, hypovolemic shock is a common accompaniment to severe injury or illness. It may develop in any situation where blood volume is reduced (through blood or fluid loss), where blood vessels are abnormally widened, or in which the heart's action is weak, in which blood flow is obstructed, or through a combination of these factors.

Signals of shock include:

- Dizziness and decreased level of consciousness /fainting
- Confusion and changes in mood or behavior including restlessness or irritability.
- Cold, clammy skin.
- Rapid, weak pulse.
- Rapid, shallow breathing.
- Going into hiding – especially dogs and cats

It is important to note that some animals when experiencing a trauma (such as being hit by a car) will hide, whether they are indoors or outdoors in nature. This is a natural instinct for animals coming from their wild roots to not become prey to another while in their state of vulnerability. Yet in hiding they can also lead to their own demise if those attempting to help cannot find them.

General Treatment for Hypovolemic Shock

- Reassure the animal with your words and energy. Be calm and peaceful. Help the animal to know he/she is safe in your care.

- Call a veterinarian if deemed necessary.

Holistic Emergency Care and Trauma Recovery for Animals / Section III

- If possible, lay the animal with its tail end elevated about 6-8 inches or what seems comfortable for her. This will improve circulation and keep the blood in the area of the vital organs. (**Do not** elevate feet if you suspect serious spinal or internal injuries.)
- Maintain the body temperature as close to normal as possible.
- Monitor breathing and pulse.

Flower Essence Treatment

- Administer Bach Rescue Remedy or FES Five Flower Remedy to assist in restoring balance.
- Arnica – repairing life energy after shock or trauma: this flower essence can be utilized after the animal is stabilized.
- Self Heal – recuperative healing from shock
- Star of Bethlehem – soothing, maintaining inner peace after trauma; healing effects of past trauma, often repressed at the time.

Homeopathy Treatment

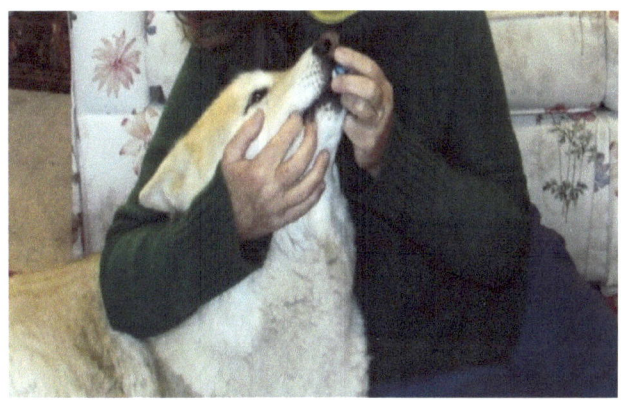

Be sure to use homeopathic tablets rather than cream in the case of shock or major trauma. The homeopathic pellets take the medicine systemically which is of vital importance. The cream is more for topical bruising and traumas.

The main homeopathic remedy for hypovolemic shock is Arnica Montana. This is specifically for shock and of course will assist with any bruising or related trauma.

Administer: Arnica Montana 6X, 30X or 30C.

Dose: 3-4 tablets every 30 minutes for the first 2 hours. Then every four hours.

Remember when giving the animal the remedies, that due to the shock and trauma the she might be confused and uncooperative. So be gentle and yet firm. Let her know what you are doing and why. Make sure she swallows all of the tablets.

These simple steps can mean the difference between life and death.

True Life Example

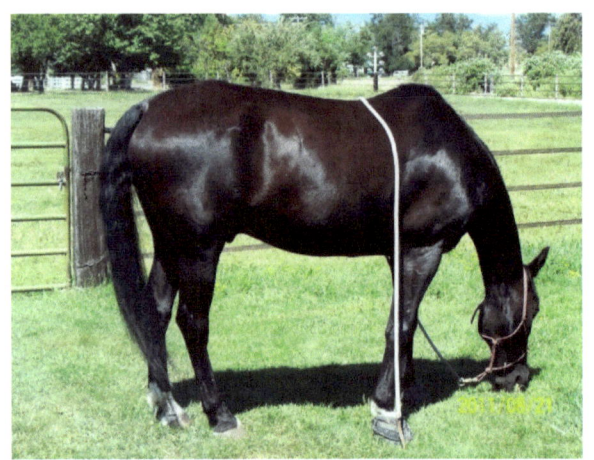

As a young woman I kept horses and showed them in the San Diego riding circuit. At this time the Del Mar Fair and Rodeo we held simultaneously. After showing my horse one evening some of the rodeo participants came through the barn areas setting off firecrackers. One was thrown into the hay bale outside my horse's (Bar Harbor) stall.

Fortunately it did not set the place on fire, which it could have easily done. However, Bar Harbor did go into shock. This predated my knowledge of holistic healing and I did not do much to assist him. The next day I went to check on him and he bit me on the hip. He was not a biter – this was a direct shock response. His action got my full attention, and I then had the vet look him over and tend to him as he saw necessary.

If this had occurred after I gained my holistic knowledge I would have administered both Rescue Remedy and Homeopathic Arnica Montana 30c to assist Bar Harbor's body in coming back into balance more easily.

Holistic Emergency Care and Trauma Recovery for Animals / Section III

CHAPTER 28
ALLERGIC REACTIONS and ANAPHYLACTIC SHOCK

*Extreme Cases of Anaphylactic Shock
Can Lead To Coma and Death If Left Untreated.*

Anaphylactic shock is the result of a <u>severe</u> allergic reaction to a food, chemical, or an insect bite or sting. This can turn very quickly into a life-threatening situation. The animal's throat can swell shut, completely blocking the airway and causing the animal to suffocate. It is very important to recognize the signals of a severe allergic reaction and act by calling your veterinarian and quickly administering remedies.

The signs and symptoms of anaphylactic shock different considerably from that of hypovolemic shock and can be described as follows:

- Hives, itching, watery eyes
- Swelling at site of bite or sting
- Decreased level of consciousness
- Nausea, vomiting
- Difficulty breathing due to a swollen voice box
- Circulatory collapse

Holistic Emergency Care and Trauma Recovery for Animals / Section III

Treatment of allergic reaction begins with recognizing the signals of an allergic reaction and acting quickly.

If the symptoms are extreme, call your veterinarian if available. At the same time, dependent upon your supplies at hand, perform one of the following:

Divine Assistance / Energy Healing

- First objective is to calm the animal down and to call in divine healing energies – Divine Love – being the most important. Like with any situation you can facilitate the calling in of Divine Love and an Divine Emergency Team (Divine 911) whether you are directly hands on with the animal(s) or assisting from a distance.

- If you are a Reiki or Theta practitioner, utilize your skills to call in Divine Assistance. If not, this simple invocation can make you a facilitator of the Divine Energies to begin bringing the animal's body back into balance.

Say silently or out loud "God/Goddess (Creator or Mother/Father/God) make me an instrument of your peace, healing and LOVE to assist this animal(s)"
(or whomever / whatever is in need)

- Breathe, connect heart to heart with the animal(s) and allow the Divine energies to be emanated through you to all in need while envisioning the Divine Highest and Best of all being served.

- Continue with other assistance as suggested below while maintaining the Divine Connection as intuitively guided.

General Treatment

- Liquid Benadryl - for children is best. Gauge according to body size.
- Monitor breathing and pulse.
- Converse with the animal intuitively and telepathically to allow a greater sense of knowing as to his condition and how best to assist.

Holistic Emergency Care and Trauma Recovery for Animals / Section III

Flower Essence Treatment

- Administer Bach Rescue Remedy either cream or liquid. If giving the liquid orally – dilute in water first: 3 drops to 1 oz water. Cream or liquid can be applied topically to pads or behind the ears.

Homeopathy Treatment

- If reaction is to a <u>medication</u>, administer *Homeopathy Remedy:* Rhus Toxicodendren 30X to 30C.

- If the allergic reaction is due to a bite or sting : Administer Apis Mel in 30c or higher

If no real improvement is noticed in short order, transport the animal to your local veterinarian having called ahead to let them know you are coming and why.

CHAPTER 29
MUSCLE, JOINT & BONE INJURIES

Fractures, sprains, strains and **dislocations** can range from mild to severe. Bones are rigid and can break. Muscles can stretch, tear or snap causing sprains and/or strains. If a joint is over-stressed, the bones that meet at that joint may get dislocated.

Unless a bone is protruding from the limb or is obviously deformed, it is difficult to tell if it is fractured without taking an x-ray. The general rule is, "when in doubt, treat as a fracture." With horses, an injury of this kind requires a veterinarian to come to your location. However, with smaller animals you may opt to take them to the veterinarian for x-rays or diagnosis. If so, stabilizing the injury beforehand is a must to prevent, or at least minimize, any further damage from occurring during the transport process.

As stated in the preface of Section III, even if you are going to treat your animal with alternative/holistic modalities, getting a diagnosis from a veterinarian, especially for traumas where breaks or severe soft tissue injuries are indicated is highly recommended.

General Treatment

Control any bleeding using direct pressure and elevation (for more details see section on Controlling Bleeding)

- Ice the affected area. (Remember to use a barrier with the ice unless the animal has a thick fur coat.)

- Monitor breathing and pulse until trained medical personnel arrive.

Homeopathy

- If heavy bleeding is present administer *Homeopathy Remedy:* Phosphorus 6X to 30X
- For bruising and shock administer Homeopathic Arnica Montana 30x or 30C

- If hypovolemic shock is suspected:
    - Administer *Bach* Rescue Remedy or FES Five Flower Remedy.
    - Administer *Homeopathy Remedy:* Arnica Montana and Rhus Toxicodendren 30X.

Herbal Treatment

- If heavy bleeding is present administer hemostatic herbs through tincture, decoction or topically. These include: yarrow, goldenseal, bayberry, blackberry, witch hazel and horsetail.

- For bruising and shock administer turmeric topically. (Note: I rely heavily on Homeopathic Arnica Montana rather than herbs for bruising in emergency situations.)

Splinting

The basic principles for splinting are:

- Splint only if you are transporting or moving the animal or if you are certain there is a break and need to keep the animal quiet or off the limb until professional assistance can be obtained.
- Splint only if you can do so without causing more pain or injury.
- Splint the injured area in the position in which you find it.
- Splint all joints above and below the injury.
- Check circulation to the limb before and after splinting.

By immobilizing the injury you can lessen pain and prevent further damage.

If you do not have access to splinting supplies, you can use many other things such as books, newspapers, pillows, blankets, branches and other body parts.

Dislocations should be treated as fractures and the first responder should not try to put the joint back into place. This could cause additional tearing of the joint capsule and injure blood vessels and nerves in the area.

For a *sprain* or *strain,* immediately apply cold compresses for 20 minutes every 3 to 4 hours for the first 72 hours while also providing homeopathic or herbal treatment every 3 to 4 hours as well.

Keep the animal quiet for 24 hours taking her/him out on a leash to go to the bathroom. For any pain that persists, seek medical attention.

CHAPTER 30
HEAD & SPINE INJURIES

Anyone who has made direct contact with dogs' heads knows how *tough* their skulls are. Horses are equally so, but not so much for cats or certainly birds. So anytime you find an animal unconscious and do not know the cause of his/her condition, suspect head, neck and/or spine injuries.

Injuries to the head and spine can cause paralysis, speech or memory problems as well as damage to bone and soft tissue, including the brain and spinal cord. Since x-rays are usually the only way to know how severe an animal's head and/or spine injury are, treat such an injury as if it were severe.

Signals of head and/or spine injuries include:
- Changes in consciousness.
- Severe pain or pressure in the head, neck or back.
- Tingling or loss of sensation in the paws, hooves, feet or toes.
- Nausea, vomiting.
- Blood or other fluids in the ears or nose.
- Partial or complete loss of movement of any body part.
- Impaired breathing or vision as a result of the injury.

Divine Assistance / Energy Healing
- First objective is to calm the animal down and to call in divine healing energies – Divine Love – being the most important. Like with any situation you can facilitate the calling in of Divine Love and an Divine Emergency Team (Divine 911) whether you are directly hands on with the animal(s) or assisting from a distance.

Holistic Emergency Care and Trauma Recovery for Animals / Section III

- If you are a Reiki or Theta practitioner, utilize your skills to call in Divine Assistance. If not, this simple invocation can make you a facilitator of the Divine Energies to begin bringing the animal's body back into balance.

Say silently or out loud "God/Goddess (Creator or Mother/Father/God) make me an instrument of your peace, healing and LOVE to assist this animal(s)"
(or whomever / whatever is in need)

- Breathe, connect heart to heart with the animal(s) and allow the Divine energies to be emanated through you to all in need while envisioning the Divine Highest and Best of all being served.

- Continue with other assistance as suggested below while maintaining the Divine Connection as intuitively guided.

General Treatment

If you suspect a head or spine injury you should:

- If you are within driving distance call your veterinarian

- If you are out in the mountains or other remote area call the forestry department, mountaineering rescue or fire department.

- In either case, call in Divine Assistance – Angels and Elementals to stabilize the animal and assist in the healing process.

Homeopathy

- Administer *Homeopathy Remedy:* Hypericum 30X and *Bach* Rescue Remedy.
- Stabilize the head and neck in the position you found them by placing your hands along both sides of the head, keeping it in line with the spine and preventing movement.

- Stay with the animal and monitor breathing and pulse until trained veterinarian personnel arrive or during transport if you are taking the animal yourself.

Herbal Treatment

Suspected head or spine injuries require special care if using herbs. Until diagnosis is acquired, it is best to keep the herbs to those that support cellular regeneration and overall healing. These include:

- Hemostatic: horsetail, bayberry, blackberry, cayenne, cranesbill, mullein, goldenseal, white oak bark, and witch hazel
- Cellular regeneration: comfrey, calendula
- Calmatives to assist in relaxing the animal and make them more comfortable: chamomile,

Note: if you suspect that surgery is imminent, then wait on the herbal treatment and instead utilize homeopathy and flower essences which do not interfere with any medications that might be given in surgery.

Holistic Emergency Care and Trauma Recovery for Animals / Section III

CHAPTER 31

BURNS

Burn Prevention

Burns can be caused by four different types of sources: heat, chemical, radiation and electrical. For the most part animals have an innate respect of fire as it occurs in nature. However, humanity has created new venues of burn hazards through chemicals and electricity that animals may not have an innate or learned awareness of and may come in contact with inadvertently or through the carelessness of a human overseeing their care.

There are many ways to avoid these painful injuries. Here are a few suggestions:

- Pay attention to what you are doing when working with any chemical, heat or electrical source and be certain that your animals and the wildlife are protected from its adverse effects.

- If an electrical storm is imminent and you are out doors with your animal companions be sure you all get up under cover and are completely out of any water bodies such as rivers, lakes or the ocean. Remember that lightning can hit water and travel through it hitting whoever is swimming.

- If you have animal companions or small children, keep protective coverings on unused electrical sockets.

- Make sure you secure chemical solution lids tightly and keep them out of the reach of anyone who could be harmed by them.

- Avoid walking your dogs, cats or any animal with paw or claws on really hot surfaces as it can burn their feet. Be aware of the temperature of the ground - be it cement, road surface or sand. Many surfaces can heat way above a safe temperature for bare feet during the hot months of summer. If you are not sure of a surface temperature, test it with your hand or take your own shoe(s) off to see before walking your animal companion upon the surface.

Burns can be very mild or life-threatening. The seriousness of a burn is determined by the size, depth and body area burned. When treating for burns, determine the depth of the most serious burn and treat the entire burned area accordingly. Immediate first aid may lessen the severity. Prompt medical attention can help prevent scarring, disability and deformity. If you are able, always call a veterinarian when burns cover more than one area of the body, burns are to the head, neck, hands, feet or genitals or the animal is very young or elderly, or the burns are chemical or electrical in nature.

Burns' severity can be difficult to discern in animals with extensive fur coats unless the hair has been burned away. If uncertain of the extent or location of the burn (in the case of electrical burns which generally have one or two entry/exit points), stabilize the animal using treatment options shown below and then gently search her/his body to determine the extent of the burn(s).

Holistic Emergency Care and Trauma Recovery for Animals / Section III

Divine Assistance And Energy Healing for All Burns

Initiating Divine Assistance in emergencies is relatively the same for all situations. The only difference is the urgency of the situation and also whether you have other tools at your disposal or not.

The great benefit of calling in Divine Assistance and performing energy healing is that these abilities you carry with you; within you, whether or not you have a other assistance in the form of healing tools or a nearby medical facility.

- First objective is to calm the animal down and to call in divine healing energies – Divine Love – being the most important. Like with any situation you can facilitate the calling in of Divine Love and an Divine Emergency Team (Divine 911) whether you are directly hands on with the animal(s) or assisting from a distance.

- If you are a Reiki or Theta practitioner, utilize your skills to call in Divine Assistance. If not, this simple invocation can make you a facilitator of the Divine Energies to begin bringing the animal's body back into balance.

Say silently or out loud "God/Goddess (Creator or Mother/Father/God) make me an instrument of your peace, healing and LOVE to assist this animal(s)"
(or whomever / whatever is in need)

- Breathe, connect heart to heart with the animal(s) and allow the Divine energies to be emanated through you to all in need while envisioning the Divine Highest and Best of all being served.

- Continue with other assistance as suggested below while maintaining the Divine Connection as intuitively guided.

FIRST DEGREE BURNS

First-degree burns are the least severe. The surface skin is lightly burned and there is no blistering.

General Treatment

- Cool the burn with cool water (no ice) for at least 10 minutes. An animal may be more receptive to a cold compress (i.e. soft rag or towel soaked in cold water) over just having water run on their skin. However, you must be careful not to damage the skin further.
- Cover with a dry, sterile, non-adhesive dressing.
- Protect from further injury and watch for infection.

Homeopathy

- Administer *Homeopathy Remedy:* Cantharis 6X or 30X, 3-4 times a day for 1-2 days, decreasing when obvious improvement is seen.

- Homeopathic Calendula can also be of assistance. Same dosing.

Herbal Treatment

- Apply Aloe Vera directly from plant or in gel form, preferably pure and alcohol free. Lily of the Desert is my brand of choice in juice or gel form. You can also give your animal this type of aloe vera orally mixed with a bit of water or organic apple juice.

- A decoction of calendula can also be mixed with aloe vera and given orally or gently on the skin for first degree burns.

Flower Essence Treatment

- Rescue Remedy is a welcome tool in any injury or emergency.

- The flower essences of aloe or calendula are also very helpful in healing the burns from the feeling body inward to the physical. If available, put 3-4 drops in a small amount of water and eye dropper it into the animal's mouth 1-2 times per day or if the animal is ambulatory and drinking on its own, just put the drops in clean fresh water in his/her water bowl or drinking station in the case of a larger animal.

SECOND DEGREE BURNS

Second-degree burns are more severe and, if extensive, require prompt medical attention. They are deeper than first degree burns and will usually have blisters.

General Treatment for Second Degree Burns
- Call veterinarian when deemed necessary.
- Remove collar, harness, halter or other attire on the burned area if it will come off easily and without pulling off any skin.
- Cool with large amounts of cool water, (not ice water) or wet towels or cloth.
- Separate burned toes with clean, sterile (if possible) dressing.
- Cover with dry, sterile, non-adhesive dressing.
- Elevate and protect the area from injury if comfortable for the animal
- Treat for hypovolemic shock if necessary.
- Monitor breathing and pulse.

Homeopathy
- Calendula 30X or 30C to begin healing of skin
- Cantharis 30X or 30C for pain reduction
- If shock is present Arnica Montana 30X or 30C is an option

Dosing: 3-4 times/day one or all as necessary, preferably with a gap of time 30 minutes or 1 hour between remedies.

Herbal Treatment

- Aloe vera juice can be given orally to assist in the healing and cooling of the damaged skin. Lily of the Desert is my brand of choice in juice or gel form. You can also give your animal this type of aloe vera orally mixed with a bit of water or organic apple juice.

- A decoction of calendula can also be mixed with aloe vera and given orally or gently on the skin for first degree burns.

- Colloidal Silver drops or in spray

- Manuka honey (made from pollen of tea tree flowers) orally as an antibiotic. Give internally liquefied in a bit of water or rub on gums.

- Yarrow (Achillea millefolium) decoction can also be given to the animal orally to promote healing and protect from infection.

Flower Essence Treatment

- As with 1st degree burns, the flower essences of aloe or calendula are also very helpful in healing the burns from the feeling body inward to the physical. If available, put 3-4 drops in a small amount of water and eye dropper it into the animal's mouth 1-2 times per day or

- If the animal is ambulatory and drinking on its own, just put the drops in clean fresh water in his/her water bowl or drinking station in the case of a larger animal.

- Bach or FES Rescue Remedy are always helpful in burn situations

THIRD DEGREE BURNS

Third Degree Burns are extremely severe and always require medical attention. Third degree burns involve all seven layers of the skin and sometimes fat, muscles and bone.

General Treatment for Third Degree Burns

- Call veterinarian or emergency help (fire/police)
- Cool the burn with cool water, wet towels or wet sheets.
- Elevate, if possible.
- Treat for hypovolemic shock
- Monitor breathing and pulse.

Flower Essence Treatment

- Bach Rescue Remedy or FES Five Flower Remedy orally
- Bach Rescue Remedy cream can be rubbed on skin in unaffected area

Homeopathy

- Calendula 30X or 30C to begin healing of skin
- Cantharis 30X or 30C for pain reduction
- If shock is present Arnica Montana 30X or 30C is an option

Dosing for Calendula and Cantharis: 3-4 times/day, one or both, as necessary, preferably with a gap of time 30 minutes or 1 hour between remedies. Arnica Montana 1-2 times or until shock symptoms have ceased.

Herbal Treatment

- Aloe vera juice can be given orally to assist in the healing and cooling of the damaged skin. Lily of the Desert is my brand of choice in juice or gel form. You can also give

Holistic Emergency Care and Trauma Recovery for Animals / Section III

your animal this type of aloe vera orally mixed with a bit of water or organic able juice.

- An decoction of calendula can also be mixed with aloe vera and given orally or gently on the skin for first degree burns.

- Colloidal Silver drops or in spray

- Manuka honey (made from pollen of tea tree flowers) orally as an antibiotic

- Yarrow (Achillea millefolium) decoction can also be given to the animal orally to promote healing and protect from infection

CHEMICAL BURNS

Chemical burns can happen in the home and at the workplace. Generally speaking, the stronger the chemical and the longer the contact, the more severe the burn is going to be. The chemical substance continues to burn as long as it is on the skin or in the hair or fur.

General Treatment

- Flush the affected area with water immediately, being sure to remove anything the animal is wearing that might have gotten the chemical(s) in or on it. Continue to flush until you are certain the area(s) are free from the chemical(s) or until emergency medical assistance arrives if you have made the call.

- Call emergency veterinarian assistance if deemed necessary
- Watch for hypovolemic shock and treat if necessary
- Monitor breathing and pulse.

Flower Essence Treatment

- Bach Rescue Remedy or FES Five Flower Remedy orally

- Bach Rescue Remedy cream can be rubbed on skin in unaffected area

Homeopathy

- Causticum is the primary homeopathic for chemical burns. If you do not have any on hand then use Cantharis
- Calendula to assist with repair of skin cells

Herbal Treatment

Herbal treatment comes in after the chemical(s) have been removed from the animal's body; fur, skin, feathers, hair, etc. The herbs used are primarily for cellular regeneration, pain relief and possible infection prevention.

- Aloe Vera, comfrey and calendula for cellular regeneration : Administer Aloe Vera (organic whole leaf or juice, orally), on its own or combined with tincture or decoction of the other herbs.
- Chamomile for pain relief
- Yarrow, Echinacea, or Plantain for infection prevention

Other Treatments

- Colloidal Silver can be used internally and externally in a spray to assist in the prevention of infections.

ELECTRICAL BURNS

Never go near an animal you think has been injured by electricity until you are sure the power source is turned off. The severity of an electrical burn depends on how long the body is in contact with the electric current, the strength of the current, the type of current and the direction it takes through the body. The animal may have multiple burns; one burn where the current entered the body and others where it left the body.

Electrical wounds may look minor, but the tissues or organs beneath may be severely damaged. In the case of an electrical burn from coming into contact with electric sparks or unprotected wire, the wounds may be local and larger.

Lightning strikes are also considered to be electrical burns in how they enter and leave the body and how they affect the body overall.

General Treatment

- Think Safety. Do not enter an unsafe area or touch someone who is still in contact with a live electrical wire in some way.

- Disconnect power source yourself if possible or have turned off by electric company.

- Check the animal for breathing and pulse.

- Check for multiple burn sites. There are usually at least two points – an entry and exit point that the energy traveled. They may be small, but the internal damage may be extensive.

- Watch for shock -- Administer *Bach* Rescue Remedy if symptoms appear.

- Monitor breathing and pulse.

Homeopathy

- Phosphorous or Phos to assist in the relief of pain from electrical burns 6X to 200X dependent upon what is available.

- Administer the remedy 3 times in 15 to 30 minutes dependent upon the pain level of the animal. If there is no notable improvement, move on to another remedy such as Cantharis or Hypericum.

- In the case of electrical burns, it is highly advised to get the animal to a veterinarian as quickly as possible to check for internal damage.

Herbal Treatment

If the burns are not life threatening there are several herbs that can be of assistance primarily in decoction form:

- Comfrey
- Elder flowers
- Calendula

Aloe vera juice can also be given orally to an animal – 1:4 ratio aloe to water or water & apple juice. These herbs all assist in calming the pain and increasing the body's ability to regenerate damaged cells.

Flower Essence Treatment

- Bach Rescue Remedy liquid or cream or
- FES Five Flower Remedy
- Aloe vera remedy
- Self-Heal Flower Remedy

CHAPTER 32

POISONING

Poisoning is something that occurs with animals far too frequently due to the amount of poisons that some people are still using in their homes and businesses. And of course there are government agencies and hurtful people who intentionally poison animals wild and domestic.

I have experienced this directly through the horror of one of my dogs eating some meat laced with poison years ago. Many animals in the neighborhood died. We were lucky, as I was home when she convulsed and the vet was close by and able to send emergency assistance.

There are four ways an animal can be poisoned. They are:

Ingested - swallowing something toxic.

Inhaled - breathing in poisonous gases or fumes.

Absorbed - touching something that poisons you on, or through the skin.

Injected - an insect bite or sting or by intravenous drugs.

Some signals to watch for which may indicate that a poisoning has occurred:

- Evidence at the scene such as empty containers or open cabinets and/or unusual odors, fumes or smoke.

- The animal is nauseated, vomits, has diarrhea, chest pain or abdominal pain, has difficulty breathing, is sweating or there are changes in consciousness level.

- Burns around the lips or tongue or on the skin.

Holistic Emergency Care and Trauma Recovery for Animals / Section III

POISON CONTROL CENTER PHONE NUMBERS

The United States has a system of Poison Control Centers as do some states including California. These centers all have websites with free information and also a free hot line phone number in case of an emergency.

In the United States - America Association of Poison Control Center. The American Association of Poison Control Centers supports the nation's 55 poison centers in their efforts to prevent and treat poison exposures. Poison centers offer free, confidential medical advice 24 hours a day, seven days a week through the **Poison Help Line at 1-800-222-1222.**

This service provides a primary resource for poisoning information and helps reduce costly emergency department visits through in-home treatment. The AAPCC's mission is to actively advance the health care role and public health mission of our members through information, advocacy, education and research. Here is their contact information:

- Phone: 1-800-222-1222
- Websites: http://www.poison.org ; http://www.aapcc.org/

The AAPCC's will answer questions regarding animals and people. And if they do not have the information needed they may refer to you to other agencies such as **ASPCA's Animal Poison Control.**

- Phone: (888) 426-4435
- Website link is: http://www.aspca.org/pet-care/animal-poison-control

The national Poison Control Center is free, but the Animal Poison Control may charge $65 for the consultation as they are staffed by veterinarians.

Another option is **Pet Poison Hotline** which charges $39 per incident:

- Phone: 800-213-8660
- Website: http://www.petpoisonhelpline.com/

Holistic Emergency Care and Trauma Recovery for Animals / Section III

TYPES OF POISONINGS AND BASIC TREATMENTS

Ingested Poisoning Examples

If you suspect one of your animals has been poisoned, immediately phone the Poison Control Center or your veterinarian. If possible, quickly find out what the substance was and when and how much was ingested. If you know what was ingested then also begin treatments as guided below. Take any containers you find with you to the phone and be prepared to answer the operator's questions.

If your animal has ingested a medication that was not meant for him, never assume you know what to do, and <u>never</u> use the antidotes listed on product containers. They are often wrong.

Holistic Emergency Care and Trauma Recovery for Animals / Section III

INGESTED POISONING

Many animals live life through taste testing their environments. It is this tendency along with humans carelessness regarding leaving poisonous substances around that makes ingested poisoning a potential hazard.

Symptoms of Ingested Poisoning

Clinical signs will vary depending on the type of poison swallowed. They can be as mild as:

- generalized lethargy
- malaise and weakness
- to gastrointestinal signs like vomiting
- diarrhea, drooling, and nausea

More severe signs can include

- agitation
- excessive sedation
- Tremors
- Twitching
- Seizures or even coma[7]

Personal experience has taught me that the ingesting of food poisons verses chemical poisons can have considerably different symptoms. Dogs who have eaten grapes or raisins can have symptoms of kidney failure, while a chemical poison can show up as seizures or worse. I have experienced both with animals (dogs and cats). The food poisoning I could care for at home. The chemical poisoning (meat laced with poison and thrown around our

---

[7] http://www.petmd.com/dog/emergency/poisoning-toxicity/e_dg_swallowed_poisons

neighborhood) sent my dog into seizures and required immediate veterinarian intervention which saved her life.

Key to treatment is the awareness of what has been ingested. Note: Using syrup of ipecac to Induce vomiting to remove the ingested poison used to be commonplace. This practice has been for the most part stopped.

Regardless of the means, it is critical **NOT** to induce vomiting if you suspect the animal has ingested one of the following:

- strychnine → alkalis (lye)
- strong acids → Kerosene
- fuel oil → gasoline
- coal oil → paint thinner
- cleaning fluid → anything else that is corrosive in nature

General Treatment

The most important tool to keep on hand in case of poisoning is **Activated Charcoal** (which can neutralize certain poisons in the body in cases where vomiting should not be induced).

- Call Poison Control Center – See Appendix A
- Administer Activated Charcoal as directed – if directed – by poison control specialist

Flower Essence Treatment

- Bach Rescue Remedy or
- FES Five Flower Remedy
- If poison contained radioactive material or metals, the FES Yarrow Environmental formula is suggested.

Homeopathy

These remedies are specifically in reference to **food poisoning** situations.[8]

- **Arsenicum**:- No. 1 homeopathic medicine for food poisoning, especially after meat, when there is vomiting and diarrhea. Those who need Arsenicum feel physically very weak, but they are so anxious they can't help but be restless. They are nervous at the thought of being left alone and when feeling at their worst actually feel they are going to die. Symptoms are often most severe from midnight - 3am.

- **Pulsatilla**: Is helpful after eating bad fish. It's also good for upsets brought on by too much ice cream.

- **Lycopodium**: Is better suited to poisoning from shellfish.

- **China**: No. 1 homeopathic medicine to promote recovery after dehydration. Sometimes even after diarrhea and vomiting has stopped, a terrible feeling of weakness remains, due to the effects of dehydration. China can be extremely helpful in these circumstances.

Herbal Treatment

Herbal treatment for poisoning – ingested or otherwise is generally done after any life threatening symptoms are handled through homeopathy, flower essences, a veterinarian intervention or a combination thereof.

---

[8] http://www.homeopathyworld.com/foodpoison.htm

ABSORBED POISONS

Absorbed poisons can include chemicals such as acids, alkalies, phenols, and some plants including poison oak or ivy. Most animals are not susceptible to poison oak or ivy, but there are a few recorded cases. More likely they carry the oils on their hair and then transfer it to others with whom they come into contact.

A word of caution: Documentation shows that companion animals are also often poisoned by the use of flea and tick prevention medicines. Choosing natural, non-toxic options for flea and tick prevention is a much better option.

In the case of absorbed poisons, it is more likely to be a human-made poisonous substance getting on the body such as an insecticide, cleaning fluid or other substance resulting in an adverse reaction. Symptoms of absorbed poisoning include swelling, skin irritation, rash, blisters and burning.

General Treatment

- Flush immediately with water. Follow this with a rinse of apple cider vinegar and goldenseal.

- Remove all clothing that may have the poisonous substance on it (collar, harness, vest, etc.)

- Monitor breathing and pulse. Reference vital sign chart in Appendix B. If problems with breathing or pulse arise, administer flower essence (below) and call

    - Poison Control (800-222-1200)
    - ASPCA Animal Poison Control : **888-426-4435**
    - or your veterinarian.

Flower Essence Treatment

- If severe Bach Rescue Remedy cream or tincture or
- FES Five Flower Remedy
- Also, FES Self Heal can be of great assistance

Homeopathy

- In the case of poison ivy or oak, administer *Homeopathy Remedy:* Rhus Toxicodendren if symptoms develop (i.e. itching, burning, swelling of skin)

Herbal Treatment

Herbal treatment for poisoning – ingested or otherwise is generally done after any life threatening symptoms are handled through homeopathy, flower essences, a veterinarian intervention or a combination thereof.

Holistic Emergency Care and Trauma Recovery for Animals / Section III

Inhaled Poisons

Most fumes and gases are invisible and many are odorless. Never enter an area if you suspect you may be exposed to poisonous fumes or gases. In non-lethal doses the damage that inhaled poisoning do to an animal (or person) are by irritating the lungs and overall respiratory system. In addition, as the poisons go from the lungs into the blood stream, contamination of the blood can occur damaging the hemoglobin and red blood cell quality overall.

General Treatment

If you suspect an animal has inhaled a poison such as carbon monoxide, smoke or chemical fumes and gases:

- **CALL POISON CONTROL CENTER: ASPCA ANIMAL POISON CONTROL CENTER: 888-426-4435 ; more #'s in Appendix A at the back of the book.**

- Administer Activated charcoal if recommended by poison center.

- Once treatment is underway call veterinarian if you feel the situation is going to require additional assistance. Always error on the side of caution in these situations.

Flower Essence Treatment

There are a variety of flower essences that can assist in the immediate care of poisoning and the aftercare. The basics are listed here:

- Bach Rescue Remedy
- FES Five Flower Remedy
- Love Lies Bleeding – for profound pain and suffering which moves soul beyond its personal limits

Herbal Treatment

There are many components of assisting with inhaled poisoning that can be aided through the use of herbs. Whether they are utilized in the immediate moment or after seeing a veterinarian is up to the person caring for the animal in the emergency situation itself.

Suggestions:

- Blood purification herbs are always of benefit
- Inhaled Poisons can often damage the mucous membrane of the body (throat, lungs, stomach, etc). Herbs that are demulcants in decoction form can aid in recovery

Holistic Emergency Care and Trauma Recovery for Animals / Section III

Injected Poisons

Injected poisons include insect bites and stings, snake bites or vaccines that cause a reaction an animal. In my experience they are the most prevalent of the poisons that domestic animals experienced.

Prevention – Bites and Stings

Awareness of the animals, insects and plants that can inflict poisons into your animal's or your own body is the first step preventing having a problem with them. Having awareness and a healthy respect (not fear) of who they are in the world and what environments are likely to be where they hang out allows you, and through you, your animals, to live in harmony with them more easily.

Then there is the issue of boundaries. We have ours and they have theirs. This is especially true of snakes, spiders and insects. Creating healthy boundaries in our home environments and then respecting the home boundaries of poisonous (and all) animals, insects & plants in nature can allow you, your animals, and poisonous creatures to journey through life without ever having a confrontation.

Brown Recluse: The violin pattern is not diagnostic, as other spiders can have similar markings (e.g. cellar spiders and pirate spiders). For definitive identification it is imperative to examine the eyes. While most spiders have eight eyes, recluse spiders have six eyes arranged in pairs (dyads) with one median pair and two lateral pairs. Only a few other spiders have three pairs of eyes arranged in this way (e.g., scytodids).

Recluses have no obvious coloration patterns on the abdomen or legs, and the legs lack spines.[1] The abdomen is covered with fine short hairs that, when viewed without magnification, give the appearance of soft fur. The leg joints may appear to be a slightly lighter color. (Source: http://en.wikipedia.org/wiki/Brown_recluse_spider)

Black Widow Spider : These spiders like to reside in dark quiet places. I have never seen one in the wild, on the other hand, I have seen plenty in my garage or other buildings on property in which there are spaces that do not get visited often.

Important: Keep your garage and out buildings clean and be aware when allowing your animal companions to go into spaces that have not been visited or cleaned for a while.

According to Pet MD, even though your pet may not feel it while they are being bitten, pain starts to set in immediately around the area of the bite. Pain progresses quickly and spreads to the lymph nodes nearest to the site of the bite. The pain reaches maximum intensity in one to three hours. Your pet may feel a constant pain during this time, or it may come in waves. The pain from this bite can last up to 48 hours.

Holistic Emergency Care and Trauma Recovery for Animals / Section III

Insect Bites

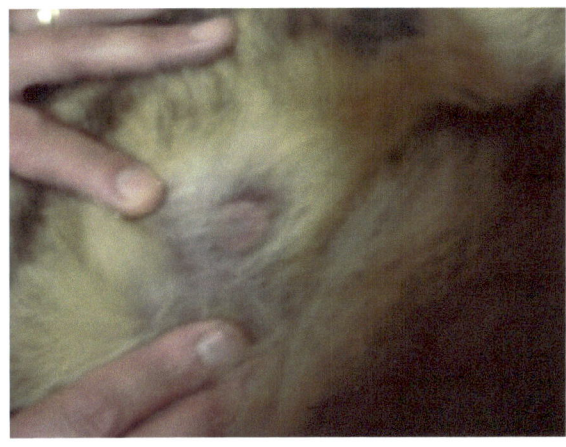

This visual is Spirithawk's leg with a spider bite. Although I was not certain, I suspected it was a Brown Recluse, and treated it accordingly. Regardless of the type of bite they can be uncomfortable and even painful; however, what to watch for are signs on of the bite being from a Brown Recluse (Fiddler Spider) or Black Widow.

Bites from these poisonous spiders must receive special attention to be sure they are resolved correctly.

Insect Bite Symptoms

- Stinger may be present
- Bite marks
- Possible allergic reaction

Pain
Swelling

Homeopathy is of key importance for successful holistic treatment of these bites. For details see **Homeopathic Treatment** below.

General Treatment

If present …

- Remove the stinger by scraping with a credit card or something similar.

- Wash area with soap and water or antiseptic solution, such as witch hazel & lavender or yarrow.

- Apply cold compresses to reduce swelling

- Watch for allergic reaction.

Holistic Emergency Care and Trauma Recovery for Animals / Section III

- If you notice signs of allergic reaction – see section on Allergic Reactions and call veterinarian if life threatening situation is developing.

Flower Essence Treatment
- Bach Rescue Remedy or FES Five Flower Remedy
- Self Heal

Homeopathy Treatment for Insect Bites

The homeopathic remedy used for bites depends upon who did the biting.
- Administer Apis Mellifica : insect bites
- Ledum Pal 30X : use for all bites and puncture wounds
- Wasp stings: Administer *Homeopathy Remedy:* Apis Mel, Calendula 30X.

Herbal Treatment for Insect Bites

Knowing the herbs that are good for insect bites and grow abundantly in nature can be very helpful. These may vary dependent upon where you live. Regardless of the herb you choose to use, I highly recommend also using Homeopathic Ledum Pal as well. (See above)

- Plantain – both common and broad leaf: If fresh is available, rub on insect bite site or administer decoction or tincture (diluted) if that form is available
- Calendula
- Aloe Vera
- Witch Hazel and lavender

[4]Chelation Therapy can be used to treat spider and snake bites. <u>Alternative Medicine. The Definitive Guide</u>, pg. 126-129.

Holistic Emergency Care and Trauma Recovery for Animals / Section III

Snake Bites

Celia Balderree

Snake bites can be a very frightening thing for everyone involved – including the snake. It is important in such instances to understand that the snake was just acting in self-defense and would much rather have gotten out of your animal's way. Until we are all (humans & animals) living in a state of peace and harmony there is going to exist a certain level of reaction that occurs between us.

This also goes for domesticated animals towards wild and vice versa. Most wild animals these days see our companion animals as an extension of the human condition and as such hesitate to trust them.

Homeopathic Treatment for Snake Bites

In addition to Ledum Pal, the main homeopathic remedies for snake bites are:

- **Aconite and Lachesis 30c, 30x or 200x or c**

  Administer 3-4 tablets every 15 to 20 minutes for 1 hour while watching for heightened or diminishing symptoms. If symptoms worsen, contact veterinarian.

Holistic Emergency Care and Trauma Recovery for Animals / Section III

CHAPTER 33

SUDDEN ILLNESS

Ishnahnay experiencing allergeic reaction to food or environment – photograph was taken before she was diagnosed

Prevention

Sudden illness within animals can manifest from an internal imbalance, an external influence, or a combination. Our health is our own responsibility, as is the health and well-being of the animals in our care. In order to attain or maintain it there are many things that we can do.

*It is the view of the author, that all animals (wild or domestic),
as well as the other kingdoms of nature are in our care and stewardship,
thus their well-being
is our responsibility to a great extent.*

Keeping the immune system of our animal(s) strong is of critical importance. This is accomplished through whole wild and organic nutrition, stress control, exercise, rest, drinking plenty of purified water, body work, restoring the environment to its naturally purified and harmonious state, and more.

Holistic Emergency Care and Trauma Recovery for Animals / Section III

It is up to us to take the very best of care of ourselves and our animals through holistic life style and prevention. This is even more so since many of the means that we have used in the past for "correcting" disease are no longer viable alternatives (such as repetitive use of antibiotics, steroids).

Learn to listen to and observe your animal's body and pay attention to the signals it is sending you. Remember to do daily checks of her body to provide you a heightened awareness of anomalies or intruders such as ticks, stickers and the like. Also, remember nutrition as a key to well-being

Providing our animals with abundant purified water is of key importance to their well-being. So be sure to refill all water bowls, baths and containers daily, if not twice a day. Also, clean the containers regularly to prevent the growth of fungus that could compromise your animals' immune systems.

Another element of key importance in preventing sudden illness is to be aware of toxins in your environment and that of animals in your care. A vast majority of toxins that are in our environments are there because humans have created them and put them there either directly or indirectly. Toxins in the air, water, on the earth and plants as well as in your home can cause sudden illness to an animal in the form of a poison or over-prolonged exposure such as pesticides, flea collar residue, cleaning solutions and more.

When choosing holistic care, expand this process to include organic gardening, natural cleaning products and pest control. You may not have control over the larger toxic issues created by government or community, however, you can at least make your home an expression of harmony and an example to your community and beyond while keeping your animals and yourself in a greater state of wellness.

Holistic Emergency Care and Trauma Recovery for Animals / Section III

When Illness Strikes

When an animal becomes suddenly ill, she will usually look and feel sick. Though there are many different types of illnesses, many have the same symptoms. In most cases, it is not necessary to know what is causing the illness to recognize when it is necessary to seek medical attention.

Exceptions to this include extreme poisoning and bloat, both of which can require immediate veterinarian assistance, and in the case of poisoning, knowledge of the causal agent.

Common signals include:

- Nausea, vomiting or diarrhea
- Sweating or change in skin color
- Dizziness, confusion, decreased consciousness or fainting
- Seizures
- Paralysis
- Severe headache, slurred speech, difficulty seeing
- Difficulty breathing
- Constant pain or pressure

If you notice any of these conditions, take immediate action as warranted by the symptoms.

General Treatment

- Call your veterinarian or a holistic animal consultant if deemed necessary.
- Care for life-threatening conditions (breathing, pulse).
- Do your best to have the animal(s) you are helping relax and keep them from becoming chilled or overheated.

Holistic Emergency Care and Trauma Recovery
for Animals / Section III

- Watch for changes in his/her condition.
- Reassure the animal and hold the vision in your mind and heart of her being well and happy again -- always be positive, even under grim circumstances

If ill, many animals will attempt in their own way to find a remedy. This is especially the case if they are outdoors with grasses and herbs accessible to them.

Internal Cleansing

If this is the case, let her eat what she feels is necessary while observing her manner. Is she really anxious and frantically looking for help, or is it a more casual process?

If she is anxious, this is a clue to you to provide assistance through other means and determine whether professional medical assistance is required.

Divine Call

Beloved Angels and Elementals who watch over my animals and me please assist (name)'s body in coming back into balance and guide me to assist in whatever way(s) I am able.
Thank you.

Vomiting

If your animal companion or an animal that you are assisting is vomiting, the first thing is to observe what kind of vomiting it is and if you can detect whether the problem is from an external or internal cause or both. If poison is suspected, refer to the chapter on Poisoning.

Most animals will intentionally eat grass and other wild herbs to cleanse themselves of unwanted toxins, parasites and to rebalance their gut. Their doing so may be a sign that they are ill. However, it is just as often a preventative measure that they take to stay well. This is a rather methodical process of their eating grass or herbs, throwing up and then repeating until they are satisfied they have completed the task.

Often in the vomit there will be grass and abdominal juices (including water). But not a whole lot else unless there is an underlying illness or problem that the animal is attempting to cleanse and balance such as having eaten something that is making them sick. If the latter is the case, there may also be an anxiety present with the animal – something like the energy of "oh, God, get it out of me!"

If you feel that the animal is actually ill, then follow the steps below. If you feel that she is doing preventative cleansing, then you can assist her by adding macro foods such as spirulina, kelp or dandelion to her food on a daily basis to assist her body in gently detoxifying.

General Treatment

- Observe the vomit and overall body action/symptoms to gain a greater understanding of what is causing it. What else is going on? Ask you animal to show you what she is feeling or experiencing.

- Look to your environment to determine if the animal has consumed something poisonous or toxic in some way.

- If you suspect bacterial or viral cause then administer a dose (eye dropper) of Colloidal Silver.

Holistic Emergency Care and Trauma Recovery
for Animals / Section III

- If vomit is violent, look to homeopathy and also flower essences for assistance, while calling veterinarian or holistic consultant for assistance.

Flower Essence Treatment

- **Bach Rescue Remedy / FES Five Flower Remedy:** This is the primary flower essence in all emergencies.

- **Arnica:** helps to heal deep-seated shock or trauma which may become locked into the body and prevent full healing recovery.

- **Self Heal**: inspires the inner healer of the body to receive the greater healing assistance from the etheric realms of Life.

- **FES Yarrow Environmental Formula:** If environmental poisoning or toxins (including metals and radioactive substances)

- **Crab Apple:** This flower essence is the cleansing remedy for toxins, pathogens, and negativity. Anytime there is impurity or contamination this essence is a great choice. It helps rid toxicity, poisoning, skin conditions, infections and body odor. [9]

Homeopathy

The homeopathy for vomiting is dependent upon the symptoms which also often (but not always) reflective of the cause.

- **Food Poisoning:** Administer Homeopathy Remedy: **Arsenicum or Veratrum Album** 30X.

- **Over-Indulgence**: Administer Homeopathy Remedy: **Nux Vomica or Pulsatilla** 30X.

- **Or vomiting With Severe Cramping**: Administer Homeopathy Remedy: **Bryonia** or Colocynthis 30X.

---

[9] http://www.blessedfloweressences.com/Blog/tag/diarrhea/

- **With persistent and Extreme Nausea**: Administer Homeopathy Remedy: **Ipecac** 30X (not to be confused with Syrup of Ipecac!)

Herbal Treatment

The herbal support for vomiting and other sudden illness really depends on the cause as well as the symptoms.

- Determine if the vomiting is due to a bacterial or viral infection or some other cause such as poisoning

- If you feel it is viral or bacterial and you are not already treating the symptoms with homeopathy then it is suggested to use one or more herbs that are antibiotic and antiviral in property. Again with animals these are best used in either tincture or decoction form.

These include:

- Echinacea
- Goldenseal
- Garlic
- Thyme

Holistic Emergency Care and Trauma Recovery
for Animals / Section III

Diarrhea

Diarrhea in animals, especially those with whom we share a home, can be a messy business. Most animals given the opportunity will go outside when they are having such a problem as they do not wish to mess their home. If they cannot exit to a yard or outside area, then the situation may become a combination of them being embarrassed or worried that you are going to get angry or distressed, as well as them having the temporary body imbalance.

So like with a child, while you are assisting your animal with coming back into balance and wellness, also be compassionate regarding the mess he may be creating for you to clean up. Being distressed about whatever mess you may have to clean up, may compound the reason for the illness with emotional dis-ease in the animal possibly prolonging the challenge at hand.

The Danger

Extreme diarrhea, especially in young or old animals, can be very dangerous due to the threat of dehydration. Like vomiting, diarrhea can sometimes be the animal's way of self-cleansing from a moderate toxin or incompatible food source and may not last long.

On the other hand, if it is being caused by a more extreme or chronic issue it may persist or reoccur until the greater imbalance is identified and removed from her environment, diet or other point of entry.

Characteristics of Diarrhea[10]

This chart is referencing dogs in particular, however can also be applied to other mammals. The term "rapid transit" refers to food or whatever the animal has ingested moving swiftly through the GI track with little or no absorption. The body is just getting rid of it as quickly as possible.

---

[10] http://pets.wcbmd.com/dogs/diarrhea-causes-treatment-dogs

Holistic Emergency Care and Trauma Recovery for Animals / Section III

COLOR	LIKELY CAUSE	POSSIBLE LOCATION
Yellow or Greenish	Rapid Transit	Small bowel
Black, tarry	Upper GI Bleeding	Stomach or small bowel
Red blood or clots	Lower CI bleeding	Colon clots
Pasty, light	Lack of bile	Liver
Large, gray, rancid	Inadequat3e digestion	Small bowel or absorption

CONSISTENCY	LIKELY CAUSE	POSSIBLE LOCATION
Watery	Rapid transit	Small bowel
Foamy	Bacterial infection	Small bowel
Greasy, often with oily hair around the anus		Malabsorption Small bowel, pancreas
Glistening or jellylike	Contains mucus	Colon

ODOR	LIKELY CAUSE	LIKELY LOCATION
Food-like, or smelling like sour milk	Rapid transit and inadequate digestion or absorption (suggests overfeeding, especially in puppies or kittens)	Small bowel
Rancid or foul	Inadequate digestion with fermentation	Small bowel, pancreas

FREQUENCY	LIKELY CAUSE	POSSIBLE LOCATION
Several small stools in an hour, with straining		Colitis Colon
Three or four large stools in a day		Inadequate digestion or absorption Small bowel, pancreas

Remember with holistic treatments your intention is to look at both the symptoms and the source to determine what treatment to provide your animal.

General Treatment

Most diarrheas will pass on its own unless it is caused from poor diet or other chronic challenges, so the main concern is to keep the animal hydrated, comfortable and provide him with proper minerals. Animals who are still in touch with their inner healer will most likely choose to fast when their body is purging in such a manner. So be aware of what she is telling you intuitively while you are facilitating her healing.

- If poor diet is the root cause, utilize Probiotics and Digestive Enzymes to strengthen the animal's digestive system.

- Apple juice for the pectin which assists in cleansing the liver and overall toxins

- Kaopectate : carried in most drug stores – utilizes pectin fiber and a mineral from clay to assist in binding bacteria and toxins.

- Seaweed, Spirulena or Chlorella to help balance the body and provide minerals lost through the diarrhea.

Homeopathy Treatment

There are a variety of homeopathic remedies for diarrhea based on the possible cause and characteristics:

- **Food Poisoning**: : Homeopathy Remedy: **Arsenicum or Veratrum Album 30X**.
- **Over-Indulgence**: Homeopathy Remedy: Nux Vomica 30X.
- **Overindulgence of Fats:** Homeopathy Remedy: Pulsatilla (especially ice cream) 30X.
- **Yellow**: Homeopathy Remedy: **Podophyllum.**
- **Green or Mucous:** Homeopathy Remedy: **Chamomile, Ipecac or Pulsatilla.**
- **Always Changing**: Homeopathy Remedy: **Pulsatilla**.
- **Like Rice Water**: Homeopathy Remedy: **Veratrum Album**.

Flower Essence Treatment

Always remember that the main focus of Flower Essences is the feeling and mental bodies of whomever are taking them. So using them in combination with herbs, homeopathy or nutritional supplements such as seaweed or probiotics is going to provide the animal with the greatest assistance.

- **Bach Rescue Remedy / FES Five Flower Remedy:** This remedy is a general assistant for any acute imbalance, or life threatening challenge.

- **Crab Apple:** This flower essence is the cleansing remedy for toxins, pathogens, and negativity. Anytime there is impurity or contamination this essence is a great choice. It helps rid toxicity, poisoning, skin conditions, infections and body odor. [11]

- **Self Heal**: Inspires the inner healer of the body to receive the greater healing assistance from the etheric realms of Life.

- **FES Yarrow Environmental Formula:** If environmental poisoning or toxins (including metals and radioactive substances)

- **Arnica**: helps to heal deep-seated shock or trauma which may become locked into the body and prevent full healing recovery.[12]

Herbal Treatment

- If you suspect viral or bacterial cause: decoction of plantain, and yarrow
- Not sure of cause: Decoction of blackberry or raspberry leaf
- Slippery elm, marshmallow or mullen are helpful in providing irritated mucous membranes with healing support.

---

[11] http://www.blessedfloweressences.com/Blog/tag/diarrhea/
[12] Flower Essence Society Repertory

Holistic Emergency Care and Trauma Recovery for Animals / Section III

CHAPTER 34
SEIZURES

Seizures - understanding what is causing one in an animal has everything to do with how you respond to the situation overall. They can be caused by a variety of things most common of which are listed below:

- Trauma, and in the case of concussions, post trauma scar tissue in the brain
- Genetic predisposition (i.e. epilepsy)
- Tumors
- Poisoning and other toxins in the body resulting in neurological dysfunction (such as rat poison, antifreeze, alcohol, pesticides, insecticides …)
- Lead
- Kidney failure

… and more

"All cases of seizures involve electrical disturbances of the brain that result in muscle contractions of variable intensity and loss of motor control. Many animals lose consciousness and bladder and bowel control during a seizure, and some may exhibit overly affectionate, frightened, or clingy behavior immediately before an epileptic episode. Digestive disorders, hair loss, neuralgia, and several other problems may also be associated with chronic convulsive disorders." [13]

As with a human, having an awareness of an animal that has a predisposition to seizures (such as in the case of epilepsy or physical trauma creating an anatomical imbalance that causes seizures) allows you much greater knowing of the best emergency response to provide. If the animal does not have a predisposition to seizures, then it is best to assume in the moment than the cause is something else – from a new trauma to poisoning, and act accordingly. In the case of poisoning, there is no time to waste! See Poisoning Chapter for directions.

> *Your ability as an intuitive communicator with animals will allow a more extensive communication between you in such traumatic times.*

Symptoms

Seizures can come on very suddenly, for instance with poisoning, or they can come on in a more gradual manner. Below is a list of some of the more common physical and emotional symptoms.

- Dazed look
- Chomping and chewing
- Seeking seclusion
- Restlessness
- Collapse
- In the case of dogs, whining and seeking attention
- In the case of cats, bursts of outrage or aggression
- Rigidity or jerking of legs
- Throwing back of head
- Loss of urine or stools
- Drooling

---

[13] Epilepsy, Convulsions, and Seizures Holistic Approaches, by Mary L. Wulff-Tilford & Gregory L. Tilford

Holistic Emergency Care and Trauma Recovery for Animals / Section III

If you are witness to an animal that is having a seizure, do not restrain her or place anything in her mouth. If you know that it is a seizure from a predisposition, then protect the animal, specially her head while allowing her body to do what it requires to express the seizure. ((Restraining can cause further damage.)

As stated, if you are not aware of a predisposition to seizures, and you do not see another immediate cause or trauma, it is wise to suspect poisoning:

- Call a poison control center : see APPENDIX A (Red tabbed pages) for numbers
- Then call your veterinarian or emergency veterinarian clinic

Divine Assistance

In these instances I always all for Divine Assistance while simultaneously speaking prayers (Hail Mary, and I AM the Resurrection and the Life of "name"'s body into its Divine perfection, are two of my favorites.

Also breathing, going inward and asking to be made an instrument of healing is easy, broad in its application and requires no real skill other than to all the Divine to work through you.

> *Mother/Father/God Please Make Me an Instrument of Your Healing for "name"*

... then relax, listen and allow your heart/mind/body to follow the intuitive instructions that you are given.

Note, all this can be done while you are cradling the animal (or person) in your arms if there is no one else to do that for you.

General Treatment

If you do not suspect poisoning:
- Clear the immediate area so the animal will not be injured by hitting something.

- If possible, cushion the animal's head.

- If the cause of the seizure is unknown or traumatic injury occurred, contact your veterinarian while administering holistic assistance to begin the healing process.

- Transport the animal to the veterinarian if required.

- If not, then stay with the animal until the animal becomes fully aware and conscious, continuing to treat the symptoms holistically as necessary.

- Monitor breathing and pulse.

- Treat for shock

Flower Essence Treatment

No matter the cause of the seizure, administering Bach Rescue Remedy or FES Five Flower Remedy can be of assistance for the animal's body to return to balance. Due to the nature of seizures, the Bach Rescue Remedy cream may be the easiest to administer as it can be rubbed on an ear, paw or other soft (hair free) spot for easy absorption.

- For the immediate trauma and shock prevention: Administer *Bach* Rescue Remedy or FES Five Flower Remedy. Topically is best .

- The Anaflora flower essences: (http://www.anaflora.com/essences/f-essences/formulas-reg.html

    o **Daily Brain Balance:** A special blend of flower essences especially created to assist in recovery from seizures. If you are upset by your animal's seizures, you can take this formula too. Use in conjunction with Anti-Seizure Daily Formula for best results.

    o **Moon Drops:** For epileptic seizures that occur or intensify at the time of the full moon. It is also helpful for other behaviors and anxiety states that intensify at the full moon. Use with Anti-Seizure Daily Formula and Post Seizure Recovery for best results.

Holistic Emergency Care and Trauma Recovery for Animals / Section III

Homeopathy Treatment

In the immediate moments after a seizure:

- Administer *Homeopathy Remedy:* **Arnica Montana 30X** for shock and bruising.
- Other remedies can be given afterward to assist with any injuries that occurred during the seizure. (See Wound care or Soft Tissue Trauma Recovery in Section IV).

Herbal Treatment

Herbs such as the nervine varieties of Skullcap have been documented to provide good results in aiding in seizures during their occurrence and also in prevention. Other herbs that can also assist are valarien root and ***

Holistic Emergency Care and Trauma Recovery for Animals / Section III

CHAPTER 35
ELEMENT EXPOSURE – HEAT EMERGENCIES

Prolonged exposure to heat and cold can also cause illness, injury or even death. When one of these illnesses appears, it can very quickly become life threatening.

Prevention of Heat Emergencies

Prevention is worth a pound of cure. This is true of most things and with element exposure emergencies, it is extremely true.

Given the opportunity animals will naturally seek to keep their body temperature in balance.

Since they cannot just take off clothes or put them on the way humans do, they must harmonize their activities with the weather and the availability of water, shelter and such things that allow them to stay comfortable.

Holistic Emergency Care and Trauma Recovery
for Animals / Section III

Following the guidelines set below will give your animal companions positive steps to stay in harmony with the weather be it hot or cold:

LEARN TO LISTEN TO and OBSERVE
YOUR ANIMAL FRIEND'S DISCOMFORT SIGNS.
When you see a problem arising,
take action to bring the animal back into balance.

- Be certain that the animals in your care, wild or domestic, have plenty of clean, cool drinking water, and that they are staying hydrated. During the heat of summer the wild animals will thank you if you also provide water for them ... bird baths to ground watering spots. *Think gentle, loving kindness ....*

- Provide your animals the option of eating plenty of high calorie/ high mineral, easily digestible foods. This provides their bodies the fuel to deal with the added stress of the extreme elements.

- Allow your animals to rest frequently. Given the opportunity they will choose a rhythm that will allow their body temperature to stay in balance.

- Avoid being outside at the hottest time of day.

- **Do not force your animals into over-activity** (adjust activity to the temperature). Look for signals of overheating (hyper) or being too cold (hypo) (see below).

- Be sure your animals have plenty of shade and/or cooled and protected places easily accessible in the heat of the day.

- **Never leave your animals in cars or closed areas in the heat (70 degrees Fahrenheit or above) for any reason.** It can only take minutes for a closed area to overheat and kill an animal (or child).

Heat Cramps

Heat cramps are the first signal of someone who has been over-exposed to heat and can be treated quickly and easily by doing the following:

General Treatment

- Get animal out of the heat and have him/her rest.
- Give water and electrolyte fluids to drink. (Gluconade, or Pedialite for children or animals.)
- Stretch and lightly massage the involved muscles.
- **Giving Salt Tablets Or Salt Water Can Make The Situation Worse.**

For Flower Essence Treatment – through Herbal Treatment

…. See Heat Exhaustion

Holistic Emergency Care and Trauma Recovery for Animals / Section III

Heat Exhaustion and Heat Stroke Prevention

More often than not, heat exhaustion and other heat emergencies are preventable. Common sense is key in supporting your animals' ability to stay in balance and harmony with the environment's temperature. Normal vital signs for dogs, cats and horses can be found in Appendix B of this book.

Common prevention steps include:

1. During the warm months of the year (which is some places is most of the year) never leave your animal or child in a car unattended, with the windows up or down. You can leave the animal in the car if the temperature is mild, 70 degrees or less, with the windows down enough to properly ventilate the car (at least ½ way), and the car is parked in the shade, and a water bowl with fresh water easily accessible to the animals.

2. In a locked car, the temperature can climb rapidly to a dangerous level. A cracked

window on a warm day will not prevent your dog, cat, etc. from overheating and suffering heat stroke.

3. Animals should have access to shade and generous amounts of fresh water while outdoors. If the temperature is very warm, outdoor access should be limited to short periods of time and the dog or cat should be housed indoors with a fan or AC running as needed to keep the temperature comfortable.

4. If your horse, dog or other animal friend is working in warm weather be prepared to offer him water at regular intervals and understand that he may drink more water than usual under these circumstances. This includes sporting activities from hiking to playing with friends at a park.

5. Use caution with animals (dogs, cats or horses) that are obese, have respiratory difficulties, are geriatric or are otherwise unhealthy. These animals may be more prone to heat exhaustion than others.

6. In addition, short-nosed (brachycephalic) breeds of dogs and cats are at higher risk of heat exhaustion than other breeds.

Holistic Emergency Care and Trauma Recovery for Animals / Section III

HEAT EXHAUSTION

Heat exhaustion is more serious than heat cramps, and with animals you have to be able to see the signals despite their hair covering much of their skin. Pay attention; be aware of the signals and requests that your animals are giving you.

Through your awareness, you will notice signals such as:

- Increased panting – sometimes labored
- Cool, moist, pale or red skin
- Restlessness
- Nausea and/or dizziness
- Weakness and/or exhaustion
- Increased heart and respiratory rates
- Increased salivation

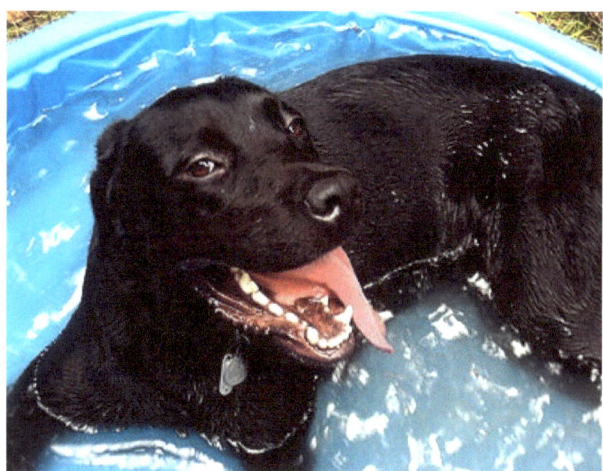

General Treatment

- First and foremost, remove the animal from the heat.
- Loosen or <u>remove</u> constrictive, collars, harnesses or other "clothing".
- For dogs or horses, if water is available:

- Either via a water hose, lake, river, pond or even swimming pool, guide the animal in the water up to her belly or chest if possible and keep her there until she shows signs of improvement.

- If the animal in distress is a cat, bird or other animal, or if there is no water body available to cool her in then:
    - Cover with cool, wet cloths and fan the animal, or if possible have person take cool shower. (Be sure he/she does not become chilled.
- If fully conscious, give water, electrolyte fluids (see Heat Cramps), and colloidal minerals

Flower Essence Treatment

As with all life threatening emergencies the primary flower essence is Rescue Remedy either Bach or the Flower Essence Society's blend (FES) which is called Five Flower Remedy.

In the case of heat emergencies you can:
- Put a few drops of the essence in water and rub it directly on the animal's skin, and
- Give a few drops in a small amount of water orally.
- Another option, if available, use the Bach Rescue Remedy cream and rub it directly on the skin.

Once the emergency is over and the animal is recovering, I suggest the Anaflora Flower Essence – Return to Joy, which assists in recovery from any type of trauma; emotional, mental or physical.

Homeopathy Treatment

In many situations the symptoms that the human or animal have are complementary, such as bruising, burns, etc. With heat and to some degree cold emergencies some of the symptoms, such as headaches, may not be as obvious unless you or someone who is assisting with the situation is an animal intuitive communicator.

If no one is present with that capacity, then it is critical for you or those helping you to use great focus of observation to determine the other symptoms that are more obvious. These are described within the following homeopathic remedy descriptions:

Also, remember that animals deal with pain differently than people to some degree. Their pain tolerance is much higher and often they go inward with the pain rather than expressing it outwardly. In some cases, checking gums and ears for heat and paws for cold can provide helpful information.

Belladona: Agonizing, sudden, shooting headache with throbbing making the individual scream in pain. Bright red face (check gums and inside ears), dilated pupils, glassy-eyed, fixed stare with no expression, no thirst but has a dry mouth.

Bryonia: Severe headache made worse by the slightest motion. Animals will tend towards guarding their heads and attempting not to move. He or she may show signs of aggression or pulling away if you attempt to touch them. The individual is extremely thirsty for large amounts of cold water.

Aconite: Faint and dizzy with headache after prolonged, direct exposure to the sun. Individual may say he feels like he is dying, be anxious and restless. Dizziness may display itself through the animal having trouble walking straight (wobbling, swerving)

Carbo Veg: Collapse from excess heat with clamminess of the skin and stomach complaints. The individual wants to be fanned and needs to feel moving air. For animals who have had heat exhaustion or heat stroke which results in their being more susceptible to ongoing problems with heat.

Gelsemium: Drowsiness, headache in back of head, no thirst, weakness, comatose and useful for sun stroke.

Glonoinum: First remedy for sun stroke. Agonizing congestive headache after exposure to sun and heat. Hot face and cold extremities, irritability and confusion. Pounding pain, compare to Belladona.

Lachesis: Excellent for treating headaches from sun exposure especially if they are worse on the left side. Individual feels worse after waking from sleep, feels faint and dizzy.

Natrum Carb: Debilitated as a result of heat exposure; is chronically affected by heat and sun stroke. Headache is worse from the slightest mental effort. *** For animals who have had heat exhaustion or heat stroke which results in their being more susceptible to ongoing problems with heat. [14]

Herbal Treatment

- Decoctions of Linden, Passionflower and Peppermint can all be helpful in cooling the body down after a heat emergency.
- Note: do not use peppermint or any type of mint if you are also giving your animal homeopathy. Remember that the mint family can neutralize homeopathic remedies.

---

[14] Referenced from: http://www.naturalnews.com/036414_heat_stroke_homeopathic_remedies.html

Holistic Emergency Care and Trauma Recovery for Animals / Section III

HEAT STROKE

Heat stroke is the most serious heat-related emergency. Call your vet and Divine Intervention immediately. An animal's body temperature rises so high that brain damage and death are possible. The signals to watch for are:

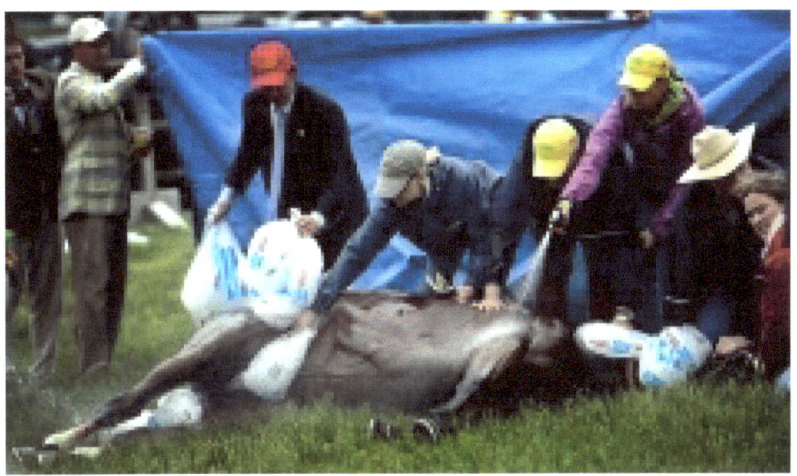

- Hot, dry, red skin
- Decreased consciousness, vomiting
- Rapid, weak pulse and breathing
- Signs of shock
- Initial restlessness leading to unconsciousness or coma

General Treatment

Your number one focus must be to get the body temperature down as quickly as possible without causing undo shock at the same time. If you are near a body of cool water lead the animal in and stay with him as she cools down in case he has a heat related seizure.

Action Steps

- Cool the animal quickly by soaking in a cool bath, wrapping in cold cloths or placing ice packs on main arteries such as the corodid or femoral arteries. (See horse photo above).
- Administer *Bach* Rescue Remedy.
- Monitor breathing and pulse.
- Do not give anything to eat or drink -- this may cause convulsions.

Flower Essence Treatment

In the case of heat emergencies you can:

- Put a few drops of the essence in water and rub it directly on the animal's skin, and
- Give a few drops in a small amount of water orally.
- Another option, if available, use the Bach Rescue Remedy cream and rub it directly on the skin.

As with Heat Exhaustion, once the emergency is over and the animal is recovering, I suggest the Anaflora Flower Essence – Return to Joy, which assists in recovery from any type of trauma; emotional, mental or physical.

Homeopathy Treatment

Also remember that animals deal with pain differently than people to some degree. Their pain tolerance is much higher and often they go inward with the pain rather than expressing it outwardly.

Glonoinum: <u>First remedy for sun stroke</u>. Agonizing congestive headache after exposure to sun and heat. Hot face and cold extremities, irritability and confusion. Pounding pain, compare to Belladona.

Belladona: Agonizing, sudden, shooting headache with throbbing making the individual scream in pain. Bright red face (check gums and inside ears), dilated pupils, glassy-eyed, fixed stare with no expression, no thirst but has a dry mouth.

Bryonia: Severe headache made worse by the slightest motion. Animals will tend towards guarding their heads and attempting not to move. He or she may show signs of aggression or pulling away if you attempt to touch them. The individual is extremely thirsty for large amounts of cold water.

Aconite: Faint and dizzy with headache after prolonged, direct exposure to the sun. Individual may say he feels like he is dying, be anxious and restless. Dizziness may display itself through the animal having trouble walking straight (wobbling, swerving)

Carbo Veg: Collapse from excess heat with clamminess of the skin and stomach complaints. The individual wants to be fanned and needs to feel moving air. *For animals who have had heat exhaustion or heat stroke which results in their being more susceptible to ongoing problems with heat.*

Gelsemium: Drowsiness, headache in back of head, no thirst, weakness, comatose and useful for sun stroke.

Lachesis: Excellent for treating headaches from sun exposure, especially if they are worse on the left side. Individual feels worse after waking from sleep, feels faint and dizzy.

Natrum Carb: Debilitated as a result of heat exposure; or if she is chronically affected by heat and sun stroke. Headache is worse from the slightest mental effort. *** For animals who have had heat exhaustion or heat stroke which results in their being more susceptible to ongoing problems with heat.

Herbal Treatment

Prolonged heat emergencies can put stress on many of the body systems, resulting in an accentuated sensitively to heat in the future unless balance is restored. In the immediacy of the emergency the following herbs can be helpful. More in depth healing is discussed in Section IV Trauma Recovery.

- Decoctions of Linden, Passionflower and Peppermint can all be helpful in cooling the body down after a heat emergency.

- Reminder: do not use peppermint or any type of mint if you are also giving your animal homeopathy. Remember that the mint family can neutralize homeopathic remedies.

CHAPTER 36
ELEMENT EXPOSURE – COLD EMERGENCIES

Prevention of Cold Emergencies

Animals may have the ability to grow winter coats for protection from the cold. Despite this they are still susceptible to frostbite and hypothermia. As animal guardians it is our responsibility that they are warm and cared for in the cold as well as the heat. Be aware of the weather outside how it affects you….

www.thumbpress.com

Prevention is the best way to avoid cold-related illness. To do so follow these guidelines:

- Be aware of animals normal vital signs (Appendix B) and have the means to measure it close at hand.

- Be sure that your animals are staying hydrated with purified water. Cold weather does not preclude the requirement for water. In many cases it creates a greater need, especially in cold/dry climates or where the animals are indoors where methods of heating are ongoing.

- Be sure to feed your animals plenty of high calorie/high mineral, easily digestible foods that are suitable to their body's requirements for well-being. Everyone's bodies require additional fuel to supply the greater burning of fuel that occurs in cold weather. This is especially true for animals that are active.

- Allow your animals to rest as they see fit if they are participating in outdoor activities. Age is a factor, as is the animal's fitness level.

- Even for animals who have warm winter coats, it is often best to avoid being outside during coldest time of day and night. Always provide your animals with warm and dry housing either inside with you or in a barn, or other structure that is appropriate to their breed and individual requirements.

- Avoid over-activity (adjust activity to the temperature).

- Be sure that your animals have adequate warm covering when out in cold weather. For some breeds this is built in – especially dogs such as huskies and long haired cats. But even they can get frostbite of the feet, ears and nose if not properly tended. Paw boots, horse blankets, and dog vests are some of the ways to keep your animals warm during the cold months of winter.

- Remove sweaty blankets or vests from your animals and replace them with dry ones as needed to assure that they stay warm efficiently.

Holistic Emergency Care and Trauma Recovery for Animals / Section III

FROSTBITE

Over-exposure to cold can cause hypothermia and frost bite. Frost bite is the freezing of body parts exposed to the cold. Severity depends on the air temperature, length of exposure and the wind.

Frostbite can mean the loss of toes, pad covering, ear and tail tips and in severe cases, paws and legs. Some animals such as dogs have pads on their feet that are built to tolerate both heat and cold that are very uncomfortable for humans. However, there is a limit to what they can take and for how long. This is why boots for dogs and horses have been developed for those who are out in the cold for long times or in temperatures (below 0 Fahrenheit) for any length of time.

Frostbite is the injury or death of tissue due to prolonged exposure to cold temperatures. Extensive cold exposure can cause the blood vessels that normally keep these areas warm to constrict, resulting in the tissue cooling and eventually dying.

Frostbitten tissue can often be recognized by its grey, waxy, discolored appearance. The area can also be cold and hard to the touch. Thawing out of an area with frostbite can display red tissue and is often very painful as the blood vessels and nerves attempt to function normally again.

Never rub the frost bitten area. This will cause more damage.[15] To care for frost bite:

General Treatment

- Get the animal(s) out of the cold and into a comfortable location (if possible) to begin the warming process.
- Warm the body parts SLOWLY either through soaking in warm water (no warmer than 105 degrees) or very gently applying warm clothes, <u>making sure you are not rubbing the area as this can cause further damage</u> until the area is warm to the touch.
- Also check for and treat hypothermia (details below) if required.
- If appropriate, bandage loosely, separating toes with cotton or gauze (don't break blisters).

Flower Essence Treatment

- If the animal is in shock or struggling with pain, administer Bach Rescue Remedy or FES Five Flower Remedy orally in a small amount of water.

Homeopathy

From Materia Medica:

- **Agaricus Muscarius** is the first remedy that comes to mind for chilblains, as it produces the stinging and itchy sensations in the toes and feet that are characteristic of frostbite. If no other remedy is specifically indicated, use Agaricus.

  Agaricus features the swelling, burning, redness, cramping, and skin eruptions that itch and burn. Some patients experience lasting redness after frostbite and symptoms of rosacea; some experience swollen veins with the cold skin. It is also good to keep in mind that the more serious effects of hypothermia are addressed by this remedy,

---

[15] Photo credit: http://www.dogids.com/blog/do-dogs-need-boots-in-the-cold/

Holistic Emergency Care and Trauma Recovery for Animals / Section III

namely the irregular, tumultuous palpitation of the heart, which can take place when hypothermia has progressed.

- Administer Homeopathy Remedy: Hypericum to assist in healing nerve damage

Herbal Treatment

Herbal treatment comes more into play in the healing of the tissue. However there are also herbs that can be utilized to assist in warming the body.

Warming of Body: ginger, cayenne pepper and cinnamon can be given in decoction to assist in warming the body and Hawthorne berry; also in decoction or non-alcohol tincture can be given to improve overall circulation.

Healing of Damage Tissue: yarrow, comfrey, calendula are three of the most common herbs that can be used to assist in healing and regenerating tissue. Yarrow also aids in preventing infection.

Administer in decoction or diluted tincture. Dosing: Tincture quantity depends upon animal size. ~ 3 drops for cat to 15 for horses; repeat every four hours until obvious improvement in tissue is observed.

Dosing: Decoction quantity also depends upon the animal's size. I encourage you to develop intuitive abilities to receive how much to utilize in any given situation. ***

HYPOTHERMIA

In hypothermia the body loses its ability to keep warm. In animals, this is usually a result of prolonged exposure to cold temperatures, especially but not exclusively, when complicated by their being wet. In mammals of all types our circulatory system is utilized along with clothing (humans), hair, or fur to keep the body warm.

When an animal is subject to cold temperatures, snow or ice cold water beyond his body's ability to keep him warm, the circulatory system may begin to constrict in the extremities withdrawing its greater energy into the body's organs as a survival mechanism. This however, will only serve as a temporary solution and if the animal is not warmed she will drop into advanced levels of hypothermia and then death (spirit and body separation).

Hypothermia Prevention

Unless unavoidable due to some circumstance out of your control, never allow animals under your care to be out in cold temperatures for prolonged periods of time – temperatures that their bodies are not built to handle. This is different for individuals. However, even if you think your animals enjoy being out in the cold (sleeping in the snow), always provide them with shelter and better yet bring them inside when cold weather strikes. Keeping your intuitive communication channels open with your animals will always assist you in knowing how your animal(s) is handling the weather.

Holistic Emergency Care and Trauma Recovery
for Animals / Section III

- One of the elements that can increase the chances of hypothermia is when your animals with paws are out in the snow in conditions where snow balls up in their paws (between their toes) and on their bellies and chest. This action compromises their natural insulting abilities and can cause their body temperature to drop more quickly than expected.
- Be very watchful of your animals around water and ice – especially partly frozen water where there is potential for the animal to fall through.

Hypothermia is recognized by the following signals:

- Shivering and numbness
- Stiff muscles
- Decreased consciousness, glassy stare
- Apathy and incoherence
- Lowered body temperatures:

Horse: Below 99 degree F; Newborn below 99.5 degrees F.

Dog: Below 101 degrees: Normal is between 100.5 – 102 degrees F

Cat: Below 101 degrees: Normal is between 100.5 – 102 degrees F

General Treatment

In any kind of cold exposure the number one action for you in assisting the animal(s) is to get her out of the cold and get her body warm once again. Everything that you do is towards this goal.

- Get the animal(s) out of the cold into a warm dry place
- Wrap him or them in blankets and at a safe place by a heater of some kind
- Place hot water bottles inside the blanket if you have them available
- Administer warm fluids orally
- Administer homeopathic and/or herbs as explained below

Flower Essence Treatment

If there are signs of hypovolemic shock, administer Rescue Remedy or FES Five Flower Remedy either topically or orally diluted in a small about of water.

Homeopathy Treatment

Remedies as written in the Materia Medica Homeopathic Reference:

- **Agaricus Muscarius** is the first remedy that comes to mind for chilblains, as it produces the stinging and itchy sensations in the toes and feet that are characteristic of frostbite. If no other remedy is specifically indicated, use Agaricus.

Agaricus features the swelling, burning, redness, cramping, and skin eruptions that itch and burn. Some patients experience lasting redness after frostbite and symptoms of rosacea; some experience swollen veins with the cold skin. <u>It is good to keep in mind that the more serious effects of hypothermia are addressed by this remedy</u>, namely the irregular, tumultuous palpitation of the heart, which can take place when hypothermia has progressed.

Herbal Treatment

There are some herbs that can assist in warming the body and are fairly easy to administer. These include the following:

- Ginger tea
- Cayenne pepper in warm water
- Cinnamon in warm water or tea

The use of these herbs to help reverse hypothermia must be done in conjunction with taking other steps as listed in the General Treatment -> Homeopathic Treatments.

CHAPTER 37
FOXTAILS, STICKERS AND SEEDS ….

Summertime and early fall is propagation time within the plant kingdom worldwide. It is the time when nature plant sends out her seeds to continue her life cycle. During this time animals that move around in nature are all subject to being carriers of these seeds in their various forms, especially those animals that live close to the ground.

As part of this dynamic seeds and stickers can find their way into animal's eyes, ears, noses, as well as in between toes and imbedded in their fur. Prevention plays an intricate part in avoiding problems with these foreign and yet naturally important objects getting into the sensitive areas of animals in your care.

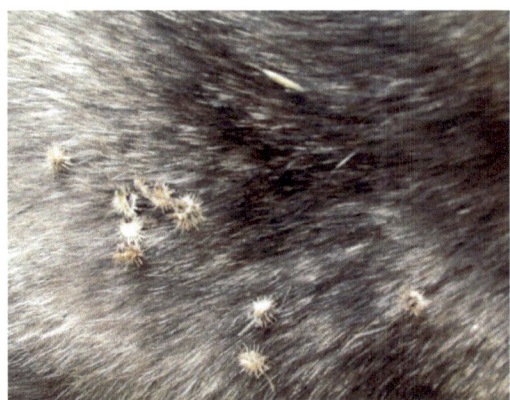

- Awareness of the environment in both your garden and in the more wild areas where your animal(s) – with or without you - spend time.
- When possible, keep your animals out of areas that are heavily seeding especially those that are free floating or that have barbs – like foxtails.
- Check animals in your care daily and after nature outings
- If you are with them in nature then be aware of signs that something has gotten in an eye, ear or other area of the body and tend to it quickly.

Holistic Emergency Care and Trauma Recovery for Animals / Section III

"Foxtails", seedpods or other foreign objects in the eyes or nose can be very dangerous, even life threatening especially regarding barbed seeds that get inhaled into the nasal passage, causing violent sneezing.

Foreign Object Awareness – The Hands on Approach

Generally speaking, animals will let you know when they have a foreign object in the hair or fur that is bothering them. If the object is being a nuisance but not immediately destructive to their body, the animal may come to you and say in her own way "hey I have a sticker in my fur, would you mind digging in there and getting it out for me?"

The furrier the animal is, the more you may have to dig to find the perpetrator. Using a combination of fingers and a good brush is the best way to be sure that you animal friend is sticker free. Important: be aware that stickers that are lodged in the fur or between toes and not found quickly can get imbedded in the skin resulting in the body attempting to protect itself by developing an abscess.

Holistic Emergency Care and Trauma Recovery for Animals / Section III

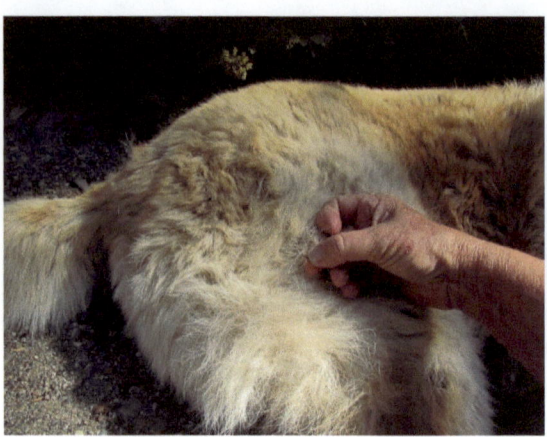

Recognizing Foreign Object Emergencies

Getting a sticker or other foreign object in an eye, nose or other sensitive place is not only uncomfortable, but it can also be life altering or threatening if not corrected quickly and completely.

- **Nasal Passage** : Rapid and often continuous sneezing; often violent; perhaps with blood

- **Inside Ears**: Shaking of head often combined with frustrated scratching of the ear (dogs/cats). Also the animal might tilt her head to the side where the problem is.

- **Eyes**: Watering, rubbing, parts of sticker or seeds protruding; mucous build-up in eye as body's defense mechanism.

- **Between Toes**: If a sticker or other foreign object gets between an animal's toes she is likely to chew around the toe areas and possibly favor the foot.

Taking Action

Anytime that an animal gets something like a sticker in an eye, nose, ear or other part of the body, human and possible Divine intervention are of key importance to prevent permanent vision or hearing damage.

Holistic Emergency Care and Trauma Recovery for Animals / Section III

Nasal Passage Obstruction

If an animal in your care develops a severe sneezing attack or other symptoms of a foreign object in the nasal passage, pay attention. Nasal passage obstructions can be fatal. As such, they require your immediate attention.

The first thing is to determine if the obstruction is mucous, a blood clot or some kind of foreign object such as a foxtail. Although all can cause great distress, blockage from mucous or dried blood can be easier to release or dissolve using saline spray.

In my life, these emergencies have always shown up when I was out walking with my dogs in nature. Once again trust in calling for Divine Assistance has been of great benefit and importance to the recovery of the one in trouble.

I suggest that you follow these steps:

Divine Assistance & Energy Healing

1. Take the animal's face in your hands, close your eyes, and request (Command) God/Goddess/All That Is to remove the object quickly and gently.

2. Breathe and send Love to the animal, seeing her well and in peace.

3. Listen for intuitive instructions of what to do next. These may include:

    - Continuing to stay present with what you are already doing.

    - Spraying saline spray or diluted aloe vera juice gently in the nasal passage. (This can assist in washing the object out the nose or down the throat to be digested or coughed out.)

- And, *Get to the vet – Fast!* may also be the message. If this is the case, call your vet's office and let them know you are coming in with an emergency – give details and get moving.

In my years living and recreating with dogs and other animals I have never had to take one to the veterinarian for a foreign object of this nature. Rather I have been blessed with great success in utilizing steps 1-3 completely resolving the situation. For this, I am to this day, deeply grateful, especially since most of these incidences have occurred when my animals and I have been in the wild, making a trip to the veterinarian challenging at best.

*** *However, it is important to keep in mind that foreign objects in the nasal passage can sometimes be life threatening. So <u>never</u> hesitate to take your animal into a veterinarian if the sneezing or other symptoms continue after you have done steps 1-3.*

Section IV
Trauma Recovery

CHAPTER 38
TRAUMA RECOVERY INTRODUCTION

My Philosophy on Trauma Recovery

There is much to learn and understand regarding how animals cope with and heal from trauma, especially trauma created through abuse of some kind. For me, it is a new type of conversation and blossoming awareness. This conversation is largely the result of the awakening consciousness of humans and our departure from the thought forms that animals are *just animals*, to the truth that they are our equals, divine and intelligent in incredible ways.

This blossoming awareness, along with a greater understanding of our innate ability to communicate with animals, is lending itself to our assisting them in healing from all kinds of trauma (physical, mental and emotional). In my journey thus far in this life, I now know more than ever that as we facilitate the healing of our animal family and kingdom as a whole, we open the door widely to our own ability to heal and return to the divine innocence within our being.

The innate innocence within all life is based in unconditional love (henceforth written as LOVE in this book). Animals embody this fully, as do human children unless they are taught otherwise. LOVE, is a major resource within animals that they utilize to such a great extent in their own coping with trauma and healing from it. When they do not receive this from the humans that are in their lives, then they open themselves more fully to receiving LOVE directly from the Divine. But the power within the journey of facilitating the healing of animals through our own LOVE and compassion cannot be undervalued.

My sense is that this journey back into LOVE and assisting each other (all kingdoms) to heal through it is a key component to all humans returning to wholeness and peace. This has much to do with the healing and respecting of the feminine aspect of God in form, that Mother Earth and all her kingdoms are aspects of the Mother energy expressed, *Goddess*.[16]

In the years that I have lived with various animals, most of whom have been rescues, I have learned great skills of inner strength, perseverance and healing from each one as they allowed me to assist them with their own journeys of healing, physical or emotional. These skills I have utilized in recent years to allow my own inner and physical healing against what seemed to me to be great adversity. It is from my experiences that I now facilitate healing and returning to wisdom within others. And it is from this wisdom that the content of Section IV has been written. Om Shanti, Namaste.

From Emergency to Recovery

With the immediate emergencies or rescues behind you and your animal(s), it is time to breathe more slowly and shift your attention to holistically facilitating the healing of the trauma(s) left in the wake of what has transpired. Trauma recovery takes on many forms depending upon the cause, effect (physical, mental and feelings) and the coping mechanism (if any) the animal is using to maintain life.

With a trauma such as a planned surgery, you have the opportunity to prepare yourself and your animal friend for the initial discomfort and the rehabilitation, whether it is for a long or short duration. Unexpected physical traumas are different due to the abruptness of their nature. Traumas of this type can require a considerable shift within both the animal and the animal's primary family members or caretaker(s) to align with the best holistic healing methods, as well as the temporary (hopefully) change in lifestyle. Generally speaking animals are terrific at aligning with various healing challenges, using innate wisdom. They are also more in the flow regarding making decisions of whether to stay in the body or leave, in the case of severe trauma.

---

[16] There are many references of this ideology that Mother Earth and her kingdoms are Goddess in form. Tom Kenyon's new movie "Songs of the Earth" speaks into this to some degree. Song of the New Earth?

Those who bring animals that are rescues into their home or lives are likely to be dealing with emotional, mental and possibly physical traumas (old or new). In the case of rescues it is even more important to utilize the skills of one who can communicate with her to assist you in knowing what has occurred in the past and the animal's overall disposition to healing from its effects.

The trauma in these cases can be obvious and easy to determine, or it can be hidden under the surface, to the degree the animal is capable, as part of her coping mechanism. What is important through all is to understand there are lessons to learn from every experience, and purpose directing it all.

The Attitude Around Healing

Wild animals that live their lives apart from humanity recover or embrace their demise as a result of trauma dependent upon their own inner strength, support, Divine assistance from God/Goddess, including other animals with which they associate. Their journey into life or death from a trauma is very personal.

Domesticated animals, however, will heal as well as they can with the support or lack of support of their human guardian(s). Research and observation show that the emotional or mind set of the human(s) that an animal associates with can greatly influence the speed and correctness of an animal's healing. One example of this dynamic is if a person sees and/or feels their animal is crippled or dying; unable to heal, their emotional energy and beliefs can impede an animal's healing. This focus can even lead to premature death either directly (putting him to sleep unnecessarily) or indirectly by interfering with the animal's inner healer.

One the other hand, if it is indeed the desire of your animal friend to recover fully, then by seeing him well and living life as he had before the injury (or disease) you are then combining your energy of achievement with his creating greater inertia towards the goal; An example of this was when I was facilitating Ishnahnay, my Wolfdog companion, to heal after she had been broadsided by a car and almost killed. She would often remind me to focus on seeing her well, running, playing and enjoying her life fully again.

Holistic Emergency Care and Trauma Recovery for Animals / Section IV

She explained to me on a more personal level how any energy I had of her not recovering was interfering with her chosen journey to recovery. So we joined together in seeing her enjoying her full athletic abilities again, and despite her having lower back damage, she accomplished her goals. (See Case Study – Ishnahnay for details).

Photograph by Julie Colt

Additional documentation shows that animals that are neglected, abused or seen as less than humans in value, often suffer greatly at the hands of those with these beliefs. The result for the animal can be physical injuries, emotional, mental trauma as well as poorly healed physical injuries. On the other hand, animals who are healing with the support of humans (and other animals) who love them and vision their complete and grace-filled return to balance, are much more successful overall in attaining whole body wellness once again.

Over the years of assisting rescued animals (both wild and domestic) in trauma recovery I have seen that the absolutely most powerful tool of their healing is LOVE partnered with seeing their Spirit/Soul and their individual path in life being fulfilled. It is here again that the attitude of who an animal is as Spirit/Soul plays an enormous role. Ultimately, seeing the animal or animals in your life as partners of life and learning that are on their own path, and yet sharing a path with you for a greater purpose, will lend a great deal to assisting you all in healing from trauma of any kind – into or out of death.

CHAPTER 39
UNDERSTANDING AND SUPPORTING THE INNER HEALER

In today's world of medicine there exists a great misconception regarding doctors, veterinarians, healers, and healing as an outside to inside activity: the idea that others—doctors and drugs, or healers and holistic modalities—are actually healing the one who is out of balance, whether the patient is animal, plant, or human. Yet, in truth, this is not so. The true healer is within each and every one, no matter their body type. The inner healer is the divine spark, the divine intelligence or Spirit, of the individual.

The idea that a person, doctor, or veterinarian is the healer is an idea that is beginning to shift as more people understand and embrace the Divine within us, or our animal friends and the major role it plays in everyone's lives. Everyone and everything else (medicine/healing modalities) are assisting as tools or facilitators.

The truth of this can be seen when a spirit separates from its physical form, or "dies," despite the best efforts of a doctor, veterinarian, or holistic healer, in conjunction with the tools they are using. Healing, into living or dying, is a conversation with the Divine; a conversation that occurs deeply within each and every one of us whether we are aware of it or not.

The Inner Healer, or also stated as *The Healer Within*…. What does that mean? The phrase *The Inner Healer* refers to the Divine Intelligence within every living Being. It is the intelligence and divine spark that orchestrates all that is our bodies; every system, every cell, no matter what the embodied form. It is also the relationship between our etheric body's life force and soul essence that guides our lives and enables an embodiment to recover from an imbalance, be it physical, mental, or spiritual (feeling).

Holistic Emergency Care and Trauma Recovery for Animals / Section IV

So how does understanding the existence of the Inner Healer in animals as well as ourselves alter our relationship with the medical world, allopathic and holistic alike, and the tools of healing made available through them? In my years of experience working with people, animals, and the plant kingdom I have been blessed with great teachings as a facilitator of healing and interspecies communicator combined. Time and time again when assisting another I have been shown to ask their divine self "what is it that the Inner Healer of this one requires to heal, if indeed it is his/her choice to do so?"

By addressing the healing process in this way you as a healer/facilitator are acknowledging that the healing truly is being done within the one who has the imbalance. You are simply providing the energetic support in a variety of forms from medicine, to nutrition, to loving patience, peace and quiet, and holding the space in your vision and feelings for him/her to recover and enjoy life once again.

An example of this is in providing a deeply nutritious diet for my animal companions. I am giving their bodies the nutritional tools to assist them in living vibrant joyous lives. Yet, I am not directly creating balance and joy in their lives. Neither is the food on its own doing so. But rather, it is the relationship or conversation (as I prefer to state it) between the animal, the food, and the etheric life force of both that come together to create the desired outcome.

Another example occurs in assisting in the recovery after an injury or surgery. As discussed in Sections II through IV of this book, there are many avenues of healing support that can be provided to an individual to aid in her/his healing and coming into balance. In most cases as a facilitator I am guided to begin this process with a combination of homeopathy, flower essences, and direct energetic support and prayer. Subsequently, I will move into using herbs and other modalities as guided.

Then through quiet, yet focused, observation and intuitive listening I will be shown or told by the one I am assisting whether the tools I am giving her are being helpful or not. If the communication indicates that they are helping, then how is it best to continue. If on the other hand, the communication and observation indicates that they are not helping, then what am I being guided to do instead? The body and spirit of the one being assisted are the directors; I am but facilitating the assistance.

There are other things that we have grown to understand through the acknowledgement of the Inner Healer. First, is that in the quiet reflection of the journey of healing (be it into living or dying), non-attachment is of great importance. To embrace non-attachment to the outcome, while at the same time holding space for the highest good of the one who is healing, allows the greater journey for all involved to unfold in grace. This is of key importance as we may not consciously know what the journey of the animal's spirit is or is meant to be.

Second is the acceptance that animal bodies, like those of humans, are multi-level in nature; physical, mental, feeling and spirit. The Inner Healer in partnership with the Etheric /Ethereal Life Force and Divine Spark is responsible to all bodies, not just the physical. So, as a facilitator, it is of key importance that you also focus your support upon all the bodies and provide them the best assistance that you are able.

The material in this book will provide you the opportunity to gain a working knowledge of basic holistic modalities that will enable you to more easily support the Inner Healer and its work with the spiritual, feeling, mental and physical bodies. In so doing you will be providing the inner healer of your animal friend(s) to return the entirety of your animal's bodies to a state of well-being.

Pain and suffering is an individual experience, but it also affects the direct and extended family, and the global consciousness of Life overall.

Why Does A Spirit Leave It's Body?

I recently heard a speaker talk about genetic and disease decoding. In his talk he said there are two reasons why someone leaves their body in the current paradigm that we have created and live in:

- Exhaustion
- Destruction

I will add a third here: a Soul/Spirit may also leave her body when she completes with her purpose for being embodied. Certainly in some cases the third reason may combine with

Holistic Emergency Care and Trauma Recovery for Animals / Section IV

the first two, but not always. Animals, like all life forms on Earth are Divine Spirit in form. They are here to learn, to serve, to evolve, and it is their desire to do so in peace.

Exhaustion

In the first case – exhaustion – an animal's body will just give up. One system or organ will just collapse and the Spirit will leave the body and move on. Here it is worthwhile to note that the Endocrine System of the body (animal and human) is where the etheric life force that sustains the body is stored. Like in humans, the Endocrine System of animals consists of

- Pineal Gland
- Pituitary Gland
- Adrenal Glands
- Thyroid
- Parathyroid
- Pancreas
- Ovaries or Testicles

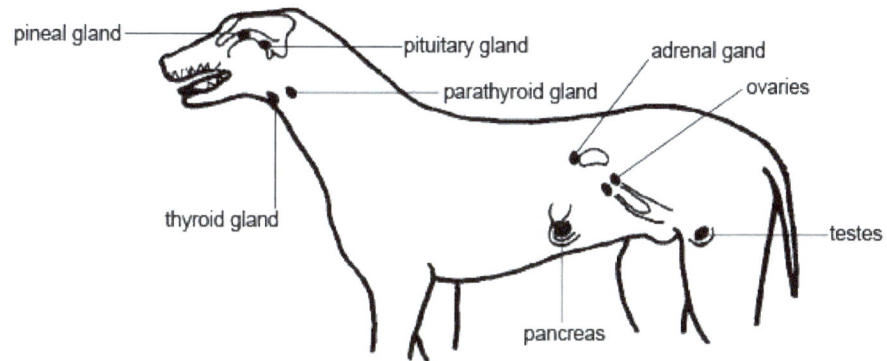

Graphic compliments of :
http://en.wikibooks.org/wiki/Anatomy_and_Physiology_of_Animals/Endocrine_System

There are many things that deplete the Endocrine System – especially in regard to the adrenals. Fear based energies which can be summed up as stress, drugs such as steroids, and poor diet. Other organs can also become exhausted such as the liver, kidneys and the heart. Exhaustion can also be brought about by the animal taking on her human's imbalances as well. This subject is discussed in length in the chapter *Animals Taking on Their Human's*

Diseases of Section IV.

Direct physical exhaustion can be brought on the animal's bodies by over exertion. This occurs more often with working animals, than through recreation, however, it can certainly occur in both. Examples of this include long distances racing, such as the Iditarod Dogsled Race, but can also occur in overdoing recreation activities such as swimming your dog in the ocean beyond his endurance, or any other sporting activity done beyond the animal's endurance levels.

The Importance of Rest and Quiet in Trauma Recovery

"Take two aspirin, drink plenty of purified water, rest and call me in the morning." This used to be common advice from a doctor to a patient. Resting and being quiet with oneself is still one of the most vital components of healing and rejuvenation. It is in the rest state that the Divine can most easily provide an animal or person the life force and re-creation support that it requires to come back into balance, and to release any trauma that would otherwise become imbedded within the multi-body system (spiritual, feeling, mental, physical) if otherwise left unattended.

Animals know innately to rest on a regular basis and will do so on their own if provided the opportunity. They have a great ability to quiet themselves and go deeply inward into a meditative rest state. In times of wellness, resting and quiet allows the life force of the body to be maintained and attention given to the body overall to stay in balance and thrive. When an injury or other trauma has occurred, rest, quiet and the outer support from their human, or if wild, their pack, flock or pod, is of utmost importance to the successful healing process.
If on the other hand, injury or illness is present in an animal's body and she is not being allowed to rest, then healing goes from a restorative process to a stressful and sometimes life threatening state of being. It is in such situations that a simple physical injury can leave great mental and emotional scarring, such as the animal not feeling safe, or exhaustion taking over and the animal giving up completely. Lack of rest and quiet can also result in incomplete healing of the physical body overall. If it is a physical injury or trauma, then it

may heal poorly, leaving deformity or heavy scaring that could with rest, quiet and support from the family have been completed restored.

Destruction and the Inner Healer

When it comes to the actual destruction of a body, the Inner Healer can be overcome and unable to regenerate the cells and body parts resulting in the Spirit/Soul of the animal leaving and returning to the ethereal world. Such destruction can occur slowly through degenerative disease or quickly by a destructive force. Examples of destructive forces are being hit by a car, being shot, poisoned or otherwise maimed, being hunted, being euthanized or slaughtered for food. Degenerative diseases such as cancer or diabetes can also destroy an animal's body, as can severe neglect and the overuse of vaccinations, steroids and other medicines.

Not all destructive experiences result in the demise of the animal's body. Within my animal family I have had two dogs who survived very destructive experiences. One being poisoned and the other broadsided by a car while walking out in the country. In both these cases I was present and able to immediately support their Inner Healer while engaging the assistance that they required. (*The case studies for Daunza and Ishnahnay are in Section IV of this book.*)

I have also had three cat family members who have departed due to their bodies being suddenly destroyed. All occurred when I was not present and were very violent in nature. In these cases there was no opportunity for their Inner Healer to reverse the destruction of the body and allow the Spirit to stay embodied. The Etheric Life Force disconnected from the bodies and the Inner Healer / Divine spark left along with the Spirit/Soul.

In cases such as these it is the Inner Healer of the human(s) and other animal family members who are left behind that must engage their multi-body systems in order to maintain or re-create balance and peace through the grief over the loss of a family member.

I feel prompted to say here that it is the human race that is responsible for a vast majority of domestic or wild animals being destroyed. And a majority of these destructions are completely unwarranted or necessary in any way, but rather occur due to life choices we as individuals and as a society make every day against the higher wishes of the animal spirits themselves.

THE DISCUSSION CONTINUED

The discussion regarding the Inner Healer is a broad one and will be continued in greater scope in Holistic Emergency Care and Trauma Recovery for Humans.

CHAPTER 40
FLOWER ESSENCES and TRAUMA RECOVERY

The balance within the feeling and mental bodies plays an integral role in an individual's ability to successfully travel the road from trauma to wholeness and inner peace. Flower essences can play a vital role in facilitating the return to balance in all bodies. The essences help to focus on the feeling and mental rebalancing, and in doing so, the physical body is then released from the negative influences of painful trauma energies which may have been interfering with its complete healing and balancing.

It is important to realize that some traumas can be completely in the feeling or mental body with no apparent consequence to the physical form at all; at least not in the immediate moment. An example of this type of trauma is from emotional abuse, which in animals can come from being caged; being forced to do work that they are unfit for; being yelled at forcefully and/or continuously. With wildlife one of the main causes of emotional and mental trauma is through their being hunted or persecuted in some other way.

Trauma can also occur within the family members of those who are injured or killed. Mourning or grieving within animal families has been documented repeatedly, bringing to our awareness the importance of assisting all who are directly or indirectly affected by trauma.

Where there is physical trauma it is quite likely that there is also trauma in the mental or feeling body. This is why it is so beneficial to begin using flower essences and other holistic healing tools at the onset of trauma whenever possible. In the case of your assisting an animal friend who has been traumatized in his past and is now in your care, begin with flower essences that support trauma recovery overall while you are getting to know the animal more deeply.

Once you are more familiar with the animal and have a greater understanding of how the trauma is showing up in her feeling and mental bodies, then you can expand to using more specific flower essences either through your own knowledge or with the assistance of practitioners trained in these tools.

Note: as the symptoms of the trauma change, so may the required flower essence shift. Observation and intuitive listening and communication with your animal friends or those in your care will assist you in knowing when to make a change. Please be patient, often it will require 30 or more days to see consistent improvement in the animals overall inner state of balance.

More detailed applications of flower essences in trauma recovery will be covered in specific chapters of Section IV. To learn more from other sources I suggest you begin with the following:

Resources

Anaflora's *Return to Joy* is a wonderful flower remedy blend to begin **with on** anyone who has been traumatized. See: www.anaflora.com for details about this remedy and all their other blends. Anaflora * Healing Animals Naturally with Flower Essences and Intuitive Listening contains detailed information about their flower essences and also how to commune with your animal friend(s) intuitively.

Flower Essence Society is a great resource for individual and organizational use and education of flower remedies as individuals. See: www.flowersociety.org for details including practitioners: http://www.flowersociety.org/practitioner/

Mary Ann Simonds flower remedies for horses and their humans' can be found on www.mystichorse.com

CHAPTER 41
ANIMALS TAKING ON THEIR HUMAN'S DISEASES

At times, companion animals will take on diseases and imbalances from their human(s) that would otherwise compromise or even destroy the bodies of their human guardian's body. This understanding has existed in the more intuitive human community for years. Now it is also coming forth through the science and medical world, giving it even greater global awareness.

The understanding of why animals do so is becoming clearer through a greater understanding of disease and how it manifests through our feeling bodies largely through the avenue of our words combined with our feelings. Animals, who like all the kingdoms of nature, embody unconditional love are in service to Life. Being in service is the greatest gift a soul or spirit can give to the Divine overall. It also brings forth the greatest evolution of the soul.

Animals who become diseased often do so to protect their human guardian and in doing so the family unit overall. For if the guardian and breadwinner so to speak is down, who will take care of the rest of the family? Many people who have animal companions have experienced this in some way whether they were aware of it or not. Over the years I have had many clients and friends who have faced such situations where their animals were taking on illness or injury to assist and protect the human who often is perceived as the alpha in the family.

Holistic Emergency Care and Trauma Recovery for Animals ./ Section IV

Although grateful, most people wish that their animals would not suffer on their behalf. Yet the animals will in turn often say, it is my choice and it is my service. They often also say that it is part of their journey of evolution to take on such a service for the greater good of the family. In recent years, my beloved Spirithawk took on the energy of bone cancer that I was drawing into my body during a very challenging time.

*What you say, think and focus upon with feeling,
you create in your reality,
whether it is wonderful or deeply painful.*

This is the Universal Law of Attraction.

When my mother completed her Bucket list she left her body through bone cancer, leaving this energy in the family energy field. When I began drawing this energy to me Spirithawk told me he would not allow this and took it into his own body resulting in his eventual demise. *I was aware of this through my abilities as an intuitive communicator and deep awareness of the divine ones who guided Spirithawk and me during our embodied journey together.*

I said I did not wish for him to carry this burden for me. The response was "It is not your choice. It is Spirithawk's choice", a very strong reminder that animals too are sovereign, sentient beings. In my years working with people and their animals I have observed animal's taking on their people's imbalances in so many ways. Some illnesses have been minor and other major, resulting in the animal leaving as Spirithawk did.

So what can you do in this regard as an animal guardian and companion? First and foremost take care of yourself holistically. Eat well, exercise and nurture yourself through quiet practices such as meditation, yoga, and just being quiet. Watch what you say, think and feel. Know that your words and thoughts combined with feelings are powerful manifestation conduits. Together they create wonderful or dire realities into your world.

Holistic Emergency Care and Trauma Recovery for Animals / Section IV

Choose to be in peace, harmony and joy. Make the choice for yourself and your family each and every day. Envision with feeling a life of joy for you and your family – two- legged and four-legged. And of utmost importance, BE GRATEFUL. Find the gifts in your life and that of your relationship with your animals and nature, and be grateful for them all. Gratitude is the stuff miracles are made of. The more that you take care of yourself and your animals, the less energy there is for a disease to find its way into your bodies and worlds.

But Are All Diseases That Animals Take On Due To Their Human?

No, of course not. Animals are individuals and sentient beings; they are on their own journey and can experience their own disease or injury. This can especially be observed with injuries to highly active animals, or with disease and trauma in abused or mistreated animals.

An example of direct injury occurred within my family when a foster family member (Braveheart) slammed into Ishnahnay tearing up her knee which then had to be rebuilt surgically. Gratefully, Ishnahnay's surgeon was skilled at this type of reconstruction. His ability, along with my knowledge of natural healing and Ishnahnay's strong inner healer, facilitated her healing and today she is easily keeping in stride with dogs half her age.

Anyone who has assisted a rescue animal that has been abused knows the great distress and disease (mentally, emotionally and physically) these animals can be in. In the cases of abuse and neglect, the causal energy generally comes from the imbalance of the human perpetrating the action, whether the animal(s) is wild or domestic. And yet, in most cases the responsible human is out of the picture, so the healing in those cases must be done directly through the animal(s), rather than on the animal and the human involved.

Holistic Emergency Care and Trauma Recovery for Animals ./ Section IV

However, incorporating forgiveness work, such as the Ho'oponopono prayer, can actually assist the human(s) responsible for the abuse to heal on many levels as well whether he/she is present or not. The Ho'oponophono Prayer to well-known and utilized in forgiveness work:

Ho'oponopono Prayer
I am sorry.
Please forgive me.
I forgive you and
I love you.
Thank you.
I release the past and embrace a peaceful future.

If you are choosing to facilitate the forgiveness process for an animal, and perhaps yourself as well (rescuers often benefit from doing this prayer as well), here are a few basic steps:

1. If you are able to receive a visual image of the person(s) responsible for the trauma either directly or through a communication with the animal you are assisting, then close your eyes, hold the picture(s) in your mind's eye (3rd eye) while reciting the prayer.
2. I you have a name(s) then more is the better. Speak the name(s) while holding the vision.
3. Recite the prayer.
4. Be sure to say thank you which anchors the prayer.
5. I add the line of *I release the past …* to assist in removing any remaining energy that might cause the experience or one's like it to be repeated for the animal or whomever the prayer is meant to assist.

It is in situations such as these that the use of flower essences and other modalities that really focus on balancing the feeling and mental bodies come in to play. Of course, volumes can and are being written on this subject. Within this section you can find more details under *Physical Rehabilitation* and *Mental and Emotional Trauma Rehabilitation*.

CHAPTER 42
POST-SURGERY TRAUMA RECOVERY

Pain Control & Transmutation

No matter the circumstance pain control and transmutation is of great importance in assisting the body to heal. Pain is an impediment to the body becoming balanced and in harmony again. This truth applied to all bodies: feeling, mental and physical.

The nervous system and feeling bodies are at the forefront of what must be calmed, healed and returned to harmony, thus allowing the remainder of the bodies to heal and come back into balance. In most cases, the veterinarian doing the surgery will send you and your animal home with pain medicine in hand. This can be helpful in the immediate time after the surgery.

However, dependent upon the severity of the surgery, your animal friend may do better in the long-term by switching to more natural pain management, including homeopathy and herbs. These administered along with flower essences can provide her with full body pain support while encouraging all bodies (feeling/spirit, mental and physical) to heal more easily.

Suggested Holistic Protocol

- Homeopathy: Hypericum perforatum, arnica montana
- Herbs: Yarrow, calendula, chamomile, willow
- Flower Essences: Self Heal; Rescue Remedy
- Nutritional: Vitamins E and C
- Ice pack application 3-4 times per day / decreasing as healing progresses

Holistic Emergency Care and Trauma Recovery for Animals ./ Section IV

The Importance of Blood Purification

Purification of our blood and that of our animal friends is of great importance. Surgery often brings drugs into the body systems, including anesthesia, pain meds, antibiotics, and associated other chemicals. These added to toxins that the animals(s) might be subject to in their living environments can compromise the physical body's blood and all that is affected directly and indirectly by the blood's function.

> Many, if not all of these herbs may grow naturally in your garden, neighborhood or surrounding parks and open spaces when left undisturbed by people who mistake them for weeds.

No matter the species of animal, blood is a primary carrier of all that enters the body, and all that leaves the body. Thus, seeing to its purification can facilitate more expedient healing in the case of trauma recovery, and greater wellness overall in the lives of the animals who you care for. Gratefully, by using holistic modalities, blood purification is relatively simple.

My suggestion is to utilize herbs that are known as Tonics and that are also blood purifiers. Due to the nature of Tonics you the option of longer use before having to switch to a different herb. In review, as stated in Section II, tonics benefit the entire body by strengthening the organs that are affected by the action of the digestive system.

Tonics are generally done over a period of time to allow time for them to work. These include: nasturtium, dandelion, comfrey, rosemary, parsley, goldenseal, burdock, lavender, mints, red clover, yarrow, raspberry, and violet. Of these, red clover is one of the best blood purifiers and anti-cancer herbs.

Blood Purifying herbs or Alteratives contain agents that gradually and favorably alter the condition of the body. Examples include: red clover, echinacea, plantain, comfrey, yarrow, burdock, chickweed, and dandelion root. The one that is chosen to utilize has to do with the other properties contained in the herb.

Although these are just a few of the herbs that are tonic and blood purifiers, looking at the examples you can see that dandelion, comfrey, red clover, and yarrow are in both. However, if you are only going to be using the blood purifier for one or two weeks at a time, then you are welcome to utilize any that are alteratives. Many, if not all of these herbs, grow naturally in your garden, neighborhood, surrounding parks and open spaces when left undisturbed by people who mistake them for weeds.

> *Aside:* If you are truly choosing to embrace holistic healing which includes using herbs, I recommend that you encourage the growth of these herbs and all those listed in Section II of the book. Also, learn when and how to harvest, store and make remedies from them so that you can stock your home and share these natural medicines within your community.

Tending to the purification of your animal friend(s) blood in such a natural way you are facilitating greater healing and providing assurance that the animal(s) also stay well once recovered from the initial trauma. Blood purification is also vitally important in the healing of arthritis and cancer. In this realm burdock (arthritis) and red clover (cancer) are the leading herbs to team up in creating desired combinations.

Administering Remedies

Zella sniffing herbal liniment

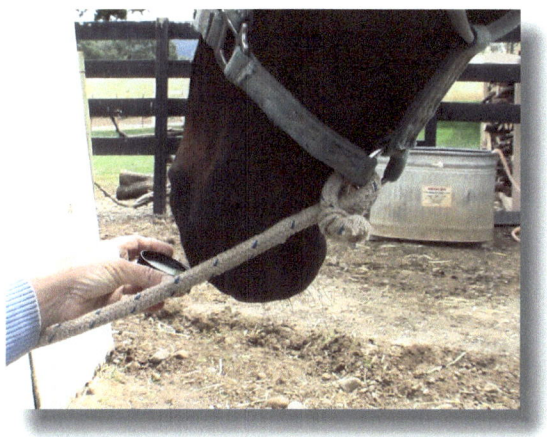

For dogs, cats and other small animals, it is often easiest to administer these herbs via infusion or decoction using an eye dropper. Some animals will enjoy having burdock and dandelion grated up in their food, especially when it has been warmed up slightly in olive oil beforehand. But other blood purifiers listed such as red clover and yarrow are better received in liquid form.

Horses and other larger animals are often

quite happy to consume these herbs when they are incorporated into their daily meals.

Feeding them directly is best done in oats or grain rather than loose foods such as hay or alfalfa. Even if the animals are being group fed, nutritive and tonic herbs such as these can be shared among them, but be sure that the animal(s) that is healing is getting enough to do him good. Tonic herbs are generally also nutritive and can be given over lengthy periods of time, thus making them safe to share among the family.

Be aware that not all tonic herbs are blood purifiers and vise verse. An example of an herb that is a blood purifier but <u>not</u> a tonic is echinacea. One of the most sought after properties of echinacea is its ability as an immune system booster at the onset of an illness. Yet, it is best only used short-term (3-4 days) before shifting to other herbs more suited for long-term use.

Holistic Emergency Care and Trauma Recovery for Animals / Section IV

CHAPTER 43
WOUND OR SURGICAL INCISION REPAIR

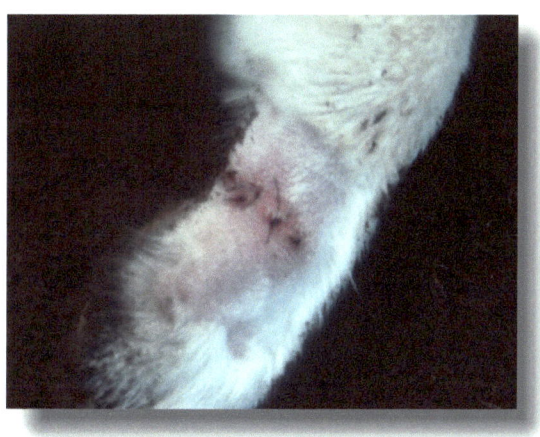

Ishnahnay's barbed wire cut with stiches

Holistic wound repair is quite simple and straight forward. The intention of what you provide your animal encompasses:

- Pain control
- Infection prevention
- Cellular regeneration
- Inflammation calming

Herbal Healing Support

I will use my Wound Repair Save as an example of herbs to utilize for wound repair in a cooperative manner. (The details and photos of these herbs can be found in Section II) Its components include:

- Yarrow: Its qualities as a hemostatic, anti-inflammatory herb and tonic (blood purification). This herb assists in the healing of wounds and guards against infection.

Holistic Emergency Care and Trauma Recovery for Animals ./ Section IV

- Comfrey: The qualities of comfrey include being a tonic, demulcent, expectorant, vulnerary and astringent assist in bone repair, cellular regeneration, blood purification and more.

- Calendula: Its properties include vulnerary, diaphoretic and astringent, which make this herb wonderful for cellular regeneration and calming of burns and skin eruptions.

- Chaparral: This plant's properties include being antibacterial, antiseptic, expectorant, and diuretic. Together they aid in infection prevention or healing in salves, liniments or tonics; arthritis and rheumatic pains, colds and flus, diarrhea, urinary tract infections

- Chamomile: Well known for its calmative properties, chamomile is also a nervine, antispasmodic, diaphoretic, making it a wonderful herb for healing in many situations.

- Turmeric: Commonly found in groceries stores this wonderful healer's properties include alterative, analgesic, astringent, antiseptic, blood thinner, which make it great for pain relief and also creates overall wellness as a blood purifier. Use caution as it is a blood thinner. This makes it inappropriate before any kind of surgery.

These herbs or others with the same properties can be administered as a salve, poultice, or in an infusion or tincture. If the surgery or injuries were extensive I recommend taking a systemic approach rather than local or to do both. In the case of local application, always utilize herbs that are safe if the animal ingests them, as many are prone to licking off whatever you might put on their skin.

Herbs to avoid include Arnica montana which can cause bruising or worse when ingested in its herbal form. **Use homeopathic Arnica montana instead**, as it heals bruises. The flower essence Arnica is also safe to use internally as are all flower remedies.

Application: Be gentle in your application or administering orally to the animal(s). Explain to her through words, feeling and visual pictures (also called visual packages), what you are giving her and why. If you are comfortable in doing so, you may also ask (call in) the animal's angelic and elemental support to assist in the communication and healing.

Homeopathic Healing Support

Homeopathic healing support for wounds or incisions is simple and straightforward. This makes using it a good choice for you if you are new to holistic and natural healing methods. Simple, effective and stress free:

- For bruising and shock: Arnica Montana – 6x to 30c
- For nerve repair : Hypericum perforatum – 6x to 30c

Flower Essence Support

Like homeopathy, flower essences are simple to administer and there are no worries about conflicting with medications prescribed by the veterinarian. If your animal friend is mobile and drinking out of her own water bowl, then the simplest method is to put 3-4 drops in the water each time you clean and refill the bowl. This should be at least once per day.

Suggested remedies include the following:

- Rescue Remedy
- Self Heal
- Arnica
- Anaflora's (www.anaflora.com) Return to Joy blend
- Also obtaining a custom blend for your animal is recommended. See Appendix C – References for recommendations.

CHAPTER 44
DISEASE RELATED SURGERIES

Recovering from surgery is no picnic whether it is you or your animal friend at the receiving end. The energies can run the gamut from physical to emotional pain, worry, grief, and for the human, financial stresses. In most cases, the intention of surgery is improved health, or at the least, greater comfort and quality of life. And the ultimate question is how best to successfully fulfill this intention.

Both holistic and wholistic[17] surgery recovery for disease or any other cause has been proven to be much more effective than simply treating the physical body and its imbalance. The question to be asking regarding the recovering – the whole recovery – is what is causing the cancer or disease in the first place?

Common causes of cancer and other disease in animals include:

- Environmental toxins

- Poor Diet (See Section II Prevention – A Major Step in Wholistic Care)
- Stressful living situations
- Repeated use of steroids compromising the immune system
- Companion animals taking on disease to assist their human guardian from being disabled by a similar disease. Note: when an animal sees their human friend as the head or alpha of the pack he may take on illness energy that otherwise would manifest in the human.

When a surgery is done in an attempt to eradicate disease such as cancer from an animal's body there are many steps that can be taken to bring about balance and wholeness of body, mind & spirit. As part of this process, it is recommended that the human guardian(s) and other indirectly affected animal family members also be given whole body support (spirit, mind & body). This is especially true in regards to nutrition and flower essence support.

No matter the family/species makeup, when one member is down due to injury or illness, everyone is affected. This is true, whether the human members are consciously aware of it or not. Those who have this greater awareness are leaps and bounds ahead in the healing

---

[17] Holistic refers to the modalities. Wholistic refers to the multiple bodies: physical, mental, feeling, spiritual

process of those who do not as it provides them greater motivation to address the causes of the imbalance(s) on a family level and beyond.

Recovery

When disease is the cause of a surgery, there is also often the wonder – will the surgery correct the challenge or will it persist? The full healing of an animal from such a surgery and the disease itself has many influences including:

- As mentioned above, <u>what caused the disease in the first place?</u>

- <u>How engaged is the animal's Inner Healer?</u> It has been my experience that the more domesticated and "inbred" an animal is, the poorer his Inner Healer may function. In addition to breeding, this is also a function of diet and overall immune system condition.

- <u>How supported are the animal's inner healer and her whole body system</u>: spirit, mind & body? Does the animal wish to live, or is he tired, depressed and ready to leave? Flower essences can play a great role in bringing new energy to an animal who is struggling with his healing process.

- <u>Is it the animal's choice to get well and stay well</u>, or is it his choice are part of his soul's journey to experience this disease to the point of it causing his spirit to leave the body (die)?

- <u>Is the human guardian(s) willing to do what it takes</u> to support the animal's full return to balance through holistic healing and/or integrative medicine?

Thus the initial steps are recovery from the surgery itself and the determination of how best to proceed with assisting your animal friend to the highest level of her journey. If you are unsure of how to proceed, obtaining the assistance of an animal communicator or intuitive is highly recommended. Even the best of animal communicators often get the assistance of another when it comes to sensitive decisions, such as facilitating for a very ill or recovering animal friend.

Having a clear sense of your animal friend's desires and goals for her healing and full recovery (or not) is extremely important in doing the best to facilitate for her, just as you would do for yourself. When you understand the desires of your animal, you can easily create a partnership for healing and wellness together.

Resting and Support

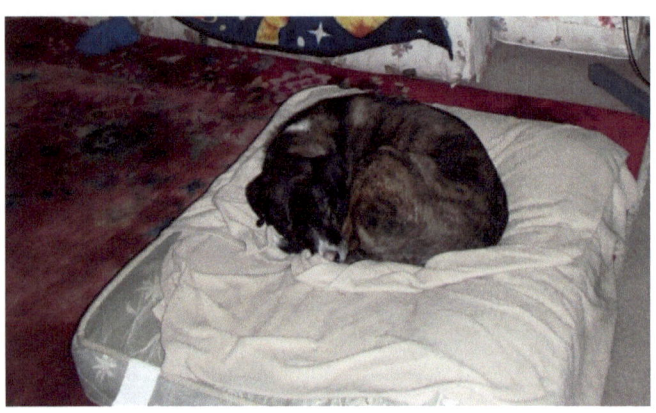

As most people acknowledge, resting is at the top of the list in importance to allow the multi-body system to heal. While it is absolutely true for the physical body, rest also plays an important role in the healing and balancing of a traumatized mind or feeling body. For it is in the rest state that animals, as well as humans, commune most deeply with the Divine. It is also the state where the greatest receiving of Divine assistance and healing can be received and assimilated.

In major physical traumas, most animals will cooperate with being quiet and resting. Yet it is when they begin feeling better, and their body can support them sufficiently in moving about, that a new conversation of rest and support must come from you or the animal(s) guardian/caregivers. With dogs, cats and other smaller animals, this time is often complicated when other animals /playmates are present who are just as anxious as the rehabilitating animal to see her back to her full self. Play time!

This is especially true if the other animals are younger, and to date injury free. These sweet ones often do not have a point of reference from which to assist, hold space or even protect the one who is healing from dangers in the immediate environment.

Holistic Emergency Care and Trauma Recovery for Animals ./ Section IV

CHAPTER 45
PHYSICAL REHABILITATION

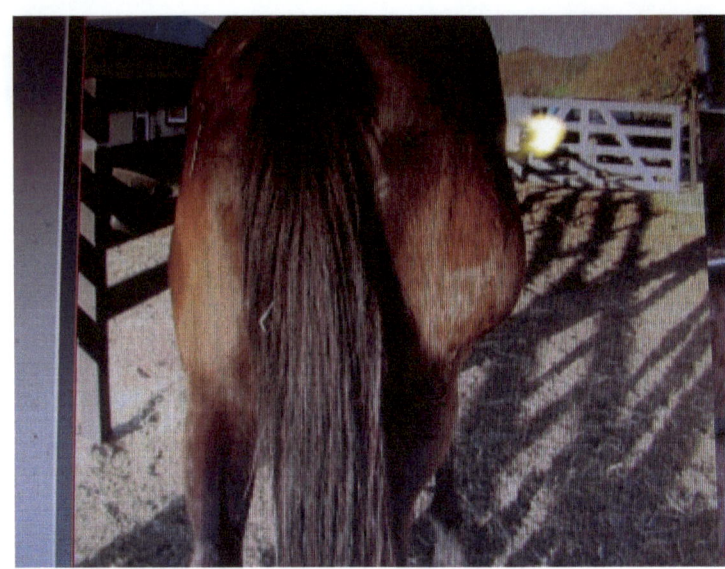

Zella After Fall on Ice (Case Study 6)

The quality of the physical rehabilitation that must come after an injury or surgery is of utmost importance. It is not uncommon for surgeons (veterinarian or human) to say "Mine was the easy part, the rehabilitation is up to you – or your animal and you" This is especially true when it is an injury/structural correction through surgery.

Another truth is all of the lower bodies (physical, mental and spirt/feeling) will be involved in the rehabilitation being fully successful. The physical healing is a deep conversation between spirit and form as the blueprint of each cell in every body system affected is rebuilt and healed.

This communion requires a balance of rest, activity, powerful, organic nutrition, and overall positive energetic support by all who are a part of the recovering animal's family and environment. Anyone who has injured herself or had surgery knows that attitude is key in the whole-healing process. This is no less true for our animal friends.

Holistic Emergency Care and Trauma Recovery for Animals / Section IV

- *Yes I Can!*

- Breathe and be peace

- Visioning → see your animal friend strong and well again – walking, running, playing. Talk and meditate with him about his vision. What is the desired outcome? Staying and being strong and well, or leaving his body and being free in Spirit?

- What are the necessary steps to accomplish this?

- Is full recovery possible?

- Be compassionate regarding the potential of minor or even major disabilities; either short or long term.

The Importance Of Pain Relief

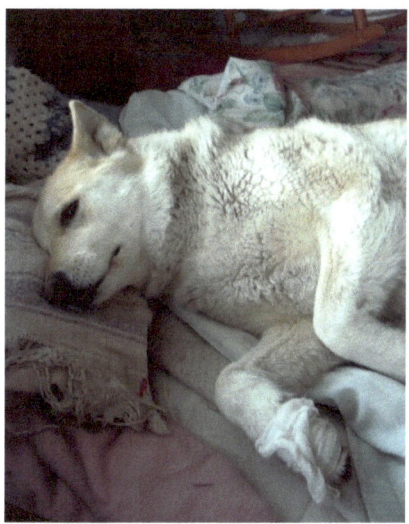

Ishnahnay Experiencing Pain After Surgery – Before Holistic Pain Management

In order for healing and cellular regeneration to occur the pain cycle within the body must be interrupted or stopped completely. Thus other than creating comfort in the animal (or human) healing, this is the primary reason for pain relievers being given during recovery

Holistic Emergency Care and Trauma Recovery for Animals ./ Section IV

from surgery or injury.

Animals have a much greater pain tolerance than humans, the extent of which was demonstrated to me years ago when my dear German Shorthair Pointer, Spencer, developed Bloat while we were out hiking. Due to the distance we were away from our car and then the emergency vet, he was in great distress by the time we arrived. It was in that moment of the veterinarian practically yelling at me that I had to let him put Spencer down right then because he was in so much pain – pain that was unimaginable to a human – that my awareness of animals' great courage opened dramatically.

From that day forward, my observation of animals shifted to a much deeper level of communication which has allowed me to understand the subtle actions animals often display when they are in pain – especially when they are attempting to downplay it for one reason or another. Whether you are a caretaker, guardian, rescuer or healer of some type, a skilled awareness of animal behavior, communication skills and the animal's personal pain management will serve you to assist them in a much greater way.

For animals, hiding pain and dysfunction is a natural instinct; one of self-protection and preservation. In the wild, pain and disability often means death. Unlike humans who can call in sick to daytime activities and stay in a warm, safe bed while healing, animals who are down, must hide, heal or die either through the elements or by the actions of another creature; human or animal.

Thus many animals downplay their pain, often making it difficult for the untrained eye or ear (communicator) to understand the depth of the discomfort that they are experiencing. Again, I encourage everyone to develop greater intuitive and direct communication abilities with animals and the Angelic and Elemental being who watch over them. The greater your abilities in these areas, the greater your ability to assist animals heal and live healthy and joy-filled lives.

Animal communication skills can be developed in many ways. There are also communicators worldwide who can be of assistance. Please see *AppendixC– References*, and our websites (Earthwise.Institute, http://www.holisticemergencycare.com, and www.kathrynshantiariel.com for more details)

Whole Body Support

Multi-body healing support, both short and long term is always of great benefit to the one who is healing, and can also be of benefit to her extended family.

Flower Remedies

As mentioned in previous sections there are several main flower remedies that I recommend for whole body rehabilitation when an animal is choosing to stay in body and heal after a trauma. These include:

- Bach Rescue Remedy or FES Five Flower Remedy (initially)
- FES Self Heal
- Arnica
- Anaflora's Return to Joy

However, many others can be helpful for specific issues. In review I suggest you go to *Section II, Flower Remedies Most Used for Emergencies & Trauma Care*, to obtain more details. Also you may find more suggestions in the Appendix C – References, at the end of the book.

Homeopathy

Herbs

For long term trauma care and general health, it is best to focus on the use of herbs that are considered Tonics. Such herbs can be utilized continuously over long periods with only beneficial results. Herbs that considered to be tonics include:

- **Circulatory System:** Hawthorn berry, Cayenne pepper, Ginger, Garlic, Motherwort and Red Clover (blood purifier)
- **Digestive system**: Chamomile, Clove, Comfrey, Dandelion, Ginger, Rue, Turmeric
- **Immune system**: Echinacea, garlic, ginger, ginseng, liquorice,
- **Muscles and Skeleton:** Alfalfa, angelica, black cohosh, comfrey, nettles
- **Nervous system:** Skullcap, Black cohosh, lemon balm, motherwort, mugwort

- **Respiratory system**: Angelica, aniseed, coltsfoot, comfrey, garlic, hyssop, licorice root, thyme, yarrow
- **Urinary system**: Dandelion, Parsley, Plantain, Yarrow
- **Skin**: Calendula, Comfrey, Echinacea, Dandelion, Nettles, Turmeric

Energy Healing Options

Theta Healing, and Reiki are both wonderful tools for providing any life form; animal, human, plant …with whole body support. As I have previously noted, I wholeheartedly encourage you to take the training for these techniques if you in the world of healing or emergency care on any level. That said, there are tools available without extensive training. Below is an example:

Healing Touch Quick Steps

Healing Touch Quick Steps - Powerful Things You Can Do Instantly to Bring Your Body into Harmony®: From holistic health pioneer and integrative healing arts practitioner Barbara J. Semple, here are two ultra-simple Quick Steps to easily help someone (animal or person) in deep need.

Quick Steps Overview

"I have used this dynamic self-help for my own healing challenges (as well as my cats) over the last 30 years. Through recovery from surgeries, stitches, aches and pains, digestive, respiratory or elimination concerns and just for the sake of unburdening and uplifting my circulation (our circulation) and vitality, everything is better with the self-help of Healing Touch Quick Steps. This natural gift passed down through the ages, is my 'go to' option for animal or person alike because I have experienced the happy benefits thousands of times myself and witnessed it in others too.

Years ago a dear friend's golden retriever was so ill that my friend thought she'd have to let

Holistic Emergency Care and Trauma Recovery for Animals / Section IV

the dog go. My friend felt very sad and helpless. Doctors couldn't help. I suggested she gently hold a forepaw in one of her hands and hold the opposite back paw in her other hand. After a minute or less I suggested she switch sides and hold the other front paw and opposite back paw. She did this twice a day and after the first day, her sweet dog began to perk up, wanted to eat and drink and became happier.

My friend continued to apply the "opposite fingers and toes" Quick Step for a few more days twice a day until she felt her pet was back to its old self. Here are two of the easiest, simplest Quick Steps for trauma and emergency recovery care of your pet in addition to your medical professional's advice. Healing Touch Quick Steps stress relief are a valuable complement, never a replacement for professional medical care." Barbara J. Semple

1. This Quick Step called "Breathe from Toes to Head," helps the whole body breathe easier. Whether animal person is sitting or lying, go to the animal's feet or paws and simply and GENTLY hold his or her BIG toes for a minute or two. When someone is seriously ill, apply for a minute or two only twice a day. Less energy healing touching is better when someone is seriously ill. No more than twice a day, morning and evening.

2. This Quick Step called "Magnificent Circulation," helps to improve overall circulation especially for someone who is recovering from surgery, as well as arthritic joints and general well-being. This Quick Step is adapted here for animals.

While your animal friend is lying down, sit at its side and GENTLY hold your animal's front paw in one of your hands and the animal's OPPOSITE back paw in your other hand. Your animal will let you know when she/he has had enough energy healing for the moment by moving a paw away from you. The diagonal connection of front paw and opposite back paw is essential.

After a minute or two (or less if your dear one moves its foot or hand away) switch to the other side and gently hold the other front paw and the opposite other back paw for a minute or so. Again, if your friend moves her paw away from your hold, she is saying she has had enough for now.

This is an excellent natural healing helper for animals or humans. For humans, you hold a finger and an opposite toe. See the Instant Healing book or HEAL NOW Cards for how-to pictures.

3. EMT Quick Step: Place right hand palm at the base of the tail (or coccyx) and your left hand palm gently at heart center. Simply be in that hand placement for a while. This is very helpful for fast, in the moment emergency need.

MAP

I am also a huge advocate of using MAP for trauma recovery and maintaining general health. (see Chapter 14 for more details)

Holistic Emergency Care and Trauma Recovery for Animals / Section IV

CHAPTER 46
MENTAL AND EMOTIONAL TRAUMA REHABILITATION

Over the past few decades more and more attention within the medical and healing communities has been placed on types of imbalances caused by extreme trauma. Intentional abuse, violence and extreme physical injury from disasters top the list of causes. Post-Traumatic Stress Disorder (PTSD) is one of the terms that have become most popular in defining these imbalances. And yet the word "disorder" within this label gives one the sense of a disease rather than an imbalance within a person, or in the context of this book, an animal.

It is important for people who assist animals as rescuers, foster guardians, healers, shelter personnel, etc. be aware of the characteristics of mentally or emotionally traumatized animals and holistic options for assisting them to return to balance and peace, *if it is the animal's choice to do so*. Much of this chapter and section overall is dedicated to such people. (((Gratitude)))

Mental or emotional imbalances "disorders" can be the response of an animal to repeated physical or emotional abuse, neglect, extreme physical trauma and other such experiences. An example of this is depicted in the book and movie "The Horse Whisperer". In this story both horse and his guardian are severely injured being hit by a semi-truck, the resulting physical trauma impacting their minds and emotions in addition to their physical bodies.

Animals often respond to such experiences by withdrawing or becoming hypersensitive to stimulus of many kinds. If the trauma is based in the physical body and then extending into the mental or emotional bodies, animals in general will often respond through avoidance, or if trapped, through aggression. In most cases, both of these responses are meant to protect the animal from whatever he may see as a threat in the world due to his current condition.

It has been my experience that the underlying energies of such responses include a lack of trust in others, or in their own ability to cope with the demands of a certain situations, such as pack or herd dynamics. The lack of trust can be specifically with people or other animals and is often a direct response to a place, activity, person, or animal was responsible or that triggers the memory in the animal of the trauma in some way.

Animals can also have trauma memories from past lives of their Spirit/Soul self, and in some cases they can embody trauma memory responses from a greater group consciousness. For example, Ishnahnay my current Wolfdog friend and teacher is extremely sensitive and overtly concerned of gun shots or any other noises that sound like guns or war. This is partly from her being killed in a past life embodiment as a wolf, and partly due to the trauma energy in nature and the animal kingdom as a whole regarding gunfire and warfare.

Trauma in Rescued Animals

Whether wild or domestic, animals that are rescued directly or through shelters often have experienced some kind of trauma or another. If the rescuer is fortunate enough to receive the history of the animal at the time of fostering, rehabilitation or adoption, then care based on knowledge is much easier to create. Yet, more often than not, the history of the animal is unclear.

In cases where the history is unknown, the animal may be willing to provide you with details directly through the use of animal communication skills. If you (the rescuer) have not developed these skills, then I highly recommend connecting with a professional animal communicator & holistic healer to be the communication bridge. What you learn may make the difference in the animal healing into balance and joy or continuing a life of uncertainty, dependent upon the severity of the trauma on the mental/emotional body level.

Case in Point: Braveheart came to join us as a foster dog just after he was dropped at the Humane Society. He was young, and passive aggressive on many levels due to trauma. I received minimal information about him from the family that dropped him off. My communication skills provided me information regarding his fear of fire, guns, men with tool belts and also provided a glimpse into why he was either on alert or hiding when we were at home.

The fear of fire came from Braveheart being tied up and confined where he lived in the country a year when wild fires were blazing out of control for months. The symptoms of *nowhere to run, nowhere to hide* were very apparent whenever we were around a fire – whether it was a camp fire or wild fire did not matter. Even the smell of fire would cause him to go into a fear and flight response. Also, men, or sometimes even women, carrying something looking like a weapon could trigger him into a passive aggressive pattern.

Once at our home, he was given wonderful nutrition, daily opportunities to socialize and a safe home and yard to rest in. The information of what he was afraid of and why provided me the ability to be proactive with him, teaching him discernment and positive life experiences, while also providing him with flower essences and herbs to assist in bringing his mind & emotions back into balance.

Over time our communications, along with healing therapies, allowed him to heal many of his imbalances while showing me those which he was not ready to release. With this knowledge I was able to find his forever home and provide his new human a great amount of information on how to provide him a quiet, safe home and how to be proactive with him when necessary.

Without clear communication and intuition, it would have been much more difficult for me to understand Braveheart's trigger points, and subsequently to assist in his healing. *Thus again, I encourage all who are working with traumatized animals to seek the assistance of skilled animal communicators, intuitives and holistic healers.*

Main Sources of Stress or Trauma in Animals

When working with animals, especially rescues experiencing trauma, it is important to consider that humans are often the source of the trauma, directly or indirectly. Therefore the animal may often initially display distrust towards humans in general.

As a result, abuse and neglect towards animals may be done on a conscious intention level, or they may be activities coming from unconscious ideas or beliefs (Examples: seeing animals as less that human "just a dog", seeing animals as animals as unfeeling, unintelligent beings to dominate, etc.). There are many examples of this behavior including:

1. Direct abuse, torture or neglect

2. Indirect stress or abuse from living in a family where abuse, unrest or stress is prominent

3. Emotional or mental trauma resulting from or part of, a physical trauma.

4. Uncaring or ignorant behaviors towards animals based on beliefs that they are lesser in value than humans.

5. Interference of the animal's journey due to the human(s) involved not hearing, understanding or supporting its accomplishment. This is applicable to wild or domestic animal individuals or groups.

6. In addition, trauma symptoms can develop anytime in the life of an animal when she has experienced trauma. They can be triggered by some present experience, even if the trauma occurred as far back as in her Mother's womb. Research has shown for animals and humans that undue stress or trauma of some sort during the pregnancy can result in physical or mental/emotional trauma in the babies.

Post-Traumatic Stress Syndrome

Post-Traumatic Stress Syndrome within animals, it is often a response to a set of traumatic situations; coping mechanisms of protection, rather than a disorder. However in the case of mental/emotional combined with physical trauma, there may also be actual neurological or other physiological/anatomical damage requiring more expanded knowledge and application of trauma recovery techniques.

PTSD can be exhibited in everything from avoidance and hiding, to passive aggression, to severe neediness and abandonment issues. The coping mechanisms that the animal displays are keenly connected to the original cause of the trauma.

- Neediness and fear of being left alone → Neglect or abandonment

- Physical and/or mental abuse → Passive aggression toward people or things that trigger memories of the abuse

- Abuse or severe neglect of some type → Avoidance or hiding due to a strong distrust of humans the animals does not know to be loving and supportive (strangers).

- Abuse can also lead to an unwillingness of animals to respond to a human when called. Again this is a trust issue, unless the animal is a husky, Wolfdog or other independent and sovereign breed, which requires that you earn their respect.

Recovery Necessities

There are many factors to assisting an animal in recovery, healing, from abuse based trauma. LOVE and Compassion are of course at the center of these, as there truly is nothing more powerful than unconditional love (LOVE) when it comes to healing and returning to balance. However, there are other pieces to the puzzle that play a key part in the journey as well. In my experience, these include:

1. Recognition of animals as intelligent, soulful, feeling beings.
2. Realization that many behavior anomalies in animals are symptoms of their response to previous or ongoing trauma.

Trauma and the Nervous System

While all parts of the physical body can be compromised by trauma, it is the nervous system and its intricate relationship with the feeling body that can oftentimes retain deep scars or memories that impede a full return to balance and wholeness. This is true whether the primary trauma was based in the physical, mental or feeling bodies.

However it has been my experience that those traumas based primarily in the physical body generally heal more thoroughly than those based in the mental or feeling bodies. This is providing the healing is accomplished through the purposeful engagement of the entire multibody system of the animal. *There is almost always some emotional engagement in physical trauma abet temporary.*

Yet if a focus of pain, sorrow, or other such energy is *engaged* then the feeling imbalance can settle into the physical body either its physiology or anatomy, possibly becoming a chronic disability.

Holistic Emergency Care and Trauma Recovery for Animals / Section IV

CHAPTER 47
CASE STUDIES

This is a compilation of a few case studies that I have written as part of facilitating healing for some animals who have lived with me and others who are clients. It is my intention, through sharing these studies, to provide you with a greater sense of how to successfully apply the information in this book to real life situations. These and additional case studies will also be shared on our website: www.holisticemergencycare.com under Educational Materials category Case Studies.

Case 1: Ishnahnay's Car Incident

Location – Shasta Vista Residential District; 35 miles from Mt. Shasta, CA

When: 5:30 pm ; *No emergency assistance available within 60 miles*

Ishnahnay before Being Hit by Car

A Day of Miracles

Fall 2006: The *events of this day were life changing for me in bringing an awareness of the power of Alternative/Integrative medicine combined with calling for Divine Assistance in emergencies as well as in our day to day lives. Had I not done so, it is possible that Ishnahnay would not have survived this day. Read on to understand why.*

Holistic Emergency Care and Trauma Recovery for Animals ./ Section IV

My two Wolfdog companions, Ishnahnay, Spirithawk and I were about 1 mile from home, hiking in the juniper forest in which we lived. Ishnahnay was ahead of Spirithawk and me, and temporarily out of our visual sight, but within hearing distance. Hares (cousins to rabbits) were abundant in this high desert forest. Ishnahnay spotted one and gave chase.

The hare dashed across a nearby dirt road. Ishnahnay followed at a dead run oblivious to anything but the chase. There were few houses in the area, and therefore little car traffic. On a busy day perhaps 5-6 cars would go by. However, Ishnahnay, crossed just as one of our neighbors came around the same corner. The timing was such that in focused chase, Ishnahnay did not see the car until it was too late. The impact was sudden.

All I heard was Ishnahnay yelp loudly one time. Then there was silence. Rushing to the scene we met our visibly upset neighbor who stopped to tell me he had just hit Ishnahnay and was going home to get his truck so he could help me take her home. Meanwhile Spirithawk and I went to find her. Moving into her instinctual behavior of a wounded animal, Ishnahnay had curled up under some bushes and then became quiet, hiding from prospective predators who might take advantage of her condition.

Spirithawk honed in on her location with some difficulty, since Ishnahnay had pulled in her energy and was in hypovolemic shock. However, with Divine Grace as our ally we located her under the tree where she had hidden herself. Once we found her, I called in an etheric healing team (*Calling Divine 911, emergency, please help*), and set to work stabilizing her while waiting for our neighbor's return. (See <u>Calling in Divine Assistance</u>). He came and gently placed her in his truck, but there was no room for Spirithawk, so we followed quickly on foot. Upon arrival at our home, Ishnahnay was lying on the porch, but upon our arrival managed to enter the house before collapsing.

All the while her healing team comprised primarily of Angels and Elementals, prompted me to get to work on her physical, mental and emotional bodies (lower bodies) while they went to work on her subtle bodies; stabilizing her life force.. Fortunately, I had just taught an Emergency Care Class and my materials & gear were still out and easily accessible. Ishnahnay was in critical condition. Yet feeling the support of the angels and elementals

Holistic Emergency Care and Trauma Recovery for Animals / Section IV

there to assist, I settled into what had to be done for her with confident focus.

Important Note: we were about 1 ½ hours from an emergency animal hospital as our local ones were closed already and even those were 40 minutes away from our home. So I had to act with the authority and wisdom that I had gained through my years of training.
Now since there were several components of this process I will break them down into sections.

First: Assessing the Situation: Ishnahnay's injuries:

- Extensive internal and external bruising, including vital organs (life threatening)
- Road rash on her belly and inner thighs
- Dis-alignment of left shoulder and spinal column from upper thoracic vertebrae through sacrum and tail.
- Extensive damage to nervous system and GI track; resulting in no bladder or fecal control.
- Diaphragm was pushed up into lung cavity, impairing Ishnahnay's breathing among other things.
- Extensive hypovolemic shock set in and was a danger for over 24 hours (life threatening)

Second: Once her injuries were determined and prioritized according to severity, my real treatment of her began.

It is important to note that since I had already called in a Divine Emergency Healing Team, they were already at work on her subtle bodies while I was assessing her emotional - physical and beginning assistance there. Again, this was key to her survival.

- Rescue Remedy (Five Flower Remedy – FES), given internally and rubbed on paws and ears to stabilize the shock reaction.
- Homeopathic phosphorus and arnica montana 30c for internal bleeding and shock (arnica). Dosed her orally every 20 minutes for 1st hour, then down to once every three hours for first 12 hours; dropping to twice a day for three days.

- Ishnahnay requested the Wound Repair Salve that I make which she ate from my hand 50 ml – 100 ml at a time over a period of days. Ingredients:

  - Yarrow
  - Chaparral
  - Comfrey
  - Lavender
  - Calendula
  - Self-heal
  - Olive oil
  - Bees wax
  - Tincture of Benzoin (preservative)

  (For ease of use in emergencies, I have since created a trauma recovery tincture to complement the salve's effectiveness.

- Homeopathic Hypericum for nerve damage was administered every hour for first four hours, augmenting the wound salve components. Dosage was dropped to twice a day beginning third day and dropped to once a day beginning day five for an additional two days.
- Working in conjunction with Ishnahnay's Divine Healing Team, I invoked Theta Healing (www.theatahealing.com) as I worked to scan her physical, mental and emotional bodies, requesting healing of whatever I was shown on an ongoing basis.
- Surface injuries (road rash) were cleansed with my witch hazel tincture and then wound salve was gently applied where advisable. (Some areas were too raw for a salve.
- So, as time allowed, I created a herbal poultice of yarrow, comfrey, lavender, calendula and selfheal which I placed on the affected areas for 10 minutes intervals to sooth and heal the raw areas.

Third, Emergency Assistance through Divine Healing Team

Holistic Emergency Care and Trauma Recovery for Animals / Section IV

As previously stated, I called in a Divine Healing Team for Ishnahnay at the accident site, knowing that they could immediately begin working on her while we were in movement and I was setting up the healing station at my home to care for her fully. It was at this time, when I was kneeling before Ishnahnay's body and tending to her, that I became fully aware of the Angelic and Elemental Team that knelt beside me to my left as we worked on her in tandem.

What I remember most about this time was how seamlessly we worked together – gratitude and grace flowing between us and Ishnahnay who was the recipient of our care. In this instance, I was gifted with visual awareness of the energies that they were weaving into her complete body system (etheric to physical) to remove the trauma and heal all that was ready to be healed.

It was during this time and since that I have been reminded of the great assistance that is available to anyone who truly and gratefully requests such assistance while being fully in faith that it does exist.

During the next 12 hours, we supported Ishnahnay through this critical time. Spirithawk did his part by holding space in the background and assisting me with communications as needed. The morning after, Ishnahnay was able to go outside and gently move about. She was still in a low level of shock. But she desired to be on the earth rather than in the house, as she knew the healing power that the Earth provides us all.

Obtaining Assistance from other Professionals

In most cases, I would have taken Ishnahnay to a veterinarian after she was stabilized. However in this instance, I was guided instead to take her to two body work professionals who could assist in realigning her body systems. First was a Feldenkrais and Osteopathic practitioner who had worked on me repeatedly, and whom I trusted implicitly. Over three appointments, she was able to pull down Ishnahnay's diaphragm and stabilize it while also assisting the realignment of her shoulder and back, the latter of which was essential in bringing the intestinal tract and bladder function back online.

After a month's time and through the following year, Ishnahnay also had regular appointments with one of our local chiropractors who worked on animals as well as people. He focused his skill to releasing the contracted places in Ishnahnay's body, which allowed the healing energies still being supplied to her to penetrate her bodies (physical, emotional, mental) effectively.

Ishnahnay's Body after Healing from Being Hit by Car

Photo by Julie Colt

Ishnahnay's Long Term Healing

As with any injury that leaves our body somewhat altered – emotionally, mentally or physically - Ishnahnay has required ongoing care and attention from me and through me in subtle ways. My support has come in an array of ways dependent upon her body's state of balance.

As can be seen in the above photograph, her lower spine down to her tail was damaged altering the positioning of her tail. To this day, there remains some damage to the nervous system in her lower back and intestinal tract leading to some heightened sensitivity in her back. Her left shoulder also requires regular attention, especially after she has been playing chase with her friends. To assist her ongoing health I provide her with macro foods (chlorella, spirulena and kelp) as well as homeopathy and herbal support as needed on a day to day basis.

Recently, a friend stated to me that when she looks into Ishnahnay's eyes, she sees a very soulful being who emanates great determination and strength of purpose, such as that required of anyone who has endured such trauma and yet is embracing as fully as possible a life of joy and peace.

Animals in all forms share this Great Spirit and ability to overcome adversity. Their deep and constant connection with the Divine – God within – has much to do with this ability. They never question who or what is God/Goddess or the Divine. They just know. And they know they are an integral part of her expression.

Case Two: Daunza's Poisoning & Recovery Case Study

Synopsis: 1998 - Ingested piece of meat laced with poison found in open field behind our home while we were out for our morning walk before I left for work. I did not realize that what she had eaten was a problem until she went into a full grand mal seizure.

Daunza's legs went rigid and upon closer check I could see her entire body was rigid. I immediately called my veterinarian, whose office was only a couple of miles away. She sent two technicians and a body board to come and get Daunza and transport her back to the clinic as I could not move her myself.
According to the vet, the type of poison that Daunza had ingested results in brain spasms that if not subdued cause the vessels in the brain to explode. She put Daunza on a valium to keep her in a deep rest state for three days to allow the poison to move through her body without destroying it.

Holistically what I was allowed to do was sit with Daunza rub Rescue Remedy on her paws, offer energy healing, and hold her paw providing her with loving support – heart to heart; breath to breath. Once she was out of danger I took her home and began the deeper work on healing her body. Besides her brain being affected, also Daunza's stomach and intestines (GI track) were damaged, affecting her ability to digest and tolerate certain foods.

My holistic regime to facilitate her healing was as follows:

Flower Essences - Rescue Remedy, Self Heal, Aloe Vera

Holistic Emergency Care and Trauma Recovery for Animals / Section IV

Herbal Support
- Infusion of mullein, chamomile, yarrow, calendula, skullcap and raw honey provided 3-4 times per day over three weeks.

- Aloe vera juice in food ongoing throughout the remainder of her life.

Homeopathic Support –

- Arnica montana for 3 days after returning home

Nutritional Support –
- Spirulena

- Digestive Enzymes

- Probiotics

Energy Healing –
- Loving energy transference in meditative state directly to Daunza's brain; every day for first month of recovery, then dropping to a few times per week.

- " " to abdominal area "

Case Three: Mitchel's Abuse → Rescue → Severe Trauma Rehabilitation: Avoidance as a coping mechanism – Mitchel

Mitchel came to live with Ishnahnay and me approximately five years after being rescued from an extreme abuse situation. His initial rescue in Tucson, Arizona, took him to a shelter where he met "Michael" who eventually adopted him when his number was up (it was a kill shelter). I learned from Michael that the first few weeks Mitchel was in the shelter, he hid in the back of his kennel with his front legs over his head for protection.

This new partnership with Michael provided Mitchel with peaceful companionship, food, a safe home and basic exercise. However Michael was very busy, leaving Mitchel at home alone much of the time. He also did not have the skills required to move Mitchel out of the trauma management stage that he lived in and into a true state of peace. After boarding Mitchel short-term with Ishnahnay, Mitchel and Michael both asked if I would take him in to live with us as a foster, or possibly permanent, member of our family. Thus our journey of healing together began.

From what Michael shared with me, Mitchel had experienced server emotional and physical abuse. *The first few weeks he was in the shelter, Mitchel hid in his kennel with his feet over his head, shaking in fear.* The symptoms of Mitchel's abuse could be categorized as Post Traumatic Stress Syndrome (PTSD) in his emotional and mental bodies. Physically he also had damage to his shoulders and his cervical vertebrae, which I found out a bit too late had given his a weakness that lead to seizures.

Mitchel's case is a complex one some of which I am sharing here and the rest will be in posts on our website (www.holisticemergencycare.com). Despite his abuse, Mitchel is a peaceful, loving individual. However, he is understandably wary of people in many ways choosing to let individuals earn his trust rather than giving it to them blindly.

Avoidance as a Coping Mechanism

Holistic Emergency Care and Trauma Recovery for Animals / Section IV

Mitchel's wariness showed up in a very intense way as avoidance when he first came to live with us – especially when we were out hiking. We are fortunate to live in an area where having dogs off leash is the norm in most places. The advantage of this for Mitchel was when we was uncomfortable about someone coming down the trail, he was able to just go off to the side far enough to feel safe.

Avoidance such as displayed by Mitchel can be very strong energy/action utilized by animals which have been traumatized through serve injury such as those that occur in car accidents or other disasters as well as in abusive situations. It can be seen in the realities of domestic animals which have been abused and also wild animals towards humans do to the centuries of hunting.

Rehabilitation

Love is the answer. Love, patience, good nutrition and flower essences have all been of prime importance in assisting Mitchel to find a space of peace within his being. Once I became aware that Mitchel was using avoidance to manage his sphere of activity around people, I was able to explain to those we met what he was doing and why. This allowed others to be supportive and understanding of him, while keeping their distance.

Ishnahnay (wolfdog companion) has also be of great support to Mitchel. Helping him to learn discernment around people (who to trust and who to avoid), and also how to play again. He thinks the world of her and is very grateful for her inner peace, joy and courage. They have become great friends and Mitchel has become a part of our family.

Nutrition

Improving Mitchel's diet has been both a joy and healing aid for him. Providing daily doses of greens from spirulina and c8horella, fresh leafy greens and carrots have placed an important role in supporting his nervous system and body overall from the effects of stress. B complex is known to be very in the support of the nervous system and are water soluble, thus requiring to be added to everyone's diet on a daily basis for best results.

Flower Remedies

Due to the complexity of Mitchel's challenges I have utilized a series of different flower remedies for him; some premade and also one custom. The premade ones that I have used successfully include:

- Anaflora : Return to Joy
- Anaflora : Courage with Buttercup added
- and after Mitchel's had a grand mal seizure : Daily Brain Balancing Remedy

Herbal Remedies

I began added an herbal tonic for the nervous system to Mitchel's daily regime also after he had the seizure. Up to when he had the seizure I had no knowledge of any preexisting condition. The grand mal seizure was very extreme and set him back quite a bit.

The Nerve Tonic that I am now giving him has Skullcap as its main ingredient. Skullcap is known for its abilities to assist in healing or at least minimizing imbalances that cause seizures.

It is important to note here that due to the extreme shock Mitchel experienced through this seizure his body and spirit connection was greatly compromised. He began a conversation with myself and others of the possibility that he might leave his body permanently if the connection could not be restored to a greater degree. This was before the Nerve Tonic was added to his regime. At this time he is doing much better, however both Ishnahnay and I are aware that he may leave if another seizure takes control of his body.

Understanding that there is an ongoing conversation with all animals – just was we humans – between Spirit and body can allow great insights to come to you as a guardian and caregiver to animals. They too have their own journey. It is important to allow them to fulfill it without intervening and ended it through unnatural ways, unless they specifically ask for the assistance.

Case Forth: Tuska – Kitten With Broken Vertebrae

8-12 weeks, feral mother, living on friend's horse ranch. I was adopting Tuska's brother Seth and upon arriving to pick him up I was informed that Seth's brother had been stepped on or clipped by a horse during the night and Tuska's back appeared to be broken. My friend, Jenay then asked me to take him as well as Seth, feeling that I could facilitate his healing. The following is a synopsis of what transpired:

- First I meditated and did a Theta session to receive what the damage was and how to facilitate its correction and the return to harmony of Tuska's body.

- I began administering homeopathic Hypericum and Arnica montana 30x, 3x a day for 3 days.

- I performed hands on energy transmission while envisioning Tuska's spine being healed. This was done again in Theta (www.thetahealing.com).

- Herbal decoction : comfrey, yarrow, horsetail.

- The severing of Tuska's vertebrae T3 or T4 damaged his spinal cord but did not sever it. Therefore he still had feeling in his back legs but could not stand on them due to the lack of support in his back.

Tuska's spirit was strong and he had full intention of keeping up with his brother Seth who was ever on the move. To keep up, Tuska would walk on his front legs but drag his rear. So, to create support and traction, I was guided to hold onto his tail at its tip and pull it up to allow Tuska's back legs and feet to be on the ground and moving as they would if his back was healed.

Chuckle, so there we would walk with Seth, Spirithawk, Tuska and me trotting alongside holding Tuska's tail up and allowing his body to walk, trot and in time run. In time, Tuska's muscles, tendons and ligaments strengthened and became a natural support for his separated vertebrae. When I held him it was obvious the vertebrae had not healed, yet Tuska ran, played and climbed tress with just as much finesse as his athletic brother Seth.

Case Five: Case Study / Testimonial :: Zella & Freebe

Maryann Frisbee's Testimonial for Katherine Ariel

I have known Kathryn for 10 years. Over the years she has helped me and my horses with various issues. She healed by stitch I had in my right side with one long distance healing. It was remarkable. I was in so much pain, it was amazing that the next day after the healing the evening before, my pain was gone.

Another instance of her remarkable healing abilities was with my thoroughbred gelding, Freebe. He suddenly could not walk without wobbling. I had the vet and a Chiropractor look at him. He was diagnosed with West Nile, which is usually fatal for horses. Katherine worked on him on two occasions and within a few day all of his symptoms disappeared. He is still alive and kicking at 24 years old.

My thoroughbred mare, Zella, got out of the pasture and was running around the property and fell on the neighbor's bricked driveway. I was not at home and my son's got her and Freebe back in the paddock. By the time I arrived home I knew my mare had suffered a serious injury and was in extreme pain. As you can see by the pictures below the damage that ensued from the fall. She could not get out of her stall. I called Kathryn. After her long distance scan, Kathryn determined Zella had a fracture in the stifle area.

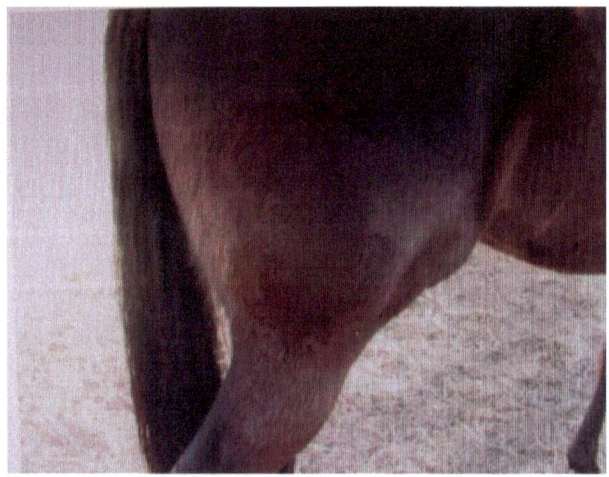

After Kathryn's initial healing, Zella was able to get in and out of the stall. Kathryn recommended I pick up several herbs, infuse them and give the concoction to Zella over the next few weeks. She also recommended that I make a tincture and rub down the entire injured area. It took a few months for the injury to heal. Zella has fully recovered from the fracture. Generally speaking a fracture can take a year to heal, but with Kathryn's knowledge of herbs that heal fractures and of herbs that reduce hematomas my mare recovered in weeks.

I have only praise for Kathryn's healing abilities and knowledge of herbs that assist in healing of all species.

CHAPTER 48
UNDERSTANDING THE LESSONS

Everything in life occurs for a reason. This is part of living in a cause and effect Universe. *For every action there is an equal and opposite reaction ...* Even so, not everything happens for a positive reason, as we create what we think with feeling, whether it is a positive focus or a negative one.

Since humans are what is called a creator race, all of our actions as individuals and as a global community have an effect upon all life around us, - again be they positive or negative. As such, we have a great responsibility to the Earth and her kingdoms as stewards and guardians of their lives and realities. It can be seen everywhere that what we create through our thoughts and actions does indeed have an impact on the other kingdoms of the earth (everyone & everything).

More and more teachings have brought forth that the cry from humans of "why me" brings with it the response – because you created it either directly or indirectly through your thoughts and actions, or lack thereof. When something appears in my outer reality that I do not consciously understand I ask my Godself or Mother/Father/God, "What is it you wish for me to know and understand from this situation?"

This question can be asked whether it concerns me personally, a family member (four-legged or two) or the world at large. I find that when I ask this question in a peaceful desire of truly understanding, the wisdom will be revealed to me in a form that I can understand and learn from. It also gives me the conscious awareness required for me to make new and better choices (if desired) as well as helping my animal family members to do the same.

When an individual understands what causes a physical manifestation of something that you either like or dislike, then you can change your behavior to create it again (like) or something new (dislike). Animals who walk with us assist us to learn through their behaviors, and they through ours. Be conscious of the cause and effect and our role in its all provides a terrific means to empower all involved to choose a life of peace and well-being over trauma and fear.

Acceptance and Gratitude

The Power of Now, world altering book by Ekart Tolle, creating a global conversation regarding the power and importance of being in the NOW moment at all times. The past is the past. What we have to work with is the NOW. And it is from NOW that the future is created. It is a simple fact, and it is an incredibly powerful one as well.

The past is the past. Letting go of the pain and embracing the wisdom give us the power to move forward, to heal and help our loved ones to do the same.

> *Gratitude and Forgiveness are two of the most powerful energies in the world*

Why be grateful for a trauma you might ask? Sometimes it is necessary to dig deep to find the gift that has come with the pain. And in some cases it may seem quite minute compared to the trauma itself. What I have learned over the years is the gift of calling for our life experiences to come through Divine Love and Grace, rather than pain and trauma. Even just that lesson, that awareness that we can choose peace, Love and grace, and through our doing so bring great blessings to the world is a mighty gift indeed!

CHAPTER 49
THE JOURNEY, THE CHOICES AND THE LESSONS

Everyone and everything is on a journey of learning and advancement of their Spirit/Soul through the embodiment (physical form) that God and they have chosen to learn the next step of their spiritual evolution. No matter what form of expression, every life form is here to learn, to serve and to advance along their spiritual pathway. Beloved Earth is a schoolhouse of sorts. She is a school to remember how to live in unconditional love, peace, harmony, while advancing through service.

So, if LOVE is the lesson, then why are there so many traumas in the world?

Simply put, the traumas are the result of the pathway of separation from the Divine that humans took a very long time ago; a decision that was made by our race to learn what it would be like to be separate from Mother/Father/God within us and upon high. It was a choice that rather backfired and we dropped ourselves and all life on Earth into a journey of fear and destruction with conditional love and pleasure on the other.

Traumas have been (and are) the outplaying of the fear based energies (fear, anger, hatred, control, dominance …) that resulted from our choice as a race, and that we have been outpicturing since that time. The outpicturing (manifesting into physical reality) has occurred into our personal lives, and into all the other kingdoms of life sharing Mother Earth with us with much pain and suffering experienced by all.

As such, we as a race are responsible to a large degree for all the suffering and trauma in the world, trauma to our own bodies and to others in all forms and expressions. The good news is that we can also be the stewards of returning our global journey back to unconditional love (LOVE), peace, harmony and well-being for all life, by making new choices.

Part of the new choices must include shedding old beliefs of judgment, inequality, dominance and of course separation from the Divine that is in all of life. The Divine within us knows what to choose to make this shift. Our inner to outer journey is to listen to the Divine promptings – also known as intuition, and act these inner promptings that are given in what is often referred to as Divine Right Action and Divine Right Timing.

In this Universe of cause and effect, free will and learning through experience, there really is no such thing as an *accident*. All actions are effects of thoughts, feelings, focus, intentions, mindfulness or mindlessness in the case of intentionally doing others harm. So as I have said previously, there is really no such thing as an accident, however trauma and emergencies do not have to be a part of our lives. We can choose as individuals and as a global race by each day making a verbal, mental and emotional choice for peace …

I Choose Peace – Mind, Body & Spirit

We are all drops creating ripples in the pond that is the consciousness of humanity and all of Life upon and including Earth herself.

Be Mindful, Peace-filled and Courageous

Your animals & all Life with thank you. Namaste.

Appendices

APPENDIX A
POISON CONTROL CENTERS

The United States has a system of Poison Control Centers as do some states including California. These centers all have websites with free information and also a free hot line phone number in case of an emergency.

In the United States - America Association of Poison Control Center. The American Association of Poison Control Centers supports the nation's 55 poison centers in their efforts to prevent and treat poison exposures. Poison centers offer free, confidential medical advice 24 hours a day, seven days a week through the **Poison Help Line at 1-800-222-1222.**

This service provides a primary resource for poisoning information and helps reduce costly emergency department visits through in-home treatment.

The AAPCC's mission is to actively advance the health care role and public health mission of our members through information, advocacy, education and research. Here is their contact information:

- Phone: 1-800-222-1222
- Websites: http://www.poison.org ; http://www.aapcc.org/

The AAPCC's will answer questions regarding animals and people. And if they do not have the information needed they may refer to you to other agencies such as **ASPCA's Animal Poison Control.**

- Phone: (888) 426-4435
- Website link is: http://www.aspca.org/pet-care/animal-poison-control

The national Poison Control Center is free, but the Animal Poison Control may charge $65 for the consultation as they are staffed by veterinarians.

Another option is **Pet Poison Hotline** who charges $39 per incident:

- Phone: 800-213-8660
- Website: http://www.petpoisonhelpline.com/

Keep these numbers in your phone, first aid kit and wherever else you keep your emergency numbers.

Holistic Emergency Care and Trauma Recovery for Animals / Appendices

APPENDIX B

VITAL SIGNS FOR DOGS, CATS & HORSES
VITAL SIGN DETAILS

Overview of Normal heart rate for dogs and cats:

The normal heart sound should consist of 2 separate beats with a silent interval between them and a regular rhythm; LUB DUB, LUB TUB (like a drum). If you have any doubts about your animal's heart or if the heart rate is not normal treat as an emergency and seek veterinary care.

The heart rate can also be taken by locating the animal's pulse along the femoral artery (inner thigh) or under the arm.

 *Vital Signs for Cats*

Normal Heart Rate:
- Cats 110-130- beats/minute

Normal Respiratory Rate:
- Cats - 20-30 breaths /minute
- Cats panting - up to 300 pants/minute
- Cats do not usually pant unless they are in a stressful situation (going to the vets), frightened, in hot weather. They should not pant for more than a few minutes at a time. If panting persists and animal cannot return to normal breathing treat as an emergency.

Normal Temperature:
- Normal Temperature: 100.5F -102.5 F (38.0 C- 39.1 C)
- Abnormal; Hypothermia (T<37.5 C); Hyperthermia (T>39.1 C)

Holistic Emergency Care and Trauma Recovery for Animals

Vital Signs for Dogs

Normal Heart Rate:
- Puppies 70-120 beats/minute
- Dogs 70-180 beats/minute
- Toy breeds (small dogs) 70-220 beats/minute.

Normal Respiratory Rate:
- Puppies 15-40 breaths/minute
- Dogs 10-30 breaths/minute
- Toy breeds (small dogs) 15-40 breaths/minute
- Dogs that are panting - up to 200 pants/minute

Normal Temperature:
- Normal Temperature: 100.5F -102.5 F (38.0 C- 39.1 C)
- Abnormal; Hypothermia (T<37.5 C); Hyperthermia (T>39.1 C)

Vital Signs for Horses

Normal Heart Rate:
- Adult : 28 - 44 beats per minute
- Newborn: 80-100 beats per minute

Normal Respiratory Rate:
- Adult: 10-24 breaths per minute
- Newborn : 20-40 breaths per minute

Holistic Emergency Care and Trauma Recovery
for Animals / Appendices

Normal Temperature:
- Adult : 99-101°F (37.2-38.3°C)
- Newborn: 99.5-102.1°F (37.5-38.9°C)

Mucous Membrane: Moist, healthy pink color
Capillary Refill Time*: Two seconds or less
Gut Sounds : Gurgling, gas like growls, "tinkling" sounds (fluid), and occasionally "roars"

Resources for Vital Sign Data:

1. First aid for pets
   By Chantale Robinson
   Biologist Veterinary Technician

2. http://www.thehorse.com/articles/31854/normal-horse-vitals-signs-and-health-indicators

APPENDIX C
REFERENCES

Books/Ebooks

- Callahan, Sharon. <u>Healing Animals Naturally with Flower Essences and Intuitive Listening</u>, Sacred Spirit Publishing, Mount Shasta, CA. 2001.

- Grieve, Mrs. M. <u>A Modern Herbal</u> (in two volumes), Dover Publications, INC., New York, 1971.

- Linda Tellington-Jones with Sybil Taylor. <u>The Tellington TTouch</u>, Penguin Books, USA, Inc. 1992.

- Moore, Michael, Drawing and photographs by Mimi Kamp. <u>Medicinal Plants of the Pacific West,</u> Red Crane Books, Santa Fe, NM, USA. 1993.

- Stein, Diane. <u>The Natural Remedy Book for Dogs & Cats,</u> The Crossing Press, Freedom, CA. 1994.

- Stein, Diane. <u>Natural Healing for Dogs & Cats</u>, The Crossing Press, Freedom, CA. 1993.

- Tierra, Michael. <u>The Way of Herbs,</u> Washington Square Press, published by Pocket Books, Copyright 1998.

- Wright, Machaelle Small. <u>MAP The Co-Creative White Brotherhood Medical Assistance Program</u>, Published by Perelandra, Ltd. Warrenton, VA 20188.

Websites

- http://www.maryannsimonds.com/
- www.anaflora.com

Holistic Emergency Care and Trauma Recovery for Animals / Appendices

- www.pets.webmd.com

Educational / Training Products

- Author Barbara J. Semple recommends the Healing Touch Quick Steps discussed here as well the First Aid Helper Cards in her HEAL NOW Cards, when you or your pet are in immediate healing need. The Healing Touch Quick Steps pictures in this card deck are a compliment rather than a replacement for professional medical help. Always seek the professional advice from your physician. HEAL NOW Cards are available at http://amzn.to/1DVf3fu

Healing Products

- Homeopathy –
    - Hylands: http://www.hylands.com/
    - Boiron: http://www.boironusa.com/

Herbal Products

- (mine)
- Herb Farm (?)
- Bulk Herb websites:

Flower Essence Products

- Flower Essence Society (FES): www.flowersociety.org
- Anaflora: http://www.anaflora.com
- Mystic Horse Products : http://mystichorse.com/

Bibliography and Attribution

Photographs

1. Tabebuia heptaphylla (Pao de Arco): By mauroguanandi [CC-BY-2.0 (http://creativecommons.org/licenses/by/2.0)], via Wikimedia Commons
2. Arctium lappa (Giant Burdock) : Christian Fischer [CC-BY-SA-3.0 (http://creativecommons.org/licenses/by-sa/3.0)], via Wikimedia Commons
3. Tummeric : J.M. Garg, via Wikimedia Commons
4. Equine Anatomy chart: www.topdefinitions.com
5. Flower Essence Repertory, by Patricia Kaminski and Richard Katz
6. http://plants.usda.gov/java/

Documentation

1. http://www.thehorse.com/articles/31854/normal-horse-vitals-signs-and-health-indicators
2. http://plants.usda.gov/java/
3. http://pets.webmd.com/dogs/dog-seizure-disorders
4. The Way of Herbs, Michael Tierra
5. Epilepsy, Convulsions, and Seizures, by Mary L. Wulff-Tilford & Gregory L. Tilford, authors of the book :Herbs for Pets

www.ingramcontent.com/pod-product-compliance
Lightning Source LLC
Chambersburg PA
CBHW042129010526
44111CB00031B/29